THE SPANISH-AMERICAN WAR

MODERN WARS IN PERSPECTIVE
General Editors: *B.W. Collins and H.M. Scott*

ALREADY PUBLISHED

Mexico and the Spanish Conquest
Ross Hassig

The Wars of French Decolonization
Anthony Clayton

The Spanish-American War
Joseph Smith

To Margaret and Michael
with best wishes
Joe

THE SPANISH-AMERICAN WAR:
Conflict in the Caribbean and the Pacific
1895–1902

JOSEPH SMITH

LONGMAN
London and New York

Longman Group Limited,
Longman House, Burnt Mill,
Harlow, Essex CM20 2JE, England
and Associated Companies throughout the world.

Published in the United States of America
by Longman Publishing, New York

First published 1994

ISBN 0 582 04300 X CSD
ISBN 0 582 04340 9 PPR

British Library Cataloguing-in-Publication Data

A catalogue record for this book is
available from the British Library

Library of Congress Cataloging-in-Publication Data

Smith, Joseph, 1945–
The Spanish-American War : conflict in the Caribbean and the Pacific,
    1895-1902 / Joseph Smith.
    p.   cm. -- (Modern wars in perspective)
Includes bibliographical references and index.
ISBN 0-582-04300-X (cased). -- ISBN 0-582-04340-9 (paper)
1. Spanish-American War, 1898. I Title. II. Series.
E715.S74 1995   93-44809
973.8'9--dc20   CIP

Set 7 in Sabon 10/12
Produced by Longman Singapore Publishers (Pte) Ltd
Printed in Singapore

CONTENTS

ACKNOWLEDGEMENTS

Over several years my undergraduate course on U.S. History has dutifully included a discussion of the events of 1898. From the kindness of the late Harold Blakemore, who regularly asked me to review books on this subject for the *Journal of Latin American Studies*, I became aware of changing historical interpretations and the need for an up-to-date synthesis designed for student use. To my surprize and delight, Harry Hearder suggested that I write a general study for Longman. I am indebted to him that he chose me to do this. The timing was propitious because the task of research was enormously assisted by my spending 1990-91 in the U.S.A. as a Visiting Professor at the University of Colorado at Denver. My work was later greatly facilitated by a travel grant from the British Academy which enabled me to visit Havana and Santiago de Cuba in 1992. I wish also to thank the Departmental Research Fund of the Department of History and Archaeology at the University of Exeter for financial assistance to make research trips to London and to attend overseas conferences.

Among the individuals who have helped me complete this project, I am grateful to Mark Foster for giving me the opportunity to teach a graduate course on the Spanish-American War at the University of Colorado at Denver. My special thanks go also to Michael Garcia for his many personal kindnesses and to John Lynch for his invaluable counsel. The editorial stage of publication had been expedited by the efficiency of Bruce Collins and Longmans. I am also grateful to Sean Goddard for supplying the maps. Most of all, however, I must once again thank Rachael for her encouragement and enduring support.

LIST OF MAPS

I THE SPANISH-CUBAN WAR (1895-98)

THE 'EVER-FAITHFUL ISLE'

During the latter half of the nineteenth century Spain cut a sorry figure in comparison to the expanding great powers of Europe. The monarchy, the traditional symbol of Spanish unity, was overthrown in 1868 and only restored in December 1874 by a military *coup*. The untimely death of King Alfonso XII in 1885 resulted in an infant successor and the regency of the Habsburg princess, María Cristina. Beset not only by Carlist pretenders to the throne but also by persistent criticism from republicans and socialists, the monarchy faced an increasingly uncertain future as the century drew to a close. Paradoxically, however, Spanish political life during 'the Restoration' projected an image of relative calm and stability. This was achieved by *caciquismo*, a system of scheming and manipulation which enabled the political bosses known as *caciques* in alliance with the wealthy landowners, military leaders and government officials to rule the state for their own personal advantage. At the national level, politics were dominated by the Conservative and Liberal parties who took it in turns to share periods in government office. The two foremost practitioners of *caciquismo* were Antonio Cánovas del Castillo, who headed the Conservatives, and Práxedes Mateo Sagasta, the leader of the Liberals. Behind the democratic veneer of elections, debates in the Cortes (national parliament), and regular changes of government, Spanish politics were controlled by a network of corrupt and selfish cliques. Political life was so barren that Spain was said to be marooned in 'the Dead Sea of politics'.[1]

The curious mood of self-deception so evident in Spanish internal politics also applied to the country's relationship with its

---

1 *El Imparcial* (Madrid), 14 October 1877, cited in Earl R. Beck, *A Time of Triumph and Sorrow: Spanish Politics during the Reign of Alfonso XII, 1874–1885* (Carbondale, IL 1979), p. 99.

overseas colonies. There was no denying the fact that the once great empire of Charles V and Philip II had shrunk by the middle of the nineteenth century to include only Cuba, Puerto Rico, the Philippine Islands, and a few small territories in the Pacific Ocean and North Africa. However meagre they were in size, the continued retention of these possessions assuaged the sense of national loss and humiliation caused by the breaking away of the Latin American colonies at the beginning of the nineteenth century. In this context, Cuba was accorded special significance in the Spanish psyche. Not only was Cuba the largest and richest island of the West Indies, but it had also remained loyal to the mother country. Cuba was affectionately described by Spaniards as the 'ever-faithful isle' and was perceived as living proof that God's blessing continued to shine on Spain's imperial status.

Long and narrow like a crocodile, Cuba stretches more than 700 miles in length from west to east and varies in width from 20 to 50 miles across, though at one point the island is more than 100 miles from north to south. Its geographical position astride the Atlantic Ocean and Caribbean Sea had historically made the island a frequent port of call for Europeans *en route* from the Old World to the New World of Mexico and Central America. The Spaniards first came as conquerors in search of gold and silver, but some chose to settle in Cuba and thereby established a pattern of emigration which continued right up to the end of the nineteenth century. Spanish emigrants arriving in Cuba were known as *'peninsulares'* because they had been born in the Iberian peninsula. Their 'white' children who were born in Cuba and the New World were called 'creoles'. The distinction was crucially important because *peninsulares* regarded themselves as 'pure-blooded' and therefore superior to creoles. Moreover, Spanish imperial rule was dedicated to ensuring that the *peninsulares* retained a privileged status and dominated the government, the Church, the military and commerce.

The steady flow of emigrants from Spain to Cuba during the nineteenth century ensured that the *peninsulares* remained a substantial and highly powerful element of Cuban society. In fact, the number of *peninsulares* was actually boosted during the 1880s as a result of the introduction of government financial assistance for unemployed Spaniards emigrating to Cuba. Of the island's 1.6 million population listed in the census of 1887, about 150,000 were *peninsulares* and 950,000 were creoles. Whites therefore comprised almost 70 per cent of the population. The remainder were mostly blacks and mulattos who were descended from Africans brought as slaves to work on the plantations.[2] The institution of slavery was maintained for almost the whole of the nineteenth century. A sizeable free coloured population existed, but it was economically and socially consigned to the bottom of society. Life was harsh for the people of colour. Discontent showed itself in occasional slave uprisings but more commonly in a general lawlessness and banditry that was such a feature of rural areas especially during the latter half of the nineteenth century. One calming influence for *peninsulares* and creoles was the presence of a permanently strong garrison of 20,000 Spanish troops in Cuba. Indeed, whites – whether *peninsulares* or creoles – considered the maintenance of Spanish authority as the best guarantee of protecting property and social order.

If subjection to Spain brought advantages for creoles in Cuba, there were also serious disadvantages, including the perpetuation of the special privileges accorded *peninsulares* from the Captain General at the top to the most humble government official. Moreover, the restrictive policy of mercantilism sought to give Spanish shipping and products a virtual monopoly of colonial trade. In addition, the Spanish crown levied high taxes on profitable local industries such as sugar and tobacco. Consequently, the nineteenth century witnessed frequent complaints from the creoles in Cuba against what they considered to be shameless exploitation by a reactionary and corrupt imperial system. On occasion, discontent erupted into violence and revolt. This was particularly evident in the eastern province of Oriente which was more racially mixed and economically less developed than the wealthy western provinces of Occidente (which included the capital, Havana), Las Villas, and Camagüey. It was the Orientales, comprising not only creoles but also even larger numbers of blacks and mulattos,[3] who took the lead in declaring that Cuba should separate itself from Spain and become independent. This radical objective was publicly proclaimed in the village of Yara on 10 October 1868. Such pronouncements were known as 'gritos', and it was therefore the 'grito of Yara' which marked the beginning of the Ten Years' War of 1868–78.

For a decade the roving bands of Orientales referred to

---

2 1887 Census figures are taken from US War Department, *Report on the Census of Cuba* (Washington DC, 1900), p. 173.

3 The Chinese also served with distinction in the fight for independence. See Juan Jiménez Pastrana, *Los chinos en la historia de Cuba, 1847–1930* (Havana, 1983), pp. 118–27.

derogatorily by the creoles as *'mambises'*[4] fought a guerrilla war against numerically superior Spanish forces. The most celebrated rebel chiefs were Máximo Gómez y Báez, a veteran professional soldier born in Santo Domingo (the present-day Dominican Republic) who rose from sergeant to the rank of major-general, and Antonio Maceo, the mulatto leader from Santiago de Cuba, former mule-driver and hero of the peasants. Hampered by mountainous terrain, lack of roads and a rainy season which stretched from May to October, the Spanish army was unable to pursue and destroy the insurgents. However, the Spanish forces retained control of the cities and towns, and by sheer weight of numbers they successfully confined the rebels to the mountains. In so doing, they prevented the revolt from spreading beyond Oriente. The rich sugar plantations of the west therefore escaped the war and most of its destructive effects. The military stalemate was broken in 1876 by the arrival from Spain of General Arsenio Martínez Campos. Acting more like a politician than a general, Martínez Campos astutely exploited the divisions and war-weariness among the Orientales by offering amnesty and the prospect of political concessions. An agreement to end the fighting was eventually signed at Zanjón in Camagüey on 10 February 1878.

Although neither side had achieved a clear military victory during the Ten Years' War, the Pact of Zanjón was generally interpreted in Cuba as a Spanish triumph. The amnesty for the rebels was honoured, but Spanish politicians, operating within the system of *caciquismo*, subsequently showed little interest in implementing political or administrative reforms. The notable exceptions to this were the abolition of slavery in 1886 and the negotiation of a commercial agreement with the United States in 1891. The likelihood of significant political change was, however, severely constrained so long as Cuban representation in the Spanish Cortes was effectively limited to 6 out of 430 members. Moreover, the right to vote for the Cuban delegates was based on the payment of a high poll tax which restricted the suffrage to 53,000 voters or 3

---

4 The term originated from Juan Mamby, a black officer, who was active in the 1846 revolt against Spanish rule in the Dominican Republic. Although the majority of *mambises* were men, women played an important role as *mambisas*. See K. Lynn Stoner, *From the House to the Streets: The Cuban Woman's Movement for Legal Reform, 1898–1940* (Durham, NC, 1991). Various formal descriptions were used by contemporaries and ranged from 'separatist', 'insurrectionist', 'rebel' and 'insurgent'. For convenience I have tended to use 'insurgent' in this study.

per cent of the island's population.[5] The fact that the majority of these voters were *peninsulares* merely reinforced and highlighted the latter's continued monopoly of office and privilege in Cuba.

Despite their unhappiness over the slow pace of political change, most Cuban creoles were loyal to Spain. They identified themselves with the mother country rather than the nebulous idea of 'Cuba'. Thoughts of independence were not only regarded as treason, but were also associated with the Ten Years' War and its attendant racial disharmony and destruction of property. In fact, creoles who advocated reform were hopeful that it could be achieved by traditional political methods. For this purpose the Liberal Party was formed in August 1878. Its stated objective was 'autonomy', which meant in practice the granting of wide powers of local self-government, increased Cuban representation in the Cortes and the freedom to trade. The Autonomists adopted the slogan of 'Home Rule' and frequently cited as their model Britain's granting of 'dominion' status to Canada. Indeed, the idea of autonomy for Cuba found increasing support among Spanish liberals. At the beginning of 1895, prompted by the Liberal government of Sagasta, the Cortes was on the point of enacting measures to increase Cuban membership in the national parliament, but action was deferred by the outbreak of revolt in Cuba.

Steadfast against autonomy and resolutely opposed to the separation of Cuba from Spain was the Constitutional Union Party. Founded in November 1878, this party consisted mostly of *peninsulares* who favoured what was popularly known as '*Cuba española*' ('Spanish Cuba'). Starting with the premise that God had willed Spain to discover and civilize Cuba, the Unionists were utterly convinced that the continuation of Spanish rule was essential for the island's prosperity and survival. 'The people of Cuba are Spaniards, like those in Madrid, and the island is just as much part of Spain as is Castile,' declared a typical Unionist view.[6] By utilizing the voting power of the *peninsulares* and the support of the local militia force of volunteers, the Unionists effectively stifled the efforts of the Autonomists to secure political and administrative reforms. Similar close links with government officials and business interests in Spain gave the Unionists considerable political influence in the Cortes on any legislation relating to Cuba. A particularly prominent supporter was the Conservative Party leader, Cánovas, who characteristically

5   Enrique José Varona, *Cuba vs. Spain* (New York, 1895), p. 8.
6   Juan Bautista Casas, *La guerra separatista de Cuba* (Madrid, 1896), p. 2.

affirmed in July 1891 that 'no Spanish [political] party will ever abandon the island of Cuba'. In what would become a famous phrase he declared that, if necessary, Spain would fight to 'the last man and the last peso' to retain the island.[7]

Cánovas's remark indicated the deep-seated anxiety held by many Spaniards that a renewal of armed revolt in Cuba was seemingly inevitable. This arose primarily from the actions of a small but growing number of creoles who advocated separation from Spain. However, the concept of independence, or *'Cuba libre'* ('Free Cuba'), was considered treason and was not tolerated within Cuba. Its adherents avoided harassment and arrest either by going into hiding or seeking exile abroad, usually in the United States. Most notably, Máximo Gómez and Antonio Maceo had preferred exile rather than accept the Pact of Zanjón. Those exiles who believed that the fight for Cuban independence must be continued formed numerous clubs and juntas in Latin America and Europe and especially in the United States. During the 1880s there were a number of external attempts to launch revolts in Cuba by mobilizing the existing mass economic and social discontent on the island. But these efforts failed mostly as a result of lack of organization and leadership. The defects were remedied by José Martí.

Born in Havana in 1853, Martí was a first-generation creole. His father was an artillery sergeant from Valencia and his mother came from the Canary Islands. An ardent advocate of Cuban separation from Spain, he had been imprisoned during the Ten Years' War and exiled to Madrid at the age of eighteen in 1871. Working mainly as a writer and journalist, he travelled to various countries in Latin America and from 1881 onwards lived a life of exile in the United States. During the 1880s he rose to prominence among the Cuban exiles and gained the name of 'the Apostle' by his tireless preaching not only of *Cuba libre* but also the necessity to transform Cuban society. The idea of independence as a catalyst of economic and social revolution had great appeal to the discontented masses suffering from exploitation by the ruling political elite. Acclaimed as a poet and man of ideas, Martí was also a technician and strategist. He was convinced that the Ten Years' War had been lost through lack of central direction and organization. His answer was to establish the Cuban Revolutionary Party in January 1892. With the moral support and financial backing of thousands of

---

7 Speech in Cortes, 3 July 1891, cited in Leonor Meléndez Meléndez, *Cánovas y la política exterior española* (Madrid, 1944), p. 340.

members from within the United States and especially among the large numbers of Cuban emigrants employed as cigar-workers in Florida, Martí and the new party proceeded to plan the liberation of their homeland.

THE OUTBREAK OF WAR

Martí's revolutionary activities were aided by the onset of severe economic depression in 1893. High unemployment in Cuba fuelled resentment against Spanish rule. Consequently, Martí found little difficulty in recruiting supporters and establishing a network of juntas throughout Cuba. The task of these juntas was to prepare for a nationwide rebellion which would be timed to coincide with the landing in Oriente of a force led by the most prominent exiles. The revolt was scheduled for February 1895 and called for Martí and up to 1,000 exiles to embark from Fernandina, Florida. In Oriente they would link up with two smaller expeditions, one from Costa Rica containing Antonio Maceo and the other from Santo Domingo headed by Máximo Gómez who, despite being almost sixty years old, had agreed to assume military command of the 'Liberating Army'.

The more immediate problem for the revolutionary junta in the United States was how to keep their preparations secret. Complete secrecy proved impossible to achieve because the Spanish government habitually employed a large number of agents to monitor the activities of Cuban communities resident along the eastern seaboard. Moreover, there was also the risk that the United States government might intervene under the neutrality laws which prohibited expeditions known as 'filibusters' from using American ports as bases to attack friendly foreign governments. Similar difficulties had defeated a number of expeditions in the recent past and did so again on 14 January 1895, when federal officials at Fernandina, Florida, seized the three boats intended to transport the expedition to Cuba.

Despite the disastrous setback in Florida, Martí remained convinced that Cuba was ripe for rebellion. With only two companions he sailed for Montecristi in Santo Domingo where he successfully persuaded Máximo Gómez to persevere with his part of the original plan. The revolutionary juntas in Cuba were accordingly instructed to instigate their own national revolt in February. Once the rebellion was under way they would be joined by Martí, Máximo Gómez and Antonio Maceo. As always, the most receptive region was Oriente, where a 'revolutionary atmosphere' existed.[8] On 24 February 1895 at Baire, a remote village about 50 miles to the west of Santiago de Cuba, a small group of revolutionaries led by Saturnino Lora proclaimed 'Long Live Independence and Long Live Cuba Libre'.[9] But 'the *grito* of Baire' proved to be an isolated event. Similar proclamations were not forthcoming as expected from Havana and other large cities because the Spanish authorities were already apprised of the plot. On the same day as the *grito* of Baire, rebel leaders were arrested in Havana, Matanzas and Santa Clara. The projected nationwide revolt had collapsed before it had even started.

Towards the end of March news of the *grito* of Baire reached Santo Domingo. Martí and Máximo Gómez decided immediately to prepare to leave for Cuba. On 25 March they issued the 'Manifesto of Montecristi' in which they publicly announced their aims. The manifesto acquired significance both at the time and later because it was more than just an affirmation of *Cuba libre*. Indeed, it was a calculated revolutionary statement which envisaged an armed struggle not just for political freedom from Spain but also for the liberation of the Cuban people from economic oppression and racial discrimination.[10] While this had great appeal to the mass of the coloured population, it aroused alarm among *peninsulares* and creoles who feared that the real aim of the movement was to unleash racial strife and create a black republic like neighbouring Haiti.

On 11 April, after a stormy voyage, Martí, Máximo Gómez and four companions landed on a remote beach at Playitas on the southern coast of Oriente. Maceo and twenty-two followers had set out earlier from Costa Rica and had come ashore further to the north, near Baracoa, on 31 March. The early days in Cuba were particularly hazardous for Maceo, but he avoided capture by the Spanish authorities. Indeed, reports of the return of the charismatic

8 Testifonte Gallego y García, *La insurreción cubana* (Madrid, 1897), p. 246.

9 José Miró y Argenter, *Cuba: Crónicas de la guerra* (3 vols; Havana, 1909), vol. i p. 27.

10 See Philip S. Foner, *The Spanish-Cuban-American War and the Birth of American Imperialism, 1895–1902* (2 vols; New York, 1972), vol. i pp. 5–6. One of Martí's close companions described the manifesto as Cuba's 'first constitution'. For this comment and the Spanish text of the manifesto, see Enrique Collazo, *Cuba independiente* (Havana, 1900), pp. 61–9.

'bronze titan' soon had thousands of Orientales flocking to join their hero. By the end of April Maceo claimed to have the support of '6,000 men, well-armed, and with much artillery'.[11] On 4 May the three leaders met in the mountains at La Mejorana near Santiago de Cuba. Martí had assumed the rank of major-general and was excited by the prospect of battle. On 18 May he wrote: 'I am now, every day, in danger of giving my life for my country.'[12] The following day, while eagerly riding towards what would have been his first battle with the enemy, the 'Apostle' was killed in a Spanish ambush at Dos Ríos.

Martí's death was a bitter personal loss to the rebels, but it had little immediate impact on the course of the revolt. In fact, the removal of Martí's political influence actually strengthened the authority of the military commanders, Máximo Gómez and Maceo. Ever suspicious of politicians, Gómez and Maceo were battle-hardened veterans of the Ten Years' War who saw themselves not as reformers but primarily as soldiers resuming the struggle which they had been forced to abandon in 1878. This time they were determined to fight to the end. Their own reputations for patriotism and courage were unquestioned and attracted a steady stream of new recruits to the Liberating Army. The essential beachhead had been firmly established and the battle for *Cuba libre* was well under way.

The news of revolt in Cuba provoked an emotional outburst of patriotism in Spain. The prime minister, Práxedes Mateo Sagasta, inflamed feelings further by casting blame on outside agitators. He explained that the outbreak of violence in Oriente was the product of an externally organized conspiracy. Denouncing this interference as an affront to Spain's authority and national honour, he declared on 8 March 1895: 'The Spanish nation is disposed to sacrifice to the last peseta of its treasure and to the last drop of blood of the last Spaniard before consenting that anyone snatch from it even one piece of its sacred territory.'[13] However, within days of this speech an internal political crisis had brought about Sagasta's resignation. The Conservative Party took office, and Antonio Cánovas del Castillo became prime minister. Far from weakening Spanish resolve, the change of government signified an even greater determination to destroy the rebels. Sagasta's references to the 'last peseta' and the

---

11 Cited in Foner, *Spanish-Cuban-American War*, vol. i p. 8.
12 Cited in ibid., vol. i p. 11.
13 Speech in Cortes, 8 March 1895, cited in Meléndez, *Cánovas*, p. 365.

'last Spaniard' were very reminiscent of the celebrated speech made by Cánovas in 1891. Moreover, whereas the Liberals were known to be sympathetic to proposals for Cuban autonomy, the Conservative leader had an unambiguously clear and consistent record of support for *Cuba española*. His stated priority on taking office as prime minister was to crush the revolt and re-establish the full authority of Spain over the island.

Indeed, the talk of endless sacrifice appeared premature, as the first reports from Cuba indicated that the revolt was a minor disturbance confined to a remote region. Consequently, both the Spanish government and people initially approached the conflict secure in the conviction that Spain's superior resources would soon overwhelm the relatively small number of insurgents. The first step was to assert Spanish military power in Cuba. During March 1895 seven ships carrying more than 8,500 troops sailed from Spain to reinforce the 20,000 Spanish soldiers already stationed on the island. The following month saw the despatch of an additional 7,500 reinforcements.[14] Despite his obvious intent to inflict a decisive military defeat upon the enemy, Cánovas was an exponent of *caciquismo* and did not therefore ignore the usefulness of politics as a means of securing the desired outcome. This was demonstrated by the appointment of General Arsenio Martínez Campos as Captain General and commander of the Spanish forces in Cuba. Martínez Campos was respected and admired not only in Spain but also in Cuba, where he was regarded as sympathetic to creole aspirations for political reform. His particular mixture of firmness and conciliation had brought an end to the Ten Years' War in 1878 and it was hoped that he could be similarly successful in 1895.

Martínez Campos personally doubted whether Spain could hold on to Cuba indefinitely. However, on his arrival at Havana in March 1895 the general exuded optimism. His message was clear: the mother country would resolutely fulfil her responsibility to maintain law and order. Seeking particularly to reassure *peninsulares* and creoles of the wealthy western provinces that their privileges, jobs and property were safe, he stressed that the rebellion was confined to Oriente, a region notorious for its lawlessness and racial unrest. The general publicly described his task as merely the suppression of the activities of 'bandits' who would first be

14 For statistics on troop movements from Spain, see Ministerio de Ultramar, *Fuerzas y material sucesivamente enviados a los distritos de ultramar con motivo de las actuales campañas desde marzo de 1895 a mayo de 1897* (Madrid, 1897).

contained and isolated and then quickly destroyed by the systematic application of superior military power. Skilfully taking advantage of the favourable public mood, Martínez Campos also sought to win over his opponents peacefully by talking of reconciliation and making them a general offer of amnesty. At the same time he moved to stem the flow of recruits to the rebels by promising work for the unemployed to build army barracks and repair roads and railways.

In terms of his military strategy Martínez Campos transferred large numbers of troops to the east. Some were intended to pursue the rebels in Oriente, others to reinforce Spanish garrisons in the cities and towns, but most were assigned to man an enormous defensive line known as the '*trocha*'. Dating from the Ten Years' War the *trocha* was located to the west of the city of Camagüey and extended more than 60 miles from Júcaro in the south to Morón in the north. Its military purpose was to interdict movement between the western and eastern sections of the island. In reality, the *trocha* was basically an enormous ditch about 200 yards wide. Within it were all sorts of obstacles including trees, boulders, barbed wire and explosives. Along the perimeter at intervals of about 440 yards were a combination of forts, towers and blockhouses which were manned continuously and supplied by a separate railway line running the whole length of the *trocha*. Under General Weyler in 1897 another *trocha* was constructed in the west of the island. Extending from Mariel to Majana, this western *trocha* separated Pinar del Río from Havana. In fact, the digging of *trocha*s of varying sizes and dimensions was a common Spanish practice designed to protect cities, towns and fortified positions.

In addition to the Júcaro–Morón *trocha*, Martínez Campos maintained a naval blockade to prevent the revolt receiving assistance from outside. No rebel fleet existed so that the Spanish navy enjoyed mastery of the seas around Cuba. Consequently, whereas ships regularly arrived from Spain bringing the Spanish army troop reinforcements and material of all kinds, the military resources available to the rebels steadily dwindled. The most serious disparity between the two forces was that of weapons and ammunition. In part this arose from the historical fact that civilians in Cuba were not accustomed to possessing firearms. The Spanish authorities had always placed strict regulations upon the use and possession of firearms because of fear of slave uprising and creole rebellion. Consequently, whereas the Spanish forces were well equipped with up-to-date Mauser rifles, artillery and large quantities of ammunition, the insurgents possessed few modern rifles and were

11

always severely short of ammunition. In fact, their favourite weapon was the machete, a long knife commonly used for cutting sugar-cane and paths through the tropical jungle. In close combat, however, the skilful use of the machete was often more deadly than the bullet of the most modern rifle. Spanish soldiers were said to be terrified when they heard an insurgent commander give the order to 'draw machetes'.

Martínez Campos hoped to limit the amount of actual fighting by stamping out the rebellion while it was still in its infancy. Indeed, he had already hinted that he expected to return triumphantly to Spain in November. However, his offer of amnesty was spurned by the insurgents who defiantly made it clear that they would only enter into negotiations on the basis of Spain granting independence to Cuba. Martínez Campos had therefore to move into the field and attempt to defeat the rebels by force. Outside the major cities, however, he was dismayed to find little support from the local people. On the march from Havana to Oriente he privately informed Madrid that success would be more difficult to achieve than in 1876–78 because 'the country is more hostile to us'.[15] Just as in the Ten Years' War, the insurgents were able to draw assistance from and blend into the local population. Moreover, Spanish numerical superiority proved of little advantage so long as the enemy carefully avoided pitched battles and preferred hit-and-run cavalry tactics against weak and vulnerable targets. Consequently, the Spanish troops, most of whom were infantry rather than cavalry, found themselves forever chasing an elusive foe. An American visitor stressed the inconclusive nature of the fighting:

> A well-planned, long-sustained battle is unknown in Cuba. The Cubans if taken by surprise, scatter immediately. The Spaniards have been ambushed so often that they are very loath to follow. Unless in greatly superior numbers, they avoid trying issues with detachments they may chance to meet. In the uplands and mountains the Cuban bands are fairly secure from assault. They dash into the open country, pounce upon a column, kill a few soldiers, and get away with small loss. The Spaniards fear to pursue, lest they be led into a narrow pass and [are] shot to pieces – a fate which many a valorous column has met.[16]

15 Martínez Campos to the Minister for the Colonies, 8 July 1895, cited in Valeriano Weyler, *Mi mando en Cuba* (5 vols; Madrid, 1910–11), vol. i p. 27.

16 Thomas G. Alvord, Jr, 'Why Spain has Failed in Cuba', *The Forum* 23 (1897), p. 567.

There were also so many gaps in the overstretched Spanish lines that Máximo Gómez was able to breach the *trocha* without difficulty and enter Camagüey in July. A further blow to the strategy of Martínez Campos was the onset of the rainy season in May, which virtually precluded large Spanish offensive operations until November. Ironically, at the same time as they were reducing the scale of their military activities in the field, Spanish officers complained of an acute shortage of manpower. Faced with the need to deploy more and more troops on purely defensive duties such as protecting sugar plantations and manning the *trocha*, Martínez Campos was compelled to request additional reinforcements from Spain. Consistent with its intention proclaimed earlier of fighting to the 'last peseta' and the 'last Spaniard', the government in Madrid readily complied, so that by the end of 1895 the forces under the command of Martínez Campos had grown to 120,000 regular troops. In fact, the number of soldiers was so large that the island could be described as being virtually occupied by the Spanish army. Within the space of a few months a local disturbance had been transformed therefore into a full-scale colonial war.

The evident failure of Martínez Campos to fulfil the hopes of a quick victory which his appointment had aroused resulted in an understandable decline in the fighting spirit of his troops. Service in Cuba was never popular and was vigorously resisted by regular army officers and soldiers, who preferred to remain in Spain. Consequently, the large majority of reinforcements were young conscripts drawn from the lower classes and hurriedly despatched overseas with minimal training and preparation. In his brief visit to the Spanish forces in late 1895, Winston Churchill was greatly impressed by the 'tough Spanish peasants' and their ability to cover long distances without complaint.[17] But the grim conditions of service in the tropics soon reduced morale. Another contemporary writer described the conscripts as 'raw, ill-fed, ill-clothed, ill-treated, and badly-paid troops, the greater part of whom are mere lads'.[18] Not only were they fighting a fierce and often invisible enemy in an unfamiliar country, but they also ran the risk of contracting one of the many tropical diseases endemic during the Cuban rainy season. The most common were malaria, dysentery and yellow fever. Indeed, the Spanish forces were permanently weakened by disease and

17 Winston S. Churchill, *My Early Life: A Roving Commission* (London, 1930), p. 95.
18 Fidel G. Pierra, *Spanish Misrule in America* (New York, 1896), p. 46.

sickness. From March to December 1895 there were almost 50,000 hospital admissions of soldiers suffering from non-combat illness. During the following year the figure more than quadrupled.[19] For every single Spanish soldier killed in combat, it was estimated that ten died of disease. The corresponding losses among the insurgents were markedly different with fewer casualties resulting from disease than combat. Once when Máximo Gómez was asked who were his best generals, he replied, 'June, July, and August'.[20]

By the summer of 1895 the insurgent forces in Oriente claimed that the Liberating Army had more than 20,000 men under arms. They even boasted of a formal structure of command headed by the Commander-in-Chief, Máximo Gómez, and organized into army corps, divisions, regiments, battalions and so on. In practice, this organization was more nominal than real, and provoked the ridicule of Spanish officers who described the 'Liberating Army' as a collection of undisciplined gangs of criminals and outlaws.[21] However, Spanish contempt masked an inner insecurity because the small mobile band of between twenty and 100 men was the most dangerous and effective striking arm of the insurgents. Such groups could fight as infantry, but it was as cavalry – typically mounted on sturdy ponies – that they demonstrated their greatest skill and success. They also enjoyed the distinct advantage of usually operating within their own local terrain where they could live off the land, easily find means of escape and shelter when necessary, and acquire accurate information on the whereabouts of Spanish forces. Moreover, should the occasion arise they could join together with other similar insurgent groups and form a larger unit which might temporarily even outnumber Spanish forces in the vicinity. For example, in July 1895, *en route* to Bayamo, Martínez Campos was compelled to withdraw in some disorder after being attacked at Peralejo by 2,000 insurgents led by Antonio Maceo. 'The Spanish commander had the worst of the skirmish and was in considerable personal danger,' reported a British observer.[22]

Nevertheless, such large engagements were rare. The strategy adopted by the 'old fox', Máximo Gómez, was based on carefully avoiding frontal assaults and pitched battles against an enemy superior in numbers and equipment. Always conscious of his side's

---

19 Louis A. Pérez, Jr, *Cuba Between Empires, 1878–1902* (Pittsburgh, 1983), p. 75.
20 Cited in Foner, *Spanish-Cuban-American War*, vol. i p. 20.
21 A. Días Bento, *Pequeñeces de la guerra de Cuba* (Madrid, 1897), p. 119.
22 *The Times* (London), 24 July 1895.

lack of military resources, he was convinced that guerrilla warfare was the most effective way of compelling Spain to admit defeat. The Liberating Army was divided into separate units which were instructed to camp by day in the mountains, swamps and *manigua* (the jungle) from which they would emerge usually at night to attack 'soft' economic targets such as railway and telegraph lines and especially the sugar plantations. These tactics were highly successful. Not only did they deplete Spanish and loyalist revenue and resources but they also resulted in relatively few casualties and gave the strategic initiative to the insurgents. Moreover, so long as the Spanish commanders did not know where the next assault was coming from, they had to tie down large numbers of men to protect property and lines of communication. It was an infuriating and virtually impossible mission. Replying to Spanish criticism that 'Cuban generals don't put up a fight', Máximo Gómez astutely remarked: 'This means they don't put up a fight on the Spanish-chosen territory. They put up a fight when they want to, and they refuse to enter a combat which would favour the enemy.'[23]

Further evidence of the advance of the insurgent cause was the formation of a provisional government. On 15 July a Cuban Republic was proclaimed. Almost two months later on 13 September 20 delegates met as a constituent assembly at Jimaguayú in Camagüey and established a provisional government. A written constitution was approved on 16 September providing for a Council of Government headed by a President. Salvador Cisneros Betancourt was chosen for this office. For the important task of seeking overseas diplomatic recognition the assembly appointed Tomás Estrada Palma as the Representative of the Provisional Government of the Cuban Republic in New York. Although the army was nominally placed under civilian control, the Commander-in-Chief, Máximo Gómez, continued to enjoy complete freedom of action. Indeed, the provisional government lacked a permanent location and was constantly on the move to avoid capture by the Spaniards. Aptly described as 'a government of the woods', it played an indirect role in the military struggle that was fast unfolding at the end of 1895.[24]

---

23 Cited in Foner, *Spanish-Cuban-American War*, vol. i p. 30.
24 See the comments of the American Consul in Fitzhugh Lee to Richard Olney, 11 July 1896, Washington DC, National Archives, Records of the Department of State, Record Group [hereafter cited as RG] 59, *Havana, Cuba*, Consular Dispatches, microfilm reel 126.

Like Martí, Máximo Gómez had always recognized the crucial importance of mounting a national rather than a regional revolt. As soon as the 1895 rainy season was over he intended to break out from Oriente and extend the war into the wealthy provinces of the west. Following the maxim that attack is the best means of defence, such a move would be a pre-emptive strike against the offensive plans of Martínez Campos. It would also significantly enhance the prestige of the Liberating Army both at home and abroad. But the emphasis would still be on fast-moving guerrilla warfare. Indeed, Máximo Gómez remained absolutely convinced that economic disruption was the best way to defeat Spain. He had already issued a terse circular on 1 July: 'The sugar plantations will stop their labours, and whoever shall attempt to grind the crops, notwithstanding this order, will have their cane burned and their buildings demolished.'[25] The same policy of 'total war' would be extended to the western provinces. Mindful of the fact that sugar was the most important industry on the island, Maceo and other colleagues argued that the policy was too extreme and would prove to be self-defeating. However, Máximo Gómez was adamant that the threat to destroy property and put sugar plantations to the torch was essential to overcome the opposition of the loyalist creole landowners and sugar planters.

While Máximo Gómez gathered together his forces in Camagüey, Antonio Maceo with around 1,500 men left Baraguá in Oriente on 22 October. Calixto García assumed command of the insurgents who remained behind in Oriente. A few weeks later, on 29 November, Maceo crossed the eastern *trocha* without a single casualty even though it was reckoned that Martínez Campos had stationed 16,000 troops close by. On the following day Maceo joined Máximo Gómez at Lázaro López in Camagüey. Reviewing the assembled army of 3,000 men, Máximo Gómez declared: 'Soldiers! The war begins now. ... I predict for Martínez Campos complete destruction ... a prediction which will be fulfilled when the invaders reach the doors of Havana with the flag of victory.' With these words the 'Invading Army' began its advance into the west.[26]

As the Invading Army approached the open plains of Central Cuba Martínez Campos was confident of intercepting and destroying the insurgents. But European military tactics and even

25 Decree dated 1 July 1895, cited in Foner, *Spanish-Cuban-American War*, vol. i p. 22.
26 Cited in ibid., vol. i p. 51.

Spanish numerical superiority were no compensation for lack of mobility and skilful generalship. Instead of forcing the insurgents into a decisive battle, Martínez Campos found himself either losing contact with the enemy or involved in a series of skirmishes from which his quarry always escaped. The initiative passed completely to the insurgents as the main Spanish army was compelled to retrace its own steps back towards Havana. 'The humiliating fact remains', noted *The Times* of London, 'that Spain's greatest general, as he is called, has been completely outmanoeuvred by Máximo Gómez and the mulatto Maceo'.[27] Martínez Campos appeared incapable not only of halting the advance of the insurgents but also of preventing the widespread destruction of property symbolized by the fields of burning sugar-cane which they left in their wake. Describing the general as 'an invincible optimist', *The Times* gloomily reported that Cuba was 'lapsing into total anarchy'.[28] In December it was confirmed that the rebels had entered the province of Havana. Even the capital city was now in danger. Rumours of imminent attack by '12,000 machetes' provoked increasing panic among its citizens.[29]

On 2 January 1896 Martínez Campos declared a state of emergency throughout the western provinces of Havana and Pinar del Río. Havana itself came to resemble a besieged city as cannons were placed in all the major public squares, troops patrolled the streets and sentries maintained constant vigilance. The expected rebel assault on the capital did not occur because it was not militarily feasible and had never been part of Máximo Gómez's invasion plan. The insurgents possessed neither the numbers nor the weapons to attack an armed and fortified city with any real prospect of success. Their aim was to create maximum economic and social dislocation and thereby fatally undermine Spain's resolve to resist *Cuba libre*. In accordance with this strategy, Maceo compounded Martínez Campos's many existing problems by moving to the west of Havana. On 8 January 1896 the insurgents entered Pinar del Río, the location of the richest tobacco plantations in Cuba. Two weeks later Maceo scored the symbolic propaganda victory of reaching Mantua, the westernmost town in Cuba. In three months the 'bronze titan' had marched more than 1,000 miles. He and Máximo Gómez had achieved what had earlier seemed to be impossible: they had taken the war from the mountains of Oriente to the gates of

---

27 *The Times* (London), 20 January 1896.

28 Ibid., 5 November 1895.

29 Francisco Durante, *Salsa mambisa* (Mexico City, 1897), p. 42.

Havana and had thereby transformed a provincial revolt into the 'Spanish-Cuban War'.

The success of the Invading Army was a disaster not only for Spanish policy but also personally for Martínez Campos. His initial offer of amnesty to the rebels and his talk of reconciliation had aroused controversy, but criticism had been suppressed in order not to undermine the war effort. Now that the military situation had deteriorated so badly, it was increasingly felt both in Spain and in Cuba that Martínez Campos must be replaced preferably by a general who would prosecute the war much more vigorously and ruthlessly. Such a move was facilitated on 7 January 1896 by Martínez Campos's offer to resign. Less than two weeks later on 20 January he was relieved of his command and replaced as Captain General by Valeriano Weyler y Nicolau.

'BUTCHER' WEYLER

In keeping with the Germanic ancestry denoted by his surname, Weyler was a no-nonsense professional soldier. He had personal experience of Cuba and had served there for two years during the Ten Years' War. The ruthless pursuit of the enemy both in Cuba and during a later campaign in Catalonia in the peninsula had already earned Weyler a reputation for 'extreme cruelty', a criticism which he found personally embarrassing and sought to disavow.[30] But this did not signify soft-heartedness. Weyler believed that Martínez Campos had erred on the side of leniency in Cuba and that this had only encouraged the further spread of the revolt. Weyler let it be known that he could be relied upon not to make the same mistake. By 'fighting war with war', he predicted that the conflict would be brought to an end in less than two years.[31]

On 10 February 1896 Weyler arrived in Havana and confronted what he privately described to Madrid as 'a very grave situation'.[32] He saw his immediate task as 'reawakening the Spanish spirit', and to foster this he deliberately ended his first public proclamation with 'Long Live Spain' and 'Long Live Spanish Cuba'.[33] His ringing endorsement of *Cuba española* boosted the morale of the loyalists in

---

30 See Weyler, *Mi mando*, vol. i pp. 102–13.
31 Ibid., vol. iv p. 398.
32 Ibid., vol. i p. 129.
33 Proclamation dated 10 February 1896, cited in ibid., vol. i p. 121.

Havana and emboldened them to usher in a period of political repression. In fact, Weyler's appointment was interpreted as a serious blow not only to the policy of reconciliation but also to the prospects of autonomy. The Constitutional Union took the opportunity to single out anyone who had deviated from complete loyalty to Spain. A number of creoles whose 'crime' had been to advocate Home Rule were either imprisoned or chose exile. Some preferred to join the insurgents.

Weyler's reputation for ruthlessness was further reflected in the instructions sent to his commanders in Oriente and Camagüey to implement what would become known as the policy of 'reconcentration'. In crude terms they were empowered to empty the countryside of people, crops and livestock. The displaced Cubans would be 'reconcentrated' in fortified camps close to towns and cities with large Spanish garrisons. The policy of 'counter-insurgency' was hardly new, but its indiscriminate employment on such a large scale provoked controversy and outrage, especially in the United States. Indeed, the infamous concept of the concentration camp has long been associated with Weyler, but he was not the originator. It had been under discussion in Spanish political and military circles during 1896 and was an acknowledgement that Spain could no longer count upon the loyal cooperation and acquiescence of the mass of the rural Cuban population. However, Martínez Campos had objected to what he considered was too extreme a policy and one which was not certain to guarantee military success. Weyler was one of the foremost advocates of reconcentration. His replacement of Martínez Campos indicated that the policy was finally to be implemented.

In effect, the efficient removal of up to half a million people proved to be a task well beyond the capability and resources of the Spanish military. The serious lack of adequate housing, food, sanitation and health-care resulted in the death of up to 100,000 Cubans. The large majority of the remaining '*reconcentrados*' endured a state of destitution.[34] As a result, reconcentration proved to be a public relations disaster not only for Spain but also for Weyler, who was subsequently branded in the American press with the nickname 'butcher'. From the military point of view, however, it was claimed that the policy offered many advantages. Civilians were

34 Ernest R. May, *Imperial Democracy: The Emergence of America as a Great Power* (New York, 1961), p. 127. Contemporaries estimated that as many as 400,000 Cubans died.

suspected of disloyalty and were frequently a hindrance to operations in the field. Their removal would aid the mobility of Spanish forces and reduce the risk of ambush and surprise attack. A depopulated countryside would also significantly weaken the insurgents by depriving them of food, shelter, information and a pool of new recruits. However, few real military gains were forthcoming. The ruthless strategy of 'fighting war with war' merely increased economic devastation and further alienated the civilian population.

In conjunction with the policy of reconcentration, Weyler sought to use the *trocha* as a wedge between the insurgent forces. He ordered the construction of a strongly fortified *trocha* – sections of which were to be illuminated by electric lighting – to the west of Havana, starting at the town of Mariel and continuing for almost 20 miles to Majana on the southern coast. This western *trocha* was principally designed to isolate Antonio Maceo in Pinar del Río. A holding operation would be maintained against Máximo Gómez while Weyler mounted his main offensive in Pinar del Río. After defeating Maceo, Weyler would then concentrate on securing the central regions around Havana and Matanzas as a prelude to driving the insurgents to the Júcaro–Morón *trocha* and back into Oriente. Without supplies and aid from the rural population, Weyler reckoned that the rebels would soon disintegrate as a fighting force.

At first things went according to plan. Weyler's arrival raised Spanish morale, and life in Havana returned to 'its normal aspect'.[35] Nevertheless, the threat of the insurgents was still present. Maceo and at least 500 men were still active in Pinar del Río while Máximo Gómez continued to operate in Central Cuba. Weyler responded by reinforcing the western *trocha* and sending a succession of 'flying columns' numbering from 500 to a few thousand troops to pursue Maceo. However, the great cavalry skill of Maceo combined with the rainy season to frustrate all Spanish efforts to capture him. In October the policy of reconcentrating the civilian population was introduced into Pinar del Río. When the weather improved in November, Weyler went to the province and took personal command of a large army numbering more than 12,000 men. By this time the strain of almost constant movement and fighting had reduced the size of Maceo's own forces to around 150. Responding to Máximo Gómez's request that he return to

---

35 *Diario de la Marinha* (Havana), 9 March 1896, cited in Weyler, *Mi mando*, vol. i p. 165.

Oriente, Maceo brilliantly avoided encirclement by Weyler. On 4 December 1896 he crossed the Mariel *trocha*, but decided to linger in the vicinity of Havana perhaps with the intention of raiding the capital to score a propaganda victory against Weyler. While at Marianao, however, Maceo was ambushed and killed by Spanish forces on 6 December. Francisco Gómez, the son of Máximo Gómez, also died in this engagement.

The death of Maceo was a major triumph for Weyler and a heavy blow for the insurgents, especially Máximo Gómez, for whom the year ended 'with very sad auspices'.[36] In January 1897 Weyler moved from Pinar del Río to Central Cuba to turn his attention to Máximo Gómez. In his correspondence with Madrid Weyler noted that one year previously the Invading Army had created enormous panic in this region. He therefore felt considerable gratification that Spanish forces were now driving the insurgents in headlong retreat back to Oriente. At the end of February Weyler reached Sancti Spíritus and proudly informed Madrid that the revolt had been ended in the western provinces.[37] The claim had a good deal of foundation, but it was not wholly accurate. Small guerrilla bands continued to be active in Pinar del Río and parts of Central Cuba. Moreover, Máximo Gómez, admittedly with considerably depleted forces numbering no more than 300 men, remained at loose in the hills to the south of Sancti Spíritus. Further to the east there was the perennial problem of Oriente where the insurgent leader, Calixto García, claimed to have at least 20,000 men under his command. Indeed, as Martínez Campos had similarly experienced in 1895, the mountains of eastern Cuba made it extremely difficult for Weyler to conduct large offensive operations against the insurgents. In addition, from May onwards he had to contend with the rainy season which made roads impassable and turned streams into rivers. The heat of summer also brought the dreaded yellow fever and a higher incidence of cases of exhaustion and fatigue. A frustrated Weyler had no choice but to suspend offensive operations in June.

The unavailability of sufficient numbers of healthy troops was a serious concern for Weyler. This might seem surprising in view of the fact that 90,000 reinforcements were sent from Spain during the period from February 1896 to May 1897. Furthermore, Weyler also placed the local Corps of Volunteers on active duty so that he could

36 Máximo Gómez, *Diario de campaña, 1868–1899* (Havana, 1968), p. 314.
37 Weyler to Minister of War, 26 February 1897, cited in Weyler, *Mi mando*, vol. iii pp. 336–40.

recruit directly from the peninsular population. This meant that more than 200,000 men were under his command in the spring of 1897. Arrayed against this number were, at the most, 20,000 to 30,000 active insurgents. But Spanish numerical superiority was highly misleading. At least half of all Spanish troops remained on defensive duty protecting the *trocha*s, forts, towns, property and lines of communication. At any one time, another quarter were in hospital or too sick for active service. This left Weyler with a total fighting force of around 50,000. But such a large number of troops was never available to Weyler at any one time or in a particular place. The soldiers were dispersed in numerous garrisons spread out all over the island. Their deployment was also made difficult by the lack of good roads and a railway network which was in serious disrepair and under threat of frequent guerrilla attack. Moreover, the majority of the 'healthy' Spanish troops were recently arrived conscripts usually no more than sixteen or seventeen years old and deficient in military training and discipline. Their health and motivation were soon undermined by the climate and bad treatment. Food was invariably poor and pay was meagre. Subsisting on an inadequate diet of rice and dried meat, one infantryman in the field recalled how there was hardly a day of rest for his unit. It was not surprising that 80 per cent complained of ill-health.[38]

Despite his proclaimed intention to move aggressively against the enemy, Weyler was eventually compelled to adopt a defensive strategy not dissimilar to that pursued by Martínez Campos. It was not that Weyler was outmanouevred by the rebels. In fact, he was personally feared much more than Martínez Campos. 'Cruel' Weyler was how Máximo Gómez referred to the general in his diary.[39] The implementation of reconcentration in the eastern provinces had devastated the countryside and effectively denied the insurgents such things as food, clothing and shelter. Nevertheless, with 200,000 men – more than half of the total Spanish regular army – under his command, Weyler had signally failed to crush the rebellion and this aroused a rising groundswell of criticism in Spain. Weyler privately complained to Cánovas about 'the exaggeration' of the Madrid press and suspected that Martínez Campos was taking revenge by intriguing against him. He assured the prime minister that his forthcoming winter offensive would end the war in April or May of

38 Manuel Corral, *¡El desastre! Memorias de un voluntario en la campaña de Cuba* (Barcelona, 1899), pp. 107–10.

39 Máximo Gómez, *Diario*, p. 333.

1898.[40] However, this show of confidence could not conceal the reality that the longer the war continued, the greater the cost in Spanish lives, treasure and morale. Moreover, there was also the growing risk that the adverse publicity given to reconcentration had so inflamed American public opinion that this might result in military intervention by the United States.

THE COLLAPSE OF SPANISH POLICY

In the spring of 1897 the predicament facing Cánovas and the Spanish government was worse than at any time since the commencement of the war. The spectre of American intervention was worrying, but even more pressing was the emerging discontent within Spain itself over Weyler's inability to bring a successful end to the war. Official government statements that the military campaign was progressing well were losing their credibility. Just before the opening of the Cortes on 19 May the Liberal Party leader, Práxedes Mateo Sagasta, derided the government's policy when he observed: 'After having sent 200,000 men and having spilt so much blood, we are masters in the island only of the territory upon which our soldiers stand.'[41] As the internal political consensus in favour of the war effort crumbled, it was no longer unpatriotic to discuss the subject of Cuban Home Rule. Even Cánovas acknowledged that a greater measure of local self-government should be introduced in areas which had been pacified. Liberal Party leaders such as Sagasta and Segismundo Moret y Prendergast wanted more decisive action, and argued that autonomy was preferable to an interminable struggle which must ultimately drive Spain to bankruptcy. The adverse economic effects were visible in the national debt which had more than doubled from 180 million pesos in February 1895 to 400 million pesos in June 1897.[42] Agricultural and industrial depression were also intensified by the war. After giving an initial boost to the economy, the war had become economically wasteful and damaging especially for Catalonia, the most prosperous region of Spain and much of whose wealth was dependent on the profitable export trade to Cuba. There was also the enormous emotional cost of sending more than 200,000 men

40 Weyler, *Mi mando*, vol. iv pp. 398–400.
41 Cited in ibid., vol. iv p. 408.
42 Pablo de Alzola y Minondo, *El problema cubano* (Bilbao, 1898), p. 25.

overseas with all the attendant pain, injury and death associated with war. The number of fatalities in 1897 was reckoned to be close to 40,000. Consequently, hardly a family in Spain was immune from the personal tragedy of war. Nor did it appear that the army's demand for young men was likely to diminish. The outbreak of nationalist rebellion in the Philippines in August 1896 and rumours of disaffection in Puerto Rico compelled the despatch of more troops to seemingly endless colonial burdens. The nightmare scenario of Spain expending its 'last man' and 'last peso' was fast becoming a reality.

Quite unexpectedly, on 8 August 1897 Cánovas was assassinated by an Italian anarchist, Miguel Angiolillo. The murder was not directly connected with events in Cuba. Nevertheless, supporters of *Cuba española* were thrown into disarray by the death of the man who had personified their cause. For Weyler it was an 'irreparable loss'.[43] On 4 October Sagasta accepted the invitation of Queen María Cristina to form a new government. Sagasta appointed Moret as Minister for the Colonies and unequivocally indicated that a radical change of colonial policy was imminent when he declared: 'I will fulfil my programme, establish autonomy in Cuba and recall Weyler. ... The Liberal Party is prepared to grant Cuba all possible self-government, a broad tariff and every concession compatible with inflexible defense of Spanish rule and sovereignty in the West Indies.'[44] Within days Weyler was relieved of his command and formally replaced in November by General Ramón Blanco y Erenas, a previous Captain General of the Philippines.

Towards the end of November the Queen Regent proclaimed the ministerial decree unveiling the Liberal plan to establish an autonomist government for Cuba. The highlight was a new executive council located in Havana and consisting of thirty-five members, seventeen of whom would be elected by Cubans and the other eighteen appointed by the Spanish Captain General. Provision was also made for a separate Cuban House of Representatives in which one member would be apportioned per 25,000 inhabitants. But the right to vote in local elections was still strictly based on property qualifications. Moreover, the Captain General possessed

43 Weyler, *Mi mando*, vol. i p. 7.
44 Message dated 4 October 1897, cited in Foner, *Spanish-Cuban-American War*, vol. i p. 127. The conciliatory policy extended beyond Cuba. Similar constitutional reforms were instituted in Puerto Rico. An agreement was also reached with the Filipino insurgents in December 1897 which brought a temporary end to the fighting in the Philippines.

the power to veto bills passed by the House and to dissolve that assembly should he so wish. Sagasta and Moret obviously hoped that they had done enough to gain the support of the creoles in Cuba. However, their scheme was a decree and not a consultative document. In this sense, it was typical of the selfish and devious politics of *caciquismo*. In return for cosmetic political reforms, Spanish control over Cuba would be effectively maintained.

Nevertheless, as proof of Madrid's change of policy, Blanco immediately released a number of creole political prisoners and ordered a relaxation of the policy of reconcentration. Although he cancelled Weyler's plan for a major winter offensive against Máximo Gómez and Calixto García, Blanco still continued military operations by placing more emphasis on sending out numerous small forces to engage the enemy. To show his support for the new commander, Sagasta agreed to send 20,000 reinforcements from Spain during November. It was evident therefore that the removal of Weyler and the offer of autonomy were not to be interpreted by Cubans as an admission of Spanish military defeat or that Spain had any intention of renouncing its sovereignty over the island. In reality, Sagasta was attempting to end, if not 'win' the war by a combination of military firmness and political conciliation. It was the old and well-tried formula adopted successfully by Martínez Campos in 1878 and unsuccessfully in 1895. The important difference in 1897 was that Spain had finally been compelled to concede a measure of Home Rule for Cuba.

The change of policy, however, had come too late. The insurgent leaders were immensely gratified by the recall of Weyler, which they attributed to their own military success rather than to Spanish magnanimity. Mindful of how similar promises of reform from Madrid had undermined their resolve in 1876–78, they dismissed the offer of autonomy as a propaganda trick. Both Máximo Gómez and Calixto García made it clear that they were confident of victory and would only stop fighting when *Cuba libre* was achieved. They categorically rejected discussions with Blanco, and informed their followers that anyone breaking ranks on this question would be regarded as 'a traitor'.[45] That this was not an idle threat was demonstrated in January 1898 by Máximo Gómez's approval of the summary execution of Colonel Joaquín Ruiz, a

---

45 Order of Calixto García dated November 1897, cited in Aníbal Escalante Beatón, *Calixto García: Su campaña en el 95* (Havana, 1978), pp. 295–6.

creole emissary sent by Blanco to inform the rebels of the government's proposals for autonomy.

Meanwhile the autonomist executive council had come into being in Havana in January 1898. Perceived as the creature of a Spanish ministerial decree, the council's impact was slight so long as its exact powers and function remained uncertain. The matter of most immediate concern for loyalists in Cuba was the emerging realization that Spain could not win the war. The inability of the Spanish army to launch the customary winter offensive against the rebels contrasted with news of increased insurgent activity in Oriente and parts of Central Cuba. Indeed, Calixto García had command of forces in excess of 20,000 men in Oriente and was skilfully picking off vulnerable Spanish garrisons. At the end of August 1897 he had used the threat of artillery bombardment to compel almost 1,000 Spaniards to evacuate the city of Victoria de las Tunas. This reflected the emergence in Oriente of a common pattern in which small Spanish garrisons simply chose not to resist the insurgents. They preferred instead to withdraw to the protection offered by large cities such as Santiago de Cuba and Holguín. These negative tactics revealed the extent to which the vast Spanish army had become crippled with sickness and low morale. Its growing reluctance to fight the enemy was underlined by the fact that the large majority of Spanish units rarely ventured outside their protected forts and garrisons. As a result, control of the countryside was handed by default to the insurgents. 'This war cannot last more than a year,' predicted Máximo Gómez at the beginning of 1898.[46]

The insurgents had feared that the offer of autonomy would split their ranks. The reforms, however, were much more divisive among the loyalists. In contrast to Cánovas, Sagasta and Moret placed great emphasis on gaining the active support and cooperation of the Cuban creoles. As part of the policy of reconciliation Blanco

---

[46] Statement reported in US Press on 2 January 1898, cited in Pérez, *Cuba Between Empires*, p. 167. The view that an insurgent victory was only a matter of time has led historians to question whether American military intervention was necessary to defeat the Spaniards. Some Cuban historians have argued that the McKinley administration intervened with the ulterior motive of forestalling an insurgent victory which would have resulted in the implementation of Martí's revolutionary programme. The foremost example of this interpretation is Emilio Roig de Leuchsenring, *Cuba no debe su independencia a los Estados Unidos* (Havana, 1960). The same theme is expressed in Pérez, *Cuba Between Empires* and Foner, *Spanish-Cuban-American War*. For a guide to Cuban historical works on this subject see Duvon C. Cubitt, 'Cuban Revisionist Interpretations of Cuba's Struggle for Independence', *Hispanic American Historical Review* 43 (1963), pp. 395–404.

had therefore deliberately appointed only creoles to the new council of government. *Peninsulares* were confused and angry. They were incensed by their exclusion from office and the selection instead of creoles, some of whom had been in prison for their autonomist views and others who had only recently returned from exile. Discontent surfaced on 12 January 1898 when rioting occurred in Havana. Shouting 'Long Live Weyler' and 'Down with Blanco and Autonomy', mobs consisting mainly of *peninsulares* and some Spanish soldiers symbolically destroyed the offices of two local newspapers which were well-known critics of the army.

The Havana riots demonstrated the many difficulties facing the implementation of political reform. Weyler's dismissal had aroused controversy not only in Cuba but also in Spain, where his supporters had organized large demonstrations in his favour. Republicans and Carlists were reported to be urging him to stage a military *coup* against the government. The fact remained, however, that Weyler had been given twenty months and 200,000 men to achieve a military solution to the conflict and he had failed. His reinstatement was therefore neither militarily sensible nor politically practicable. On the other hand, the alternative policy of political reconciliation had been categorically rejected by the insurgents and had now aroused the violent disapproval of loyalists. The government in Madrid was dismayed and perplexed about how to proceed. Moreover, there was also the urgent need to consider the intentions of the government and people of the United States. In his telegram to Washington giving news of the riots, the American Consul in Havana, Fitzhugh Lee, queried whether Blanco could maintain law and order in the capital. The potential danger to American life and property was such that Lee requested the protective presence of American warships. 'Excitement and uncertainty predominate everywhere,' he summed up.[47] The evident Spanish disunity boosted the prospects of an insurgent victory, but it also increased the probability of direct military interference by the United States in the Spanish-Cuban War.

---

47 Lee to William R. Day, 13 January 1898, RG 59, *Havana, Cuba*, Consular Dispatches, microfilm reel 131.

2 AMERICAN INTERVENTION

THE 'LAWS OF GRAVITATION'

The people of the United States generally displayed a dislike and lack of respect for Spain. This was partly the consequence of an Anglo-Saxon Protestant heritage which conditioned Americans to regard Spaniards as the enemy agents of monarchical aggression, political and religious oppression and moral decay. It also reflected the rivalry and animosity arising from quarrels over territory dating back to the colonial period. These disputes had resulted in the gradual whittling away of Spanish possessions in North America. The United States was notably successful in acquiring the Louisiana Territory from France in 1803 and the Floridas in 1819. For historical, commercial and strategic reasons, it seemed that Cuba would be next. That island was only a short sailing voyage – less than 100 miles – from the Florida keys and commanded the sea routes that led to the River Mississippi and the Gulf of Mexico. In a celebrated statement made in 1823, Secretary of State John Quincy Adams added the element of scientific certainty:

> There are laws of political as well as physical gravitation; and if an apple severed by the tempest from its native tree cannot choose but fall to the ground, Cuba, forcibly disjointed from its own unnatural connection with Spain, and incapable of self-support, can gravitate only toward the North American Union, which by the same law of nature cannot cast her off from its bosom.[1]

The following decades witnessed various non-governmental American attempts to take over Cuba either by offers of purchase or filibustering expeditions. While Spain had felt compelled to retreat

---

1 John Quincy Adams to Hugh Nelson, 28 April 1823, United States Congress, 32nd Congress 1st Session, House Document no. 121, p. 7.

from the mainland of continental North America, it chose to ignore the 'laws of gravitation' and revealed no disposition to give up control of the 'ever-faithful isle'. Spanish diplomats adopted the proud and obdurate attitude known as '*pundonor*', and repeatedly told American expansionists that Cuba was an integral part of the Spanish empire. Although '*pundonor*' was frequently irritating to those who had direct diplomatic dealings with Spain, it failed to arouse much concern in the United States. The mass of the American people were simply too preoccupied with the domestic task of building a new country and showed little interest in overseas affairs. Any special significance which might be attached to Cuba's geographical proximity was offset by the fact that it was not a contiguous part of the North American continent. Cuba was perceived as an offshore island whose absorption, in contrast to Texas or California, could not be easily justified by appeals to America's 'manifest destiny'. Moreover, there was the peculiarly sensitive question of race and slavery. The controversy provoked by the desire of the Southern states to extend their economic system into Cuba during the mid-nineteenth century not only highlighted the large number of slaves and blacks in the Cuban population but also made annexation an explosive political issue. Similar considerations later prompted the Grant administration to avoid becoming directly entangled in the Ten Years' War. The 'laws of gravitation' went therefore into abeyance as American public attitudes and government policy towards Cuba implicitly acknowledged Spanish sovereignty over the island.

Although political ties remained undeveloped, there was, however, a steady growth of economic contact between the United States and Cuba. Much of the resulting trade and investment revolved around sugar, which had become Cuba's staple crop and most lucrative export from the 1830s onwards. But the export trade in sugar began to face increasingly stiff competition from European beet sugar during the last quarter of the nineteenth century. Consequently, Cuba's share of the world sugar market fell from nearly 30 per cent in 1868 to just over 10 per cent in 1888.[2] Spain could do little to reverse this trend, so that Cuban planters naturally looked to the rising economic power of the United States – the 'colossus of the north' – to provide not only a substantial outlet for exports but also the major source of new capital investment. In the

2 Louis A. Pérez, Jr, *Cuba: Between Reform and Revolution* (New York, 1988), p. 130.

process the United States replaced Spain as Cuba's largest trading partner and by the 1880s was purchasing from 80 to 90 per cent of Cuba's total exports. In return, Cuba bought around 5 to 6 per cent of total American exports. These goods were valued at less than 25 per cent of Cuba's exports to the United States.[3] The balance of trade, therefore, was firmly in Cuba's favour. Nevertheless, like its neighbours in the Caribbean and Central America, Cuba formed part of the 'informal' American economic empire that was being established in the region. Indeed, the prosperity of the Cuban economy became dangerously dependent on continued access to the American market. This was underlined in 1894 by the passage in the United States Congress of a new Tariff Act which unilaterally removed the duty-free status previously conferred on imports of Cuban sugar. The resulting collapse of the sugar industry in Cuba contributed significantly to the political and economic unrest which led to the outbreak of revolt in 1895. The development of closer economic relations also meant that American business interests in Cuba would be more directly affected than during previous uprisings.[4]

AMERICAN NEUTRALITY

The government in Madrid was fortunate that President Grover Cleveland preferred to take a detached view of events in Cuba. Although he did not doubt that Spanish rule was shortsighted and oppressive, Cleveland showed no desire to meddle in Cuban affairs nor any particular sympathy for the insurgents and their aspirations for *Cuba libre*. Already alarmed by the threat to property and order posed by social and economic agitation at home, he was suspicious of similar troubles elsewhere and appeared comfortable with the

3 Louis A. Pérez, Jr, *Cuba Between Empires, 1878–1902* (Pittsburgh, 1983), p. 31.

4 The argument that economic factors determined relations between Cuba and the United States is presented in Philip S. Foner, *The Spanish-Cuban-American War and the Birth of American Imperialism, 1895–1902* (2 vols; New York, 1972). Influential works which also stress the crucial importance upon American foreign policy of the need to search for overseas markets are Walter LaFeber, *The New Empire: An Interpretation of American Expansion, 1860–1898* (Ithaca, NY, 1963), and William A. Williams, *The Roots of the Modern American Empire: A Study of the Growth and Shaping of Social Consciousness in a Marketplace Society* (New York, 1969). For a different interpretation, see David M. Pletcher, 'Rhetoric and Results: A Pragmatic View of American Economic Expansionism, 1865–98', *Diplomatic History* 5 (1981), pp. 93–105.

official explanation of the Spanish government that the disorder in Oriente was the work of bandits and outlaws. Like many Americans he was also disturbed by reports that the real aim of the revolt was to set up a black republic. True to his conservative and legalistic mind-set, Cleveland was determined to act properly and uphold the law of nations. Consequently, on 12 June 1895 he issued a proclamation of neutrality prohibiting Americans from serving with or giving military and financial assistance to the rebellious insurgents. The Treasury Department and the American navy were instructed to enforce the neutrality laws and prevent the launching of filibusters from the United States.

The pursuit of neutrality was made extremely difficult by the close geographical proximity of Cuba and the determination of Cuban exiles and their American sympathizers in the United States to send aid to the revolt. Officials of the Treasury Department and warships of the American navy, however, were effective in stopping thirty-three filibustering expeditions from proceeding to Cuba during the period from June 1895 to November 1897. In fact, only one-third of an estimated total of seventy-one expeditions originating in the United States actually reached the island.[5] On balance, therefore, Cleveland's 'neutral' policy appeared to harm rather than help the insurgents. Nevertheless, the Spanish authorities continually condemned what they regarded as deliberately lax enforcement of the American neutrality laws. They pointed out that Martí had actually used the United States as the base from which to start the revolt and that the ships seized at Fernandina were later returned to the Cuban exiles. 'The revolution is not a popular uprising,' stated the Spanish minister at Washington, Enrique Dupuy de Lôme. He added: 'It is a filibustering movement, principally of demagogues without standing in the island, who have nothing to lose and are trying their chances.'[6] Such comments sought to put the Cleveland administration on the defensive, but they were counteracted by a steadily growing number of complaints made to the State Department from American 'citizens' – several of whom were Cuban by birth and residence – alleging wrongful arrest, mistreatment and violation of their rights by Spanish officials either in Cuba or on the high seas.

Numerous claims were also made against the Spanish govern-

---

5 Foner, *Spanish-Cuban-American War*, vol. i pp. 17–18.

6 *New York Herald*, 23 February 1896, cited in French E. Chadwick, *The Relations of the United States and Spain* (3 vols; London, 1911), vol. i p. 438.

ment for failing to prevent the destruction of American property, especially sugar plantations. The casting of blame upon Spanish officials was complicated, however, by the independent attitude and military tactics adopted by the insurgents. José Martí had always feared that a close association with Americans would compromise the fight for *Cuba libre* and ultimately result in annexation to the United States. 'To change masters', he once noted, 'is not to be free.'[7] Although appreciative of American aid, the insurgent generals stressed that the war would be won primarily by Cubans. 'Cuba is conquering her independence with the arms and souls of its sons; and she will be free shortly without any other help,' typically remarked Antonio Maceo in 1896.[8] But the proclaimed method of achieving victory aroused disquiet in Washington. In fact, the determination of Máximo Gómez to pursue a strategy of 'total war' appalled both Cleveland and his secretary of state, Richard Olney. They considered this not only a barbaric method of warfare but also conclusive evidence that the insurgents could not be trusted to respect American property and investments in Cuba. On a later occasion Cleveland privately referred to the insurgents as 'the most inhuman and barbarous cutthroats in the world'.[9] Like many Cuban creoles, Cleveland and Olney essentially held to the view that, in the present circumstances, Spanish rule was the best guarantee of maintaining law and order.

The task of dealing with claims and counter-claims arising from the war was difficult enough, but Cleveland and his successor, William McKinley, also had to take into account the excitable mood of American public opinion. Americans were naturally sympathetic towards what they perceived as one more episode in Cuba's historic struggle for freedom from Spanish tyranny. This friendly feeling was encouraged and exploited by the activities of the Provisional Government of the Cuban Republic – usually referred to as the 'Cuban junta' – which, under the leadership of Tomás Estrada Palma, vigorously lobbied the State Department and Congress and

7 Martí to Gonzalo de Quesada, 12 November 1889, cited in Pérez, *Cuba Between Empires*, p. 95. Historians have differed in their interpretation of Martí's attitude towards the United States. See John M. Kirk, 'José Martí and the United States: A Further Interpretation', *Journal of Latin American Studies* 9 (1977), pp. 275–90.

8 *Patria* (New York), 22 August 1896, cited in Gerald E. Poyo, '*With All, and For the Good of All*': *The Emergence of Popular Nationalism in the Cuban Communities of the United States, 1848–1898* (Durham, NC, 1989), p. 113.

9 Cleveland to Olney, 26 April 1898, cited in Foner, *Spanish-Cuban-American War*, vol.i p. 181.

organized public meetings and demonstrations to raise funds and express support for *Cuba libre*. A stream of information was also given to the press detailing the successes of the insurgents and the atrocities perpetrated by the Spaniards. The free news service was very welcome to the proprietors and editors of an American newspaper industry which was currently engaged in fierce competition for mass circulation. The most prominent battle was being fought out in New York between Joseph Pulitzer's *New York World* and William Randolph Hearst's *New York Journal*.

Gaining their name from a cartoon character called 'the yellow kid',[10] the 'yellow' dailies sought exciting and unusual stories, especially those containing a human-interest angle. They found abundant material in the trouble and strife of war-ravaged Cuba. Front-page banner headlines were reserved for sensational articles rather than straightforward news reporting. When the artist Frederic Remington reported from Cuba in January 1897 that everything was quiet and that there was no war to be found, Hearst despatched his famous reply from New York: 'You furnish the pictures and I'll furnish the war.'[11] For three years the readers of the yellow press were bombarded with a steady barrage of sensational and frequently exaggerated stories often accompanied by photographs and illustrations describing not so much the actual course of the war but how Spain was turning the island into a wasteland of human misery and carnage. Traditional American prejudices against Spain were reinforced by reports of torture and summary execution. 'These revolting details of unspeakable cruelty', stated the *Chicago Tribune*, 'show how close is the Spaniard of today at heart to the Spaniard of two and one-half centuries ago.'[12] Editors were especially fond of singling out 'Butcher' Weyler as the supreme symbol of Spanish cruelty. The *New York Journal* called him 'the brute, the devastator of haciendas, the destroyer of families, and the outrager of women'. To the *New York World*, he was 'a barbarian, bred in an atmosphere of medievalism'.[13] Sensational articles often provoked

10 See Joyce Milton, *The Yellow Kids: Foreign Correspondents in the Heyday of Yellow Journalism* (New York, 1989), pp. 40–3.

11 Cited in Charles H. Brown, *The Correspondents' War: Journalists in the Spanish-American War* (New York, 1967), p. 78.

12 *Chicago Tribune*, 29 November 1896, cited in Marcus M. Wilkerson, *Public Opinion and the Spanish-American War: A Study in War Propaganda* (Baton Rouge, LA, 1932), p. 48.

13 *New York Journal*, 23 February 1896, and *New York World*, 8 May 1896, cited in Joseph E. Wisan, *The Cuban Crisis as Reflected in the New York Press* (New York, 1934), p. 204.

criticism and incredulity, but they were very effective in arousing public attention and thereby ensuring that Cuba remained in the forefront of American political debate.[14]

The political ramifications were seen most visibly in Congress where numerous resolutions recommending American action to aid the insurgents were introduced in every session from December 1895 onwards. While recognizing that the conduct of foreign affairs was the constitutional responsibility of the President and his secretary of state, Congressmen believed, however, that it was also their duty to deliberate how the United States might help to resolve the crisis in Cuba. Various schemes were floated, ranging from purchase to annexation. However, the basic issue of debate revolved around whether the United States government should continue the traditional policy of neutrality or embark upon a new departure and recognize the belligerent rights of the insurgents. Such recognition would directly assist the cause of Cuban independence because it would boost the morale of the insurgents and also allow them to purchase weapons and supplies from the United States. On 6 April 1896 the Senate and the House passed a joint resolution deploring conditions in Cuba and calling on the President to grant belligerent rights to the insurgents. The sizeable majorities backing the resolution were more than simply an indication of the strength of Congressional sentiment in favour of helping the insurgents. The votes also reflected impatience with neutrality and an evident desire by Congress to participate actively in the making of the nation's foreign policy.

Concurrent Congressional resolutions, however, are not binding on the executive. Cleveland, therefore, held fast to his presidential prerogative and chose to ignore the resolution. In contrast to the majority view in Congress, he remained deeply suspicious of the motives of the insurgents and did not consider them capable of forming a stable government. He was also aware that the recognition of belligerent rights would offend Spain and release the Spanish authorities from their legal responsibility to protect American property in Cuba. Such an outcome could only lead to further damage for American interests and make it more difficult to

14 Wilkerson, *Public Opinion and the Spanish-American War*, and Wisan, *Cuban Crisis in the New York Press* were influential works published in the 1930s which emphasized the importance of the yellow press in shaping American policy towards Cuba. Robert C. Hilderbrand, *Power and the People: Executive Management of Public Opinion in Foreign Affairs, 1897–1921* (Chapel Hill, NC, 1981) argues, however, that McKinley felt able to ignore the yellow press.

claim compensation. Cleveland, therefore, believed that the existing policy of neutrality should be maintained. On the other hand, almost a year had passed by and Spain had not yet crushed the revolt. This meant not only even more destruction but also a growing possibility of intervention from the great powers of Europe. Only a few months earlier Cleveland had uncharacteristically involved himself in foreign affairs and had insisted that Britain accept American arbitration of its boundary dispute with Venezuela. He believed that the time had now arrived for a similar diplomatic initiative urging Spain to concede autonomy. By doing so, the Spanish government would not only bring peace and restore order in Cuba but also mollify Cleveland's critics in Congress. On the day after the passage of the Congressional resolution, Olney articulated the administration's views in a long note presented to the Spanish minister at Washington. While not explicitly referring to the 'laws of gravitation', the underlying premise was that the United States possessed a special relationship with Cuba and that it could not tolerate a repetition of the Ten Years' War. But the show of firmness was not meant to signify the abandonment of neutrality. This was evident in Olney's offer of American diplomatic cooperation to secure a peaceful settlement that would include autonomy for Cuba while still maintaining Spanish rights of sovereignty over the island.[15]

Although they wished it could be otherwise, Spanish political leaders were compelled to face reality and acknowledge that the United States would exercise a close interest in whatever occurred in Cuba. The suspicion also persisted that annexation was the real aim of the American government. Whatever its purpose, that government possessed an enormous capacity for interference, whether by diplomatic, economic or military means. One example, which was a constant irritant to the Spanish authorities, was the highly visible presence of the Cuban junta in the United States. Above all, the prospect of American military intervention leading inevitably to the loss of Cuba was particularly dreaded in Madrid. Such an eventuality would be forestalled, it was hoped, by Weyler succeeding in bringing a speedy end to the rebellion. In the meantime, Spain

15 Olney to Dupuy de Lôme, 4 April 1896, cited in US Department of State, *Papers Relating to the Foreign Relations of the United States, 1897* [hereafter cited as *FRUS* with year number], (Washington DC, 1862–), pp. 540–4 The note was prepared on 7 April, but was predated to three days earlier so as not to appear to have been written in response to Congressional pressure. See Foner, *Spanish-Cuban-American War*, pp. 192–3.

would adopt the time-honoured practice of haughtily avoiding discussion of the subject and, if this was not feasible, gain time by engaging the Americans in lengthy diplomatic discussions. Following this strategy, the Spanish foreign minister, Carlos O'Donnell y Abreu, the duke of Tetuán, deliberately waited several weeks before replying to Olney's note. In forthright style Tetuán then affirmed that the revolt in Cuba was an internal Spanish matter. His government had resolved to restore peace by military means and to suspend the introduction of political reforms until pacification had been achieved. American advice and diplomatic assistance were not required. Indeed, Tetuán stated that the United States would most effectively help the cause of peace by vigorously enforcing its neutrality laws and curbing the activities of the Cuban junta.[16]

Cleveland's refusal to grant belligerent rights to the insurgents had prompted Máximo Gómez to accuse the Americans of insincerity. In practice, the President's decision had little impact upon the course of events in the *manigua*. 'Recognition is like the rain; it is a good thing if it comes, and a good thing if it doesn't,' the insurgent commander quipped to an American journalist.[17] In essence, the success of Tetuán's diplomatic gambit foundered primarily on Weyler's inability to defeat the insurgents. As the war dragged on with its attendant misery and destruction affecting American as well as Cuban lives and property, diplomatic communications from Washington to Madrid assumed an increasingly critical tone. By failing to win his party's presidential nomination in 1896, Cleveland had become a 'lame-duck' President. In his final Annual Message to Congress on 7 December 1896 he publicly renewed the offer of his country's good offices to assist the pursuit of peace. But signs of frustration were clearly evident in his statement that there was 'a limit to our patient waiting for Spain to end the contest'. This implied that, if Spain could not restore order in Cuba, the United States might have to intervene in order to do so. 'It can not be reasonably assumed', ominously warned Cleveland, 'that the hitherto expectant attitude of the United States will be indefinitely maintained.'[18]

---

16 Tetuán to Dupuy de Lôme, 22 May 1896, cited in *FRUS* (1897), pp. 544–8.

17 See Grover Flint, *Marching with Gomez* (Boston, 1898), p. 189.

18 See James D. Richardson, ed., *A Compilation of the Messages and Papers of the Presidents* (10 vols; Washington DC, 1896–1899), vol. ix pp. 720–2.

DIPLOMATIC DEADLOCK

In March 1897 the responsibility for conducting American diplomacy passed to William McKinley, the former Republican Congressman and Governor of Ohio who had defeated William Jennings Bryan of Nebraska in the 1896 presidential election. The new President saw his priority as leading America out from economic depression and it was with reluctance that he turned his attention to foreign affairs. Nevertheless, he did not doubt the seriousness of affairs in Cuba and was convinced that the United States must help bring an end to hostilities. Like his predecessor, McKinley recognized Spain's sovereignty over the island and believed that it was preferable that the Spaniards and Cubans should settle the crisis by negotiation rather than force. The great danger, however, was that the United States might be dragged into the fighting. While not making any specific reference to Cuba, McKinley's commitment to seeking a peaceful solution was emphasized in his Inaugural Address on 4 March 1897. 'War should never be entered upon until every agency for peace has failed,' he declared.[19] The President had served as a Union officer during the Civil War. Though not a pacifist, he genuinely hated the human destruction and cruelty resulting from war. He was especially appalled by the death and misery inflicted upon Cuban civilians by the policy of reconcentration. The dilemma that would unfold for McKinley during the ensuing months was how his personal conviction that every effort should be made to avoid war could be reconciled with the growing pressure from Congress, the press and public opinion for American military intervention.[20]

After carefully studying despatches on affairs in Cuba and especially the fact-finding report of his personal emissary, William J. Calhoun, McKinley concluded that the Spanish army could eventually win the war but only at the cost of inflicting total ruin upon the island and its inhabitants. Even if the insurgents were

19 Ibid., vol. x p. 143.

20 The view of McKinley as a weak President pushed into war was summed up in Theodore Roosevelt's description that McKinley had 'no more backbone than a chocolate eclair'. See Walter Millis, *The Martial Spirit* (Boston, 1931), p. 114. Modern historians see McKinley as an astute and effective diplomat. For example, see Lewis L. Gould, *The Presidency of William McKinley* (Lawrence, KS, 1980). An excellent guide to the historiographical literature is Joseph A. Fry, 'William McKinley and the Coming of the Spanish-American War: A Study of the Besmirching and Redemption of an Historical Image', *Diplomatic History* 3 (1979), pp. 77–97.

victorious, it was believed that this would result in widespread class and racial conflict. For reasons of humanitarianism and national interest, the United States had a duty to act. Like Cleveland, McKinley believed that the best chance of restoring peace and prosperity lay in exerting diplomatic pressure on Spain to grant political reforms. The plan which emerged from the White House essentially stressed the achievement of three main objectives. The first was the termination of the policy of reconcentration. This would be followed by an armistice to end the fighting and then negotiations between Spaniards and Cubans leading to Home Rule. In July 1897 Stewart L. Woodford was appointed American minister to Spain and instructed to convey McKinley's views personally to the Spanish government in Madrid. Although no exact timetable was given for the implementation of the peace plan, it was understood that McKinley was thinking in terms of months rather than years. The element of deliberate vagueness was necessary because the President wished his approach to be interpreted as a sincere and constructive offer of diplomatic assistance rather than an ultimatum.[21]

Woodford's arrival in Spain in September 1897 coincided with a period of political turmoil following the assassination of Cánovas. The uncertainty ended when Práxedes Mateo Sagasta assumed the premiership with the proclaimed intention of instituting autonomy in Cuba. Weyler was subsequently recalled, and instructions were despatched to reduce the severity of the policy of reconcentration. Although Woodford claimed that these developments represented a signal triumph for American diplomacy, the desire to appease the United States was only one of several factors contributing to Sagasta's dramatic change of Spanish colonial policy. In fact, American diplomatic pressure was useful in providing the Spanish government with an additional reason to justify the urgency of enacting autonomy. On the other hand, it also served to provoke anti-American feeling in Spain. This development was encouraged by Weyler, who remarked sardonically that the United States viewed his recall with 'satisfaction'.[22]

Conveniently ignoring the negative response of the insurgents to Sagasta's offer of autonomy, government officials in both Madrid and Washington expressed confidence that tangible progress was

---

21 See Sherman to Woodford, 16 July 1897, *FRUS* (1897), pp. 558–61.
22 Valeriano Weyler, *Mi mando en Cuba* (5 vols; Madrid, 1910–11), vol. v p. 213.

finally being made. 'Slowly but surely I am coming to hope that we shall get the great ends for which you seek without war,' Woodford gratifyingly informed the President in mid-November.[23] With evident relief McKinley's first Annual Message to Congress on 6 December 1897 approvingly mentioned the promised reforms and asked that Spain 'should be given a reasonable chance' to put them into effect. However, he also stressed that, if the peace process was not completed in the 'near future', American 'intervention' could not be ruled out. What form this would take was not divulged, though McKinley carefully disavowed any American desire for the 'forcible annexation' of Cuba. Territorial conquest was declared to be unacceptable and likened by McKinley to 'criminal aggression'.[24]

The optimism of December quickly evaporated early in the New Year when anti-autonomy riots broke out in Havana. The perceived danger to American citizens and their property from possible outbreaks of further disorder led McKinley to send the *Maine* to Havana.[25] The powerful battleship left Key West and arrived in Havana harbour on 25 January. Any suggestion that the decision was intended to browbeat the Spanish authorities was dismissed by the secretary of the navy, John D. Long. He insisted that the *Maine* was simply resuming the common naval practice of making 'friendly calls at Cuban ports'.[26] Spain was not likely to object because a Spanish warship had paid a 'friendly' visit to New York as recently as April 1897. Nevertheless, the decision clearly had potentially damaging implications for the Spanish government. Reeling from the shock of the Havana riots, they feared that the warship's presence must encourage the cause of the insurgents by suggesting a deterioration in relations between the United States and Spain. The knowledge that warships of the American North Atlantic Squadron had switched the location of their winter exercises from the Atlantic to the waters off the west coast of Florida also contributed to the growing sense of Spanish unease about possible military developments in the future.

23 Woodford to McKinley, 14 November 1897, cited in John L. Offner, 'President McKinley and the Origins of the Spanish American War' (Ph.D dissertation, Pennsylvania State University, 1957), p. 165.

24 6 December 1897, cited in *FRUS* (1897), p. xx.

25 For convenience I am only listing the name of American ships and omitting 'USS' which normally precedes the name to designate that the ship is part of the United States navy.

26 Long Diary, 24 January 1898, cited in Lawrence S. Mayo, ed., *America of Yesterday: As Reflected in the Journal of John Davis Long* (Boston, 1923), pp. 154–5.

Diplomatic relations received a further jolt on 9 February when the *New York Journal* published a facsimile and translation of a private letter written by Dupuy de Lôme. The letter from de Lôme to a Spanish politician had been written late in December 1897. It came, however, into the possession of the Cuban junta which passed it on to the *Journal*. In the letter the Spanish minister critically described McKinley as 'weak and a bidder for the admiration of the crowd, besides being a would-be politician who tries to leave a door open behind himself while keeping on good terms with the jingoes of his party'.[27] Despite the *Journal*'s headline, 'The Worst Insult to the United States in Its History,'[28] the revelations were not very shocking. Nevertheless, they forced Dupuy de Lôme's resignation. The main damage of the 'De Lôme Letter' was that it contributed to a further undermining of the peace process by bringing into question Spain's good faith and whether it could be relied upon to fulfil its promises of reform.

However, the sensation caused by the De Lôme letter was brief and completely overshadowed a week later when telegraph wires buzzed with the horrific news that the *Maine* had blown up in Havana harbour on 15 February. American loss of life amounted to 266 out of a total crew of 354. The reason for the explosion was unknown, but suspicion was rife in the United States that Spain must somehow be responsible. The assistant secretary of the navy, Theodore Roosevelt, privately informed a friend that the sinking was the result of 'an act of dirty treachery on the part of the Spaniards'.[29] The same conclusion dominated the front pages of most of the yellow press. The *New York Journal* was certain that a Spanish conspiracy had destroyed the *Maine*, and offered a $50,000 reward for information identifying the culprits. 'The Whole Country Thrills With War Fever,' stated a typical headline.[30] The intensity of public interest was revealed a few weeks later when Hearst proudly disclosed that the daily circulation of morning and evening editions of the *Journal* had reached 1 million and that this represented an increase of more than 250,000 from the previous year's figure.[31] The

---

27 For the full text of the letter see H. Wayne Morgan, 'The DeLôme Letter: A New Appraisal', *The Historian* 26 (1963), pp. 38–40.

28 *New York Journal*, 9 February 1898.

29 Roosevelt to Dibblee, 16 February 1898, cited in Elting E. Morison, ed., *The Letters of Theodore Roosevelt* (8 vols; Cambridge, MA, 1951–54), vol. i p. 775.

30 *New York Journal*, 18 February 1898.

31 Wilkerson, *Public Opinion and the Spanish-American War*, p. 119.

mood of the American public for striking back at Spain was highly charged. What exact form this would take was uncertain, but war against Spain now seemed a serious possibility.

McKinley resisted the enormous political and public pressure for military retaliation. Indeed, there appeared little justification for the United States government to threaten Spain with war. It was known that the local Spanish authorities had acted swiftly and commendably to assist the survivors of the disaster. The Queen Regent and her government had also sent a formal note of sympathy. Moreover, initial reports from Captain Sigsbee, the commander of the *Maine*, and Spanish officials in Havana suggested that the explosion was more likely to be accidental rather than deliberate. Accidents to coal-fired warships were far from uncommon and were usually caused by internal defects. McKinley, therefore, sensibly sought clarification by appointing an official investigation composed of three American naval officers headed by Captain William Sampson, the commander of the battleship *Iowa*. The commission started out immediately for Havana to examine the wreckage and interview witnesses. While the members of the commission were expected to seek the cooperation of the local Spanish authorities, they were instructed to stress that their task was to conduct an independent 'American' inquiry.

In contrast to the White House, the response of Congress to the sinking of the *Maine* was much more militant. There was clear disappointment at McKinley's reluctance to take a firm stand, but talk of rushing into war was tempered by the appointment of the naval inquiry. Congressmen agreed to suspend judgement on the disaster until the official report was completed. In the meantime, however, various efforts were made to try and influence the direction of the nation's foreign policy. For example, a number of resolutions were introduced calling for recognition of Cuban independence. The jingoistic attitude was also reflected on 8 March by the rapid approval without a dissenting vote of an emergency military appropriation of $50 million. These funds had been requested by McKinley and were to be used to strengthen the nation's naval defences. The large sum was also intended to impress upon an impecunious Spain the powerful resources of the United States. On 17 March Senator Redfield Proctor of Vermont delivered an enormously influential speech reporting on his own recent visit to Cuba. He saw intervention by the United States as both urgent and necessary to assist 'a million and half of people, the entire native population of Cuba, struggling for freedom and deliverance from the worst misgovernment of which I ever had knowledge'.[32] With increasing impatience Congress looked to McKinley for decisive action.

Despite the large amount of correspondence passing between Washington and Madrid, the diplomatic peace process was effectively stalled until the cause of the *Maine*'s sinking was known. On Thursday 24 March McKinley received the advance report of the American commission of inquiry. After five weeks of investigation the commission concluded that the *Maine* had been destroyed by an external explosion, most probably a submarine mine. Although it was deemed impossible to fix the exact responsibility, the implication was that the guilty person or persons must be Spaniards.[33] Given the excitable state of American opinion it was very likely that Congress would try and use the report to compel the administration to threaten military action against Spain. But McKinley did not want to make a controversial incident the single cause of war. This was evident when he sent the report to Congress on Monday, 28 March, without attaching any recommendation for specific action. Dumbfounded members of Congress were later promised that a full presidential message dealing with the whole Cuban crisis would be forthcoming in early April.

Risking his own personal prestige and political popularity, McKinley still hoped that successful diplomacy would pre-empt a possible Congressional move to force hostilities. On Friday 25 March – three days before sending the report of the *Maine* inquiry to Congress – McKinley discussed with his cabinet what he believed was the last chance to prevent the United States from becoming entangled in war. The factor accorded most weight was not so much the sinking of the *Maine* but the awareness that the reforms announced by Sagasta in November were not working. Assistant Secretary of State William Day telegraphed McKinley's views to Woodford on Saturday 26 March:

---

32 Speech dated 17 March 1898, cited in *Congressional Record*, 55th Congress 2nd Session, p. 2919.

33 The cause of explosion has never been conclusively determined. An investigation arranged by Admiral Hyman Rickover in 1975 pointed to an internal explosion when it concluded: 'In all probability, the *Maine* was destroyed by an accident which occurred inside the ship.' See Hyman G. Rickover, *How The Battleship 'Maine' Was Destroyed* (Washington DC, 1976), p. 104. An excellent historiographical essay is Louis A. Pérez, Jr, 'The Meaning of the *Maine*: Causation and the Historiography of the Spanish-American War', *Pacific Historical Review* 58 (1989), pp. 293–322.

There is no hope of peace through Spanish arms. The Spanish Government seems unable to conquer the insurgents. More than half of the island is under control of the insurgents; for more than three years our people have been patient and forbearing; we have fully prevented the landing of any armed force on the island. The war has disturbed the peace and tranquility of our people. We do not want the island. The President has evidenced in every way his desire to preserve and continue friendly relations with Spain. He has kept every international obligation with fidelity. He wants an honorable peace. He has repeatedly urged the Government of Spain to secure such a peace. She still has the opportunity to do it, and the President appeals to her from every consideration of justice and humanity to do it.[34]

Most of all, McKinley wanted Spain to declare an armistice and thereby bring an end to the fighting in Cuba. Negotiations between the contending parties would then take place on the basis of Spain offering Cuba 'full self-government, with reasonable indemnity'. The meaning of this particular phrase puzzled Woodford and, at his request, was subsequently explained by the State Department as referring not to autonomy but to 'Cuban independence'.[35] An extremely important change of policy had therefore taken place. Now that Spain could no longer be considered as the best guarantee of maintaining order in Cuba, the McKinley administration switched from neutrality to a new stance advocating the withdrawal of Spanish sovereignty. The tougher American attitude was also indicated in the request that a reply should be received from the Spanish government by the specific date of 31 March.

Spanish political leaders did not doubt the grave turn of events during the previous weeks. They were aware of the jingoistic mood of the American Congress and had been 'stunned' by the speed of passage and size of the $50 million military appropriation voted earlier in March.[36] To go to war against such a powerful country as the United States was most undesirable. But the abandonment of the 'ever-faithful isle' was unacceptable. For the army, it would signify dishonour. High-ranking officers preferred a war with the United States rather than endure the humiliation of surrendering to the

34 Day to Woodford, 26 March 1898, *FRUS* (1898), p. 704.
35 Woodford to Day, 27 March, and Day to Woodford, 28 March 1898, ibid., 712–13.
36 Woodford to McKinley, 9 March 1898, ibid., pp. 681–5.

insurgents. For the Queen Regent and the political elite, to offer an unconditional cease-fire would almost certainly invite a military *coup* which would bring down the monarchy and *caciquismo*. 'It is pretty clear', summed up *The Times*, 'that for the moment no Spanish Government can venture much further in the direction of concession without risking a domestic explosion even more fatal to the the interests of their country than defeat at the hands of a foreign power.'[37] There was a forlorn hope of last-minute diplomatic assistance from the European powers, but appeals by María Cristina to her fellow rulers proved unsuccessful. While Austria and Germany were sympathetic, Britain was not inclined to challenge the United States in what was regarded as an 'American' question. Without British participation, there could be no effective European intervention. Despite the rumours of behind-the-scenes activity, the great powers exerted negligible influence on the diplomatic crisis and the ensuing war between Spain and the United States.[38]

On 31 March the Spanish government announced that it would accept an armistice on condition that the insurgents should ask first for one. While this was a clever means of avoiding humiliation for the Spanish army, it was tantamount to a rejection of McKinley's proposals because the insurgents would definitely not comply. 'Spanish pride will not permit the ministry to propose and offer an armistice,' explained Woodford.[39] Only the prospect of an imminent diplomatic breakthrough had enabled McKinley to restrain an increasingly jingoistic Congress. He now made it clear to the Spanish government that he must deliver what was very likely to be a 'war message' to Congress. On 3 April Spain indicated a willingness to accept the mediation of Pope Leo XIII. Woodford suggested that this might lead to Cuban independence or even the cession of the island to the United States. McKinley agreed, therefore, to delay sending his message to Congress from 6 to 11 April. Nothing of significance happened until 9 April, when Woodford telegraphed a report that Spain had declared an unconditional armistice. But past experience

37 *The Times* (London), 11 April 1898.

38 The diplomatic activities of the European powers is an interesting sub-theme and has been extensively examined. For example, see Orestes Ferrara, *The Last Spanish War: Revelations in 'Diplomacy'* (New York, 1937); R.G. Neale, *Britain and American Imperialism* (Brisbane, Queensland, 1965); Ernest R. May, *Imperial Democracy: The Emergence of America as a Great Power* (New York, 1961); and John L. Offner, *An Unwanted War: The Diplomacy of the United States and Spain over Cuba, 1895–1898* (Chapel Hill, NC, 1992).

39 Woodford to McKinley, 31 March 1898, ibid., p. 727.

had made McKinley distrustful of Spanish delaying tactics. Diplomatic deadlock had finally been reached. The President had already prepared his message to Congress and he resolved to deliver it on schedule.

On Monday 11 April McKinley's message was read out to a packed Congress. After carefully describing the evolution of the crisis in Cuba and the long succession of diplomatic efforts to reach a peaceful solution, it concluded that American intervention had become necessary to end the war: 'In the name of humanity, in the name of civilization, in behalf of endangered American interests which give us the right and the duty to speak and to act, the war in Cuba must stop.' Significantly, McKinley asked Congress not to make a declaration of war but to 'authorize and empower the President to take measures to secure a full and final termination of hostilities between the Government of Spain and the people of Cuba'. This authority would give McKinley the flexibility to delay war and continue diplomatic negotiations.[40]

Congress, however, displayed a bellicose mood. Numerous speakers expressed the traditional American distrust and hostility towards Spain. 'The history of Spain is a history of more than a thousand years of concentrated cruelty,' declared Senator Shelby Cullom of Illinois.[41] The people of Cuba were regarded as only the most recent victims of Spanish oppression and brutality. In fighting for their freedom, the Cubans were perceived not only as brave and patriotic but also as emulating the example of the American Revolution. For Senator Henry Teller of Colorado, their struggle had assumed heroic proportions. He pointed out that the insurgents had successfully resisted for three years a Spanish army four to five times greater in size than the corresponding forces sent from Britain to combat the American Revolution. 'The time has come when the American people demand and when the interests of the race demand', asserted Teller, 'that we shall say the people of that island are entitled to be free.'[42]

Although McKinley clearly disapproved of Spanish rule in Cuba, this did not mean that he automatically regarded the insurgents as formal allies in the event of a war with Spain. In fact, he still saw no reason to grant recognition to the Cuban provisional government.

40 For the text of the Presidential Message, see ibid., pp. 750–60.
41 Speech dated 15 April 1898, cited in *Congressional Record*, 55th Congress 2nd Session, p. 3879.
42 Ibid., p. 3898.

This brought him into conflict with a powerful body of opinion in Congress which favoured immediate recognition. McKinley's attitude was puzzling, and aroused the suspicion that he was really seeking a war of conquest with the ultimate aim of annexing Cuba to the United States. These misgivings were most evident in the Senate where David Turpie of Indiana introduced an amendment calling for recognition of the Cuban republic 'as the true and lawful government of the island'. McKinley let it be known that he considered the proposal an encroachment upon the executive's authority to conduct foreign policy. The President's supporters succeeded in narrowly defeating the amendment. Instead of recognizing the Cuban republic, Congress stated that 'the people of the island of Cuba are, and of right ought to be, free and independent'.[43] But a political price had to be paid by McKinley. This was the acceptance of a measure put forward by Senator Teller in which 'the United States hereby disclaims any disposition or intention to exercise sovereignty, jurisdiction, or control over said island except for the pacification thereof, and asserts its determination when that is accomplished to leave the government and control of the island to its people'.[44] Although it was accorded relatively little attention in April 1898, the disavowal of annexation contained in the 'Teller Amendment' would later prove to be extremely important in influencing the future political status of Cuba.

On 19 April, by votes of 42 to 35 in the Senate and 310 to 6 in the House, Congress passed the joint resolution recognizing the independence of the Cuban people and demanding immediate Spanish political and military withdrawal from the island. The President was empowered to use the armed forces of the United States to enforce the resolution. The measure was an ultimatum to Spain and left no room for diplomatic manoeuvre. It was signed by the President on 20 April. On the next day he ordered a naval blockade of the northern coast of Cuba. Meanwhile, Queen María Cristina had opened the Cortes on 20 April and had delivered a stirring speech stating that Spain was 'united as one man in the face of foreign aggression' and would 'triumph in the end'.[45] In Havana,

43 Resolution dated 13 April 1898, ibid., 3814–15.

44 Resolution dated 16 April 1898, ibid., 3954. The idealist motives associated with the Teller Amendment are questioned in Paul S. Holbo, 'The Convergence of Moods and the Cuban-Bond "Conspiracy" of 1898', *Journal of American History* 55 (1968), pp. 54–72.

45 *The Times* (London), 21 April 1898.

on 21 April, General Blanco told a large crowd of loyalists that approaching American warships would be 'hurled back into the sea'.[46] That same day in Madrid, Woodford was informed officially that Spain was breaking off diplomatic relations in retaliation against what it considered was America's 'evident declaration of war'.[47] The diplomatic formalities were eventually concluded on 25 April by the passage of a Congressional resolution declaring retrospectively that a state of war had existed between the United States and Spain since 21 April. It was an outcome which neither side had wished. Spain had become locked into a colonial war of attrition with a resolute enemy whom it could neither destroy nor force into negotiations to stop the fighting. Both Cleveland and McKinley had sincerely worked for peace, but their policy of exerting diplomatic pressure on Madrid had eventually collapsed in the face of Spain's inability to abandon its most valuable colonial possession.

---

46 Ibid., 23 April 1898.
47 Woodford to Sherman, 21 April 1898, *FRUS* (1898), p. 767.

3 MILITARY PREPAREDNESS

THE OPPOSING MILITARY FORCES

The declaration of war was greeted in both the United States and Spain with rousing patriotic speeches, marches, the ringing of church bells and waving of flags. However, the transatlantic battle of words over the rights and wrongs of Spanish rule in Cuba had paid minimal attention to exactly what type of war would be fought between two countries, who were not only geographically separated by 3,000 miles of ocean but were also ill-prepared for conflict with each other. In terms of population, wealth and industrial prowess, the United States was clearly the stronger nation. 'Spain is a third-rate and declining power; we are one of the mightiest in the world,' proclaimed a typically confident American view.[1] However, when translated into actual military capability and combat experience, American claims to great power status appeared much more potential rather than real. Indeed, a review of the contending forces at the outbreak of hostilities in April 1898 suggested that Spain was by no means decisively outmatched. 'I am afraid the United States are a little inclined to underrate the strength of their enemy,' noted the Havana Special Correspondent of *The Times*, and he warned that 'this tendency may prove a costly mistake if persevered in'.[2]

Contemporary military estimates varied, but it was believed that Spain had more than 400,000 men under arms. The Spanish army was therefore greatly superior in numbers to that of the United States, which listed merely 28,000. However, the Spanish forces were widely dispersed. About half the army remained permanently in Spain while the other half served overseas. Although a sizeable garrison of up to 30,000 was based in the Philippines, the biggest

---

1 *The Nation* (New York), 21 April 1898.
2 *The Times* (London), 25 April 1898.

drain on manpower was the war in Cuba. It was reckoned in April 1898 that Spain had almost 150,000 regular soldiers in Cuba and could summon the assistance of 50,000 loyalist volunteers. Of the regular troops in Cuba, 40,000 were stationed in or close to the city of Havana, up to 20,000 in Matanzas and more than 30,000 in Oriente. The neighbouring island of Puerto Rico was held by a garrison of 8,000. The deployment of Spanish troops in Cuba appeared impressive on paper, but was specifically designed to suppress domestic rebellion rather than combat a large invading army from overseas. Moreover, military effectiveness was severely restricted by poor communications, low morale, the lack of food and especially the incidence of disease. The Spanish forces also had to contend with constant pressure from the insurgents who numbered in excess of 30,000 guerrilla fighters and in 1898 exercised virtual control of the countryside in the eastern half of the island.

Separated into numerous small posts spread out over the continental United States and numbering no more than a total listed peacetime strength of 28,000 officers and enlisted men, the American army could do essentially little to change the military balance of forces in Cuba. The numbers were relatively tiny for such a large and populated country because Americans were traditionally opposed to maintaining large standing armies. The latter were considered expensive and a threat to democracy. Furthermore, the preference for a small army was facilitated and justified by the good fortune which Americans historically enjoyed in facing weak neighbours to the north and the south and being protected by vast oceans to the east and west. Such favourable conditions also rendered it unnecessary for War Department officials and American army officers to concern themselves with detailed strategic planning against possible future enemies. In the extremely unlikely event of an external invasion of the United States, it was confidently assumed that the regular army would be quickly enlarged by men drawn from the existing state militias. In 1898 these forces, based upon the individual states of the Union and collectively known as the 'National Guard', were estimated to contain more than 100,000 soldiers. The guardsmen were volunteer reservists who generally suffered from a severe lack of up-to-date equipment, training and experience of combat. Nevertheless, they provided the personnel from which the War Department and the American army could readily mobilize a powerful force to defend the national territory. But fighting overseas was a very different matter. In this respect the American experience was markedly different from that of a colonial

49

power like Spain. With the exception of the Mexican War (1846–48), the contingency involving the despatch of substantial American forces for combat duty overseas had never been given serious consideration by American political and military leaders. The subject also held little appeal to army officers, who realized that the logistics of campaigning overseas would require the army to play a subordinate role to the navy. Consequently, the outbreak of war with a maritime power such as Spain highlighted the role of the American navy as the initial military strike force of the United States.

At the commencement of hostilities in April 1898 the United States government could call on a respectable naval force consisting of at least a dozen modern well-armed warships and more than fifty smaller vessels ranging from light cruisers to gunboats and yachts. Only fifteen years earlier, however, the American navy had been woefully ill-prepared for war. 'An alphabet of floating washtubs' was one Congressman's description in 1883.[3] But public and Congressional attitudes markedly changed during the last two decades of the nineteenth century. One reason was the influence of Captain Alfred Thayer Mahan, whose seminal work, *The Influence of Sea Power on History, 1660–1783*, was published in 1890. Mahan's writings emphasized the strategic and commercial necessity of building up a powerful American navy. At the same time there was also growing public awareness that the great powers of Europe were implementing significant changes in naval design and technology. Notably, Britain and France were constructing formidable battleships armed with increasingly powerful guns and protected from bombardment by ever thicker belts of steel. In response to these developments Congress reversed its traditionally parsimonious attitude to naval spending and voted appropriations in 1883 for the construction of four new cruisers whose decks would be protected with steel armour. This initiative established the basis of what would become known as 'the new American navy'. In 1886 orders were placed for the *Maine* and *Texas* – the first American battleships. Additional appropriations were voted in 1890 for the construction of three '*Indiana* class' battleships which were intended to be the equal of the most powerful ships then afloat. Funds for an even larger battleship – the *Iowa* – were approved by Congress in 1892.

3 *The remark of Congressman John D. Long, cited in Robert Seager II, 'Ten Years Before Mahan', Mississippi Valley Historical Review 40 (1953), p. 497.*

American battleships were built in the United States and were named after states of the Union so that each ship became a source of not only national but also local pride. Renowned for their size and armament, both the *Maine* and *Texas* weighed over 6,000 tons and cost in excess of $2 million each. They were equipped with a variety of rifles and guns, including two massive 12-inch guns fired from revolving turrets. But technological developments were so rapid that both ships were rated as 'second-class' by the time they eventually came into service in 1895. The *Maine* and *Texas* were therefore almost immediately superseded in 1896 by the three *Indiana* class ships comprising the *Indiana*, *Massachusetts* and *Oregon*. Each of the latter displaced more than 10,000 tons and could reach a maximum speed of 14 knots. They were recognized as 'first-class' battleships, equivalent in structure and firepower to the impressive *Majestic* class of the British navy. Protected on the sides by belts of nickel-steel armoured plate up to 18 inches thick, the *Indiana* class battleship possessed a variety of heavy guns fired from six revolving turrets. However, the *Iowa* was even bigger and cost more than $5 million to construct. She weighed over 11,000 tons and boasted greater firepower than any other current American warship. The entry of the *Iowa* into service in 1897 meant that the United States possessed four first-class battleships and two of the second-class, and was accordingly ranked as the sixth most powerful battleship navy in the world. The destruction of the *Maine* in February 1898 reduced the number of second-class ships to one.

In addition to the battleships, the American navy contained an assortment of armoured cruisers of which the most impressive were the *New York* and *Brooklyn*. They both displaced more than 8,000 tons and with rated speeds in excess of 21 knots were much faster than the battleships. Each ship had steel plate on the sides and deck and possessed a range of weapons including 8-inch guns. The fleet also contained several 'protected' cruisers which differed from the *New York* and *Brooklyn* in having armour mainly covering the deck and not the sides. The best of these ships was considered to be the *Olympia*, which was not only well armed but could also attain an impressive maximum speed of up to 22 knots. Others in order of displacement were the *Columbia, Minneapolis, Baltimore, Philadelphia, Newark, San Francisco, Charleston, New Orleans, Cincinnati, Raleigh* and *Boston*. Older and less mobile than the cruisers were six ironclad monitors – the *Amphitrite, Miantonomoh, Monadnock, Monterey, Puritan* and *Terror*. Equipped with heavy guns firing from double turrets, the monitor had been the pride of the American navy during the Civil War. However, these ships were at their best in defensive rather than offensive operations. They were slow of speed and were notoriously difficult to handle in the open sea, especially when the weather was rough. The remainder of the Navy List was made up of more than fifty 'unprotected' vessels, including single-turreted monitors, light cruisers, gunboats, tugs, colliers and yachts. Several of these ships dated from the Civil War and were notably lacking in firepower and armour. Quite ill-suited for direct combat against a modern battleship or cruiser, their role would be to undertake the little-noticed but indispensable task of assisting and supplying the warships.[4]

For a nation whose imperial possessions spanned the world it was not surprising that the Spanish navy was larger in total numbers than that of the United States. However, in marked contrast to the latter, Spain chose to spend much more money on the army than the navy so that the majority of its ships were small, old in design and notably lacking the protection of armour plating. More significantly, while the United States possessed four first-class battleships, Spain could claim only two – the *Pelayo* and *Carlos V*. The *Pelayo* had been designed and built in Toulon, France. She displaced almost 10,000 tons and was protected by a steel belt 16 inches thick. Her substantial armament extended up to two 12.5-inch guns. The *Pelayo* was the pride of the Spanish navy, but she had been in service for almost a decade so that there was some doubt as to whether she might still be regarded as a 'first-class battleship'. Moreover, in 1897 she had returned to Toulon for extensive reconstruction and refitting. The opinion of American naval experts was that the *Pelayo* was superior to the *Texas* but inferior to the *Indiana* class. Despite the claims of the Spanish Navy List, it was widely acknowledged, however, that the *Carlos V* was definitely 'second-class'. In fact, the ship had only been launched in 1895 and had not yet officially entered service. Although she displaced an impressive 9,000 tons and had a rated speed of 20 knots, the *Carlos V* had an armoured belt only 2 to 6 inches thick and her heaviest armament was a 10-inch gun. In terms of the American fleet, a more accurate comparison would be with the armoured cruisers *New York* or *Brooklyn*.

---

4 The American naval forces are described in French E. Chadwick, *The Relations of the United States and Spain: The Spanish American War* (3 vols; London, 1911), vol. ii pp. 28–33.

Although the Spanish navy was clearly inferior to the American navy in the number of first-class battleships, this was offset by its apparent superiority in armoured cruisers. The United States listed two such ships, while Spain claimed at least five. These included the three sister ships which had been built at Bilbao – the *Oquendo*, *Vizcaya*, and *María Teresa*. In addition there was the *Cristóbal Colón*, a *Garibaldi* class armoured cruiser which had been purchased from Italy in 1897, and the *Princesa de Asturias*, which had been launched in 1896 but was not yet ready for service. Lighter than their American counterparts, the *New York* and *Brooklyn*, the Spanish cruisers were more similar in displacement and firepower to a second-class battleship like the *Texas*. Their signal advantage over the latter was speed. Although the *Texas* had a rated speed of 17 knots, the Spanish cruisers were considered capable of exceeding 20 knots. American officers were particularly impressed by reports circulated about the *Cristóbal Colón*. Recently built at Genoa, Italy, she was reputed to be faster and more heavily armed than any of the Spanish or American armoured cruisers.[5] The strategic thinking of the day suggested that Spain would form the five cruisers into a 'fleet in being' whose speed and mobility would outmanoeuvre the slower enemy battleships and, consequently, seriously disrupt and stretch American naval resources and strategy. It was a contingency which was taken very seriously in the United States. Admiral Sampson, the commander of the North Atlantic Squadron, sincerely believed that the Spanish squadron was 'the fastest in the world'.[6]

Another American cause of concern was the torpedo, which was fast being developed as a potent weapon for use against the modern battleship. While the United States had been concentrating on building bigger and more powerful battleships, it was known that Spain had been deliberately acquiring torpedo gunboats and torpedo-boat destroyers. By 1898 Spain had thirteen such ships; the American navy had none in the equivalent class. The most impressive were the destroyers – *Plutón*, *Furor* and *Terror* – which had been constructed as recently as 1896 and 1897. These British-built ships were believed to have the ability to reach speeds of up to 30 knots. Their preferred plan of action was to approach enemy ships under cover of darkness and to launch torpedoes from a

5 The Spanish naval forces are described in ibid., pp. 33–6.
6 William T. Sampson, 'The Atlantic Fleet in the Spanish War', *The Century Magazine* 57 (April, 1899), p. 889.

distance ranging from one-quarter to half a mile. The enemy would be forced either to keep its important ships out of danger or to set up a protective cordon of lighter vessels. In the case of a war with the United States, by threatening to negate America's superiority over Spain in powerful armoured ships, the torpedo was a potential 'thorn in the side of a blockading force' and cast considerable uncertainty over the outcome of the forthcoming naval battle between the two nations.[7]

AMERICAN MILITARY PREPARATIONS

To achieve its declared war aim of liberating Cuba, the United States had essentially to secure the surrender and evacuation of the Spanish forces from the island. There was no perceived need or intention to invade Spain. The limited nature of the war was summed up in the popular slogan of 'on to Havana', which implied that American troops would soon be landed in Cuba to seize the Cuban capital. In reality, such optimism was quite unfounded, because the American army initially lacked the means to launch a successful armed invasion against entrenched defensive forces numbering several thousand men. Consequently, the first direct clash between Americans and Spaniards came at sea rather than on land. Indeed, the battle at sea held crucial significance. Without naval superiority the United States could not easily land troops in Cuba or give significant material support to the insurgents. Both sides recognized that whoever commanded the waters around Cuba would dictate the course of the war and must ultimately emerge as the victor.

While the American army was unprepared for a foreign war, the 'new American navy' was ready for immediate deployment. In contrast to the duties of the land-locked army, service in the navy regularly featured travelling overseas to show the flag and even the occasional enforcement of 'gunboat diplomacy' in distant parts of the world. Moreover, the gradual dissemination of Mahan's ideas had accustomed a new generation of American naval officers to consider how the exercise of seapower could promote the national interest of the United States. In fact, the contingency of war with Spain had been a subject of frequent discussion at the Naval War College in Newport, Rhode Island. Since 1895 a succession of secret

7 *The Times* (London), 14 April 1898.

'War Plans' had been produced which predicted with some accuracy how events would unfold in 1898. The resulting 'War Plan', which is usually attributed to the work of Lieutenant William Warren Kimball, envisaged American naval forces quickly exploiting their advantages of geographical proximity and numerical superiority in warships to mount a blockade of Cuba and Puerto Rico. Separate naval raids would also be launched against Spanish merchant shipping and military targets on the coasts of Spain, the Canaries and the Philippines. The purpose of such actions was not to land troops or seize territory but to harass, divert and destroy Spanish forces and military resources. In conjunction with these naval activities there would be an armed assault upon Havana, though it was usually assumed that most of the fighting on land would be undertaken by the Cuban insurgents rather than the American army. According to the strategic thinking of the day, Spain must eventually respond by sending a fleet of its big armoured ships to attempt to lift the American blockade and win command of the seas. At all times, the American navy would hold itself ready for the arrival from Europe of the Spanish navy, knowing that the ensuing battle of the fleets would decide the outcome of the war.

So long as Cleveland and McKinley sought a diplomatic resolution to the Cuban question, 'war planning' remained an academic exercise. In fact, it was not until the Havana riots of January 1898 that officials of the Navy Department in Washington seriously began to consider the probability of war with Spain. During that month the battleships of the North Atlantic Squadron, comprising the *Iowa*, *Massachusetts*, *Indiana* and *Texas*, were sent to the Gulf of Florida for winter drills. Although the navy was long accustomed to making regular use of this warm water area, the drills had been conducted in the more distant North Atlantic during the two previous winters mainly to avoid inflaming the already contentious issue of American maritime neutrality. While the Navy Department publicly denied that the change of location in January 1898 had any aggressive intent towards Spain, confidential telegrams were later sent to the commanders of all American warships in the Atlantic and Pacific informing them of the disturbed conditions in Cuba. Since war would require the concentration of the bulk of the fleet in home waters, it was considered particularly important by officials in Washington that ships not stray too far away from the likely area of conflict. Officers in command were also requested to maintain their ships and crews at a high level of readiness.

The shock sinking of the *Maine* in February provided the

necessary impetus to further action. The *Oregon*, the only first-class battleship which was not currently in Atlantic waters, was ordered to proceed from Washington state to San Francisco and then on to Callao, Peru. On reaching Peru in early April the *Oregon* was instructed to leave for Rio de Janeiro, Brazil. The battleship thereby embarked on an arduous 16,000-mile voyage via Cape Horn that would last two entire months. However, the withdrawal of the *Oregon* from the Pacific did not rule out implementation of the two-ocean offensive strategy outlined in the War Plan. On 25 February, Assistant Secretary of the Navy Theodore Roosevelt had instructed the Asiatic Squadron under the command of Commodore George Dewey to set out from Japan for Hong Kong. This would bring the squadron within 600 miles of Manila. Should war break out, the repositioning would enable Dewey to pose a direct military threat to the Philippines and consequently serve to distract Spanish naval forces from attacking American merchant shipping or possibly launching a raid against the west coast of the United States.

In addition to the measured strategic redeployment, the Navy Department sought to increase the size of the fleet by purchasing and chartering extra ships ranging from warships to transports. The funds were provided from the $50 million emergency national defence appropriation voted by Congress in March 1898. The most notable *coup* for the United States was the arrangement with Brazil by which that country sold two protected cruisers, the *New Orleans* and *Albany*, which were nearing completion on the Tyne in England. In fact, during the period from March to August 1898, 102 ships were added to the American fleet at a cost of more than $21 million. The total number of naval personnel was also doubled, rising from almost 13,000 to more than 26,000 officers and enlisted men.[8]

The formulation of overall strategy was facilitated by the establishment in March 1898 of the Naval War Board headed by Assistant Secretary of the Navy Theodore Roosevelt and including Captain Arent S. Crowninshield, the Chief of the Bureau of Navigation, and two senior naval officers, one of whom would later be Captain Mahan. The War Board discussed various battle plans in secret session and presented its recommendations to Secretary of the Navy John D. Long. While Congress debated the War Resolution in

8 See Charles O. Paullin, 'A Half Century of Naval Administration in America, 1861–1911', *United States Naval Institute Proceedings* 40 (1914), pp. 419–20, 426.

mid-April, Long possessed therefore the necessary information and detailed planning to issue instructions organizing the navy into battle formation. Despite the public rumours of impending vigorous action to drive the Spanish navy from Cuba, the actual deployment was more defensive than offensive. This was the direct result of the sudden alarm emerging among the residents along the eastern seaboard of the United States that war would expose their homes, property and lives to surprise raids and bombardment by the reputedly fast and elusive Spanish armoured cruisers. Even the nation's capital at Washington was believed to be virtually defenceless, just as it had been in 1814 when the British had burned the White House. However, during March the army had already started work under the $50 million emergency appropriation to strengthen existing coastal fortifications and to construct new defences. Military garrisons in the East had also been increased in size. But the navy was naturally regarded as the vital first line of defence. Accordingly, a Northern Patrol Squadron consisting of five cruisers under the command of Commodore John A. Howell was set up on 20 April to patrol the coastline between the Delaware Capes and Bar Harbor, Maine. Additional assistance with coastal defence was provided by various small craft and auxiliary vessels including the stationing of some of the older single-turreted monitors at the larger ports. These ships were operated close to shore by naval militiamen and were somewhat dismissively referred to as the 'Mosquito Squadron'.

The diversion of vessels to patrol duty was inconvenient but hardly momentous. Of much more significant strategic impact was the decision to split the main Atlantic fleet into two. In response to insistent appeals from the public and their representatives in Congress that powerful warships remain close to shore in case the Spaniards appeared, a 'Flying Squadron' of several armoured ships was stationed at Hampton Roads, Virginia. The squadron, commanded by Commodore Winfield Scott Schley, included the battleships *Massachusetts* and *Texas*, the armoured cruiser *Brooklyn*, and the protected cruisers, *Columbia* and *Minneapolis*. Schley's primary task was to help allay public anxieties by protecting the east coast from Spanish attack. The detachment of the Flying Squadron considerably reduced the overall strength of the main battle fleet, but this was partly offset by its positioning at Hampton Roads rather than New York, which meant that it remained within a few days' sailing of the Caribbean. This would allow Schley the flexibility to 'fly' south and join the main American fleet in the

Caribbean Sea should the expected great battle with the Spanish fleet be in the offing. Although subordinate in rank to Sampson, Schley enjoyed an independent command. For example, if circumstances warranted, he had the authority to move eastwards across the Atlantic and strike directly at the Spanish coast.

The rest of the North Atlantic Squadron was based at Key West, which had now become the principal headquarters of the battle fleet. Its most powerful ships were the battleships *Iowa* and *Indiana*, the armoured cruiser and flagship *New York*, three armoured monitors, the *Terror*, *Amphitrite* and *Puritan*, three unprotected cruisers, the *Cincinnati*, *Detroit* and *Marblehead* and a dozen small gunboats and torpedo boats. A change of commander-in-chief was effected prior to the war when Rear-Admiral Montgomery Sicard retired due to ill-health on 26 March and was replaced by Captain William T. Sampson. Despite the fact that Sampson had been promoted over a number of more senior officers, Secretary of the Navy Long had no doubt of the significance and suitability of the appointment:

> The moment required a man of splendid judgment, quick decision, possessing intimate knowledge of the characteristics of the vessels he would have to use, and the officers and men manning them, and enjoying the esteem and confidence of his subordinates. The consensus of naval opinion was that Sampson had these qualifications ... He enjoyed the full confidence not only of the officers and men of his own ship, but of the officers and men of the entire navy.[9]

Sampson's initial orders were to maintain his ships well-stocked with coal, ammunition and provisions, and his crews at a high level of readiness. Should war be declared he was to institute an immediate blockade of Cuba and Puerto Rico and capture or destroy any enemy ships which were encountered in Caribbean waters.

The Naval War Board also endorsed the strategy of striking at Spain's imperial possessions in the Pacific. This would be the task of the Asiatic Squadron commanded by Commodore George Dewey and consisting of four vessels – the protected cruiser *Olympia*, the unprotected cruiser *Boston* and two gunboats, the *Concord* and *Petrel*. At Hong Kong Dewey acquired a Revenue Service cutter, the *McCulloch*, and two British colliers. On 22 April the squadron was

---

9 Cited in Chadwick, *United States and Spain*, vol. ii, pp. 20–1.

further strengthened by the addition of the protected cruisers *Raleigh* and *Baltimore*. The latter's arrival from Honolulu had been eagerly anticipated because she contained a large quantity of ammunition. Dewey's instructions were also confirmed that he should prepare to attack the Spanish ships at Manila and thereby establish a base from which the Asiatic Squadron could protect American shipping operating in the Pacific.

As the various elements of the War Plan began to be put into place, the calculations of officials at Washington received a jolt not from Spain but from the new American commander-in-chief. Influenced by Farragut's surprise attack on New Orleans during the Civil War in 1862, Sampson proposed that his first act of war should be a similar daring raid on Havana. From intelligence reports and personal knowledge gained from his recent residence in Havana as chairman of the commission of inquiry into the sinking of the *Maine*, he was confident that the city would surrender with little resistance. Havana was important because it was the centre and symbol of Spanish power in Cuba. A successful attack would most likely bring a speedy end to the war and thereby render further military operations unnecessary.

Two prime considerations, however, led the Navy Department to veto Sampson's proposal. First, was the strongly held conviction that a major sea battle would eventually take place between the American and Spanish fleets so that, in the meantime, precious armoured vessels should not be risked against Havana's artillery batteries and the underwater mines and torpedoes known to be placed at the entrance to the harbour. As Mahan later noted, 'no merely possible success justified risk, unless it gave a fair promise of diminishing the enemy's naval force, and so of deciding the control of the sea, upon which the issue of the war depended'.[10] Secondly, the success of the raid ultimately depended upon the landing of American troops to occupy and secure the city. Secretary of the Navy Long admitted, however, that it was unlikely that troops would be available until October. Sampson was disappointed at the rejection of a plan of which he had 'little doubt' would be successful.[11] Nevertheless, he fully accepted the logic of mounting a blockade. By depriving the Spanish forces not only of supplies of food but also reinforcements from Spain, a blockade might well be

10 Alfred T. Mahan, *Lessons of the War with Spain, and Other Articles* (Boston, 1899), p. 32.

11 Sampson to Long, 9 April 1898, cited in Chadwick, *United States and Spain*, vol. ii, p. 75.

sufficient to compel the Spaniards to surrender within a few months, if not weeks, and, it was hoped, before the end of the rainy season in October. Even if the blockade was not entirely successful, it would allow the American army time to organize an expeditionary force. On 9 April Sampson informed Long that his own preparations at Key West were going well and that 'There will be no delay in moving when the order comes'.[12] The confidence of President McKinley and the Navy Department in their commander was duly illustrated when he was promoted to the navy's highest rank, rear-admiral, on 21 April.

The build-up of the American navy during the 1880s and 1890s was not paralleled by a similar increase in the strength of the army. The construction of warships was not only beneficial for national security reasons but it also brought considerable political and economic gains for Congressmen who represented dockyards, iron and steel factories and munitions suppliers. The army had few such lucrative 'spoils' to offer and, consequently, was treated much less favourably by the politicians in Congress. Moreover, until 1898 there was little requirement or incentive for the army to undertake serious preparation for war. Cleveland and McKinley both sought a diplomatic solution to the Cuban question and studiously avoided extensive military preparations so as not to provoke Spain. Even if war should result, the army was unsure as to its exact mission. Although coastal defence was an obvious responsibility, the demands of this duty would be limited because army officers automatically assumed that the territory of the United States would not be in danger of an invasion by Spain. However, the securing of control over Cuba was likely to compel the army to adopt an unaccustomed offensive strategy. An additional complication would be the need to cooperate closely with the navy in order to transport troops overseas. However, if the strategy was pursued of emphasizing the combat role of the Cuban insurgents, the army might even be able to avoid having to undertake a major overseas military campaign.

The problem of preparing for possible war was further compounded by the longstanding administrative rivalry between the War Department and the army. The civilian officials of the War Department staffed and headed various bureaux which were in charge of spending and organizing supplies on behalf of the army. The army officers traditionally concerned themselves with issuing military orders to troops in the field. But the exact demarcation of

12 Ibid.

responsibilities was uncertain and frequently subject to conflict. During the McKinley administration, the underlying rivalry was exacerbated by the awkward personal relationship between Secretary of War Russell A. Alger and the Commanding General of the Army, Major General Nelson A. Miles. Both Alger and Miles were notoriously vain. Whereas Alger was cautious and slow to act, Miles was impulsive and opinionated. The general had a national reputation as a courageous 'Indian-fighter', but to Theodore Roosevelt he was merely a 'brave peacock'.[13] It was hardly surprising, therefore, that the War Department lagged far behind the Navy Department in preparing for the contingency of war with Spain. Moreover, while the navy was able to emulate the great European powers in parading battleships which were the equal of any in the world, the army was minuscule in comparison to the large standing forces of continental Europe and was clearly backward in size, equipment, general staff organization and combat experience.

Disorganized and lacking a coherent War Plan, the army appeared to be drifting at the mercy of events. As the likelihood of war with Spain loomed closer, a meeting of senior army and naval officers at Washington on 4 April confirmed that the principal role in the fighting would be assumed by the navy. Army officers agreed that the first step would be the mounting of a naval blockade. However, they were much less certain as to when, where and how American troops would attack Spanish forces in Cuba. Indeed, a major invasion was regarded as unnecessary because the decisive battles were expected to occur at sea. An important consideration was the determination not to expose unacclimatized American troops to the many deadly tropical diseases which were endemic in Cuba during the rainy season. Instead, the army preferred a limited role in the actual fighting and proposed the landing of a small number of soldiers to seize beachheads, most likely in Oriente, from which supplies could be directed speedily and efficiently to the insurgents. However, mindful of the public pressure for quick action and the possibility that the President might request an armed invasion, the officers felt compelled to discuss the feasibility of an attack on Havana. Army officers reckoned that this action would require 50,000 troops. They were more inclined to favour an attack on the smaller and less well-defended Spanish bases in Puerto Rico.

13 Cited in Edward Ranson, 'Nelson A. Miles as Commanding General, 1895–1903', *Military Affairs* 29 (1965–66), p. 181.

In the meantime, little substantive was being done to prepare the army for war. Part of the explanation for this was Alger's belief that the small-scale overseas operations which were being planned would require only a relatively modest increase in the size of the regular army. The major drain on manpower would come from the need to provide coastal defence, but this would be easily met by drawing 50,000 volunteers from the National Guard. Indeed, Alger was very conscious of protecting the coastline, and had narrowly interpreted the purpose of the $50 million emergency appropriation so that the bulk of the War Department's funds were devoted solely to 'national defence'. Millions of dollars were subsequently spent on strengthening coastal fortifications, but nothing was done 'in the way of accumulating material for offensive war'.[14] One example which later attracted criticism was the inadequate provision of rifles. The .30 calibre Krag-Jörgensen rifle, which originated from Denmark, was regarded as currently the best weapon for infantry duty and had only been introduced into service in 1893. But the 'Krag' and its smokeless ammunition were in such short supply that their distribution had to be restricted to the regular soldiers. Volunteers would be equipped with the older and less reliable .45 calibre Springfield rifle.

However, the movement of troops was subject to less bureaucratic constraint. While Congress debated the War Resolution, Alger sought to assemble the various detachments of the regular army. On 15 April twenty-two infantry regiments were ordered to the Gulf ports of New Orleans, Mobile and Tampa while six cavalry regiments were despatched to Camp Thomas, Tennessee, which lay within Chickamauga Park. The locations in the Southern states were chosen because of their proximity to Cuba and reputedly good railway connections within the United States. In addition, they possessed a warm climate which was not only very suitable for training purposes but also would help to acclimatize the men for service in Cuba. During the following weeks, for logistical reasons it was decided to transfer troops from Mobile and New Orleans to Chickamauga Park and Tampa, which accordingly became the two main assembly points.

The passage by Congress of the War Resolution on 19 April revived discussion of when and where the United States would attack Cuba. Secretary of War Alger was typically complacent, and implied in his meetings with the President and the press that a large

---

14 Russell A. Alger, *The Spanish-American War* (New York, 1901), p. 9.

army could quickly be put into the field. He stated that the regular forces were currently being mobilized for action and he was awaiting the President's official call for volunteers. This could only be done legally after a formal Congressional declaration of war. However, General Miles presented a conflicting viewpoint. On 20 April at a special council of war meeting at the White House, Miles disclosed that it would take at least two months to organize a credible American expeditionary force. Furthermore, he doubted the wisdom of mounting a large-scale invasion because of the threat of disease and the large numbers of Spanish forces already well-entrenched in defensive positions on the island. He was also concerned that the safe transport of his troops could not be guaranteed until the American navy had secured complete command of the seas by destroying the enemy navy. Echoing the views of the Naval War Plan, Miles had earlier written to Alger that 'by using such force as might be necessary to harass the enemy, and doing them the greatest injury with the least possible loss to ourselves, if our Navy is superior to theirs, we can compel the surrender of the [Spanish] army on the island of Cuba with very little loss of life'.[15] Secretary of the Navy Long grasped the opportunity to flaunt the superiority of the navy over the army. 'It seems', he remarked, 'as if the Army were ready for nothing at all.'[16] Although the navy would have to assume the initial operational burden, McKinley was insistent that the army prepare itself for fighting a major overseas campaign. This was demonstrated on 23 April when he issued the first call for 125,000 volunteers to join the army. Alger and his officials at the War Department turned their energies therefore to the huge task of transforming what had been a tiny peacetime force of regulars into a massive army consisting mostly of volunteer citizen-soldiers.

SPANISH MILITARY PREPARATIONS

From its formation in October 1897 the Sagasta administration became increasingly troubled by the problem of how to avoid war with the United States over the Cuban question. Although this

15 Miles to Alger, 18 April 1898, cited in Nelson A. Miles, 'The War With Spain', *North American Review* 168 (May, 1899), p. 523.
16 Long's diary entry of 20 April 1898, cited in Lawrence S. Mayo, ed., *America of Yesterday as Reflected in the Journal of John Davis Long* (Boston, 1923), p. 183.

development was not entirely unexpected, no real attempt was made to formulate strategic planning for possible hostilities against the Americans. Spanish political leaders simply hoped that war would not occur. Indeed, any extension to the fighting in Cuba was extremely undesirable because Spain's military resources were already being stretched to the limit. Few fresh troops were available for overseas duty. Even before the sinking of the *Maine* the Spanish government had virtually ceased to send out additional reinforcements to Cuba. However, should war break out with the United States, the despatch of extra troops would not make much material difference because there were already 150,000 Spanish regulars on the island. On paper, this was a more than adequate number to defend the principal cities and ports against an external assault. Up to 40,000 regular soldiers were concentrated around Havana, which was regarded as the most probable first point of attack by the Americans. Steps were also undertaken from March 1898 onwards to strengthen fortifications and land batteries facing the sea, erect searchlights to assist the artillery, and place torpedoes and mines at the entrance to the harbour. 'The Spaniards', reported Reuters news agency on 22 April, 'are confident that Havana is prepared for any eventuality, and have great faith in the strength of their forts and batteries, as well as in the effectiveness of their heavy artillery.'[17] Ironically, stronger defences meant that the Americans would be much more likely to mount a naval blockade than launch an armed invasion. The critical test, therefore, was how long the city could hold out against an effective blockade. Local authorities estimated that existing stocks of food would start to run short after two months. Few additional supplies could be expected from a countryside devastated by three years of guerrilla warfare. Consequently, Spanish hopes of ultimate success rested on the performance of their navy and its ability to break the American blockade and gain command of the seas.

On paper, the Spanish navy was an impressive fighting force and was widely regarded as the equal of the American navy. In reality, however, the majority of Spain's warships were in a sorry state. This was readily apparent to Admiral Pascual Cervera y Topete, who had been selected in October 1897 to command the main Spanish naval squadron based at Cartagena and Cádiz. Cervera succeeded Admiral Segismundo Bermejo on the latter's appointment to the post of Minister of the Marine [Navy] in

17 *The Times* (London), 25 April 1898.

Sagasta's government. The new commander's long and distinguished naval career spanned almost half a century and included service in the Caribbean during the Ten Years' War. Despite his undoubted dedication to the navy and the service of his Queen and country, Cervera personally believed that Spain had effectively lost the military struggle in Cuba and should abandon the island rather than go to war with the United States. In his opinion, the contest was so unequal that it could only result in disaster for Spain. He privately told his cousin in January 1898 that even the recent acquisition of the *Cristóbal Colón* and three torpedo-boat destroyers from England could not compare with the much more formidable build-up of the American navy. 'The relative military positions of Spain and the United States', he lamented, 'have grown worse for us, because we are reduced, absolutely penniless, and they are very rich.'[18] Moreover, he was only too well aware of the many deficiencies in the fleet under his command. Almost every ship, from the *Pelayo* and *Carlos V* down to the smallest cruiser, was urgently in need of repair, and it was extremely doubtful whether all would be ready for service by the spring. A stream of letters and telegrams sent by Cervera to Bermejo listed the serious inadequacies of the weapons systems, the shortage of coal and provisions of every kind, and even the lack of basic navigational items such as charts and maps'.[19]

Cervera was also anxious to know the specific military objectives and tactics which the government at Madrid would want him to pursue. In contrast to the United States, no Spanish 'war plans' were in existence. Indeed, nothing substantive was revealed until 15 February 1898, when Bermejo informed Cervera of the Ministry of the Marine's 'preliminary plan' to split the navy into 'two centres of resistance'. The simplistic scheme divided the navy into defensive and offensive sections. A small number of cruisers and light vessels would stay near Cádiz to protect the Spanish coastline. The bulk of the navy, however, would be sent to Cuba. This squadron would consist of the navy's finest ships, including the battleship *Pelayo*, the five armoured cruisers, the *Carlos V*, *Cristóbal Colón*, *María Teresa* and the *Vizcaya* and *Oquendo*, both of which were at that time in Havana, plus the best three destroyers and three torpedo-boats. Linking up with various other 'larger vessels' already

18 Cervera to Spottorno, 30 January 1898, cited in Chadwick, *United States and Spain*, vol. ii p. 95.
19 For example, see Cervera to Bermejo, 6 February 1898, cited in ibid., vol. ii p. 96.

at Havana, Cervera would aim first at destroying the American naval base at Key West. Once this particular object was achieved, the Spanish squadron would secure command of the seas and establish a blockade of the Atlantic coastline, thereby severing American communications and trade with Europe.[20]

A dumbfounded Cervera replied almost immediately that the naval forces assigned to his command were three times proportionately weaker than those of the United States. 'It therefore seems to me, a dream, almost a feverish fancy', he argued, 'to think that with this force, attenuated by our long wars, we can establish the blockade of any port of the United States.'[21] He did not rule out the possibility of launching raids against American merchant shipping with his fastest ships. However, a major naval battle would be ruinous. Even if his squadron was somehow successful, he noted that it would not have recourse to adequate local dockyard facilities and materials to repair and refit. By contrast, the Americans enjoyed fine harbours and abundant supplies. In similar vein one week later, Cervera pointed out to Bermejo that the displacement of the Spanish navy was 56,644 tons against the equivalent American figure of 116,445 tons. The total firepower of the Spanish ships was only 40 per cent of the armament of the American fleet. In fact, Cervera stressed that the disparities were actually greater because his statistics included the *Pelayo* and *Carlos V*, both of which he believed would not be available for service within the near future. With such inadequate resources at his disposal, Cervera concluded that he could neither conduct an effective offensive campaign nor could he hope to win command of the sea.[22] He wrote frankly to Bermejo on 26 February:

> Do we not owe to our country not only our life, if necessary, but the exposition of our beliefs? I am very uneasy about this. I ask myself if it is right for me to keep silent, make myself an accomplice in adventures which will surely cause the total ruin of Spain. And for what purpose? To defend an island which was ours, but belongs to us no more, because even if we did not lose it by right in the war we have lost it in fact, and with it all our

20 Bermejo to Cervera, 15 February 1898, cited in ibid., vol. ii p. 98. The reference to 'two centres of resistance' appears later in Bermejo's letter dated 23 February, cited in ibid., vol. ii p. 100.

21 Cervera to Bermejo, 16 February 1898, cited in ibid., vol. ii pp. 98–9.

22 Cervera to Bermejo, 23 February 1898, cited in ibid., vol. ii pp. 100–1.

wealth and an enormous number of young men, victims of the climate and the bullets, in the defence of what is no more than a romantic idea.[23]

Bermejo admitted on 4 March that Cervera's candour had caused a 'painful impression'. While acknowledging the admiral's patriotism and good intentions, he was determined, however, to assert his ministerial authority. On the fundamental issue, therefore, Bermejo stated categorically that the government would not abandon its Cuban colony. Nor was he prepared to accept Cervera's defeatist rationale. He regarded the admiral's estimate of America's superior naval strength as flawed because it did not take into account the fact that the United States would be compelled to maintain ships in the Pacific to protect the coast of California and American merchant shipping. In this respect, Bermejo cited the example of the battleship *Oregon* which was known to be in the Pacific. Consequently, the displacement of the fleets in terms of ships available for duty in the Atlantic was 66,537 tons for the Americans and 63,018 tons for the Spanish. The Americans had therefore only a slight advantage, and this was being offset by the extensive refitting which was currently being carried out at Cartagena and Cádiz.[24] Moreover, Bermejo confidently believed that Spanish sailors were better trained and braver than those of the United States. This reflected a curious notion existing in Europe that the American navy was manned by foreign 'mercenaries'. The former Minister of the Marine, General José María Beránger, stated in an interview to the press on 6 April that 'ship against ship, a failure is not to be feared' because, 'as soon as fire is opened the crews of the American ships will commence to desert, since we all know that among them are people of all nationalities'.[25]

Cervera had cogent answers to every point made by Bermejo. He was utterly convinced that war must inevitably bring disaster for Spain because the American navy enjoyed significant logistical advantages and was much more powerful than his own squadron. In a somewhat ominous reference to one of his nation's greatest naval humiliations, he noted that American sailors were recruited in the same way as 'the crews that defeated our predecessors at

---

23 Cervera to Bermejo, 26 February 1898, cited in ibid., vol. ii pp. 102.
24 Bermejo to Cervera, 4 March 1898, cited in ibid., vol. ii pp. 102–4.
25 *El Heraldo* (Madrid), 6 April 1898, cited in ibid., vol. ii p. 40.

Trafalgar'.[26] As for the strategic importance attached to the Pacific Ocean, Cervera queried whether the Americans had any reason to fear the under-strength Spanish fleet. In fact, the Sagasta government was currently in receipt of alarming reports from the Captain General of the Philippines stating that Dewey was known to be under orders to attack Manila as soon as war was declared. The response from Madrid to this news was outwardly sympathetic, but held out little prospect of providing additional military supplies or reinforcements. Consequently, Admiral Patricio Montojo at Manila faced the daunting task of deciding how his small fleet of antiquated light cruisers and gunboats might best defend the extensive coastline of the Philippines against an assault from a superior enemy naval force. Like Cervera, he hoped fervently that war would not materialize.

For Bermejo, however, the area of strategic priority was the Atlantic and the Caribbean. He sought to reassure Cervera by reminding him of the vigorous efforts currently being made to secure extra funds for supplies, weapons and new ships. 'I repeat to you what I have said before', he told the admiral on 13 March, 'namely, that the government will act prudently in order to maintain friendly relations with the United States, and try by every means to ward off any conflict, since the opinion as to our unfavourable situation is unanimous.'[27] However, on the same day as Bermejo sought to clarify government policy for Cervera, the cabinet decided to implement the strategy originally outlined by the minister on 15 February. Captain Fernando Villaamil was ordered to leave for the Canary Islands with a flotilla consisting of three torpedo-boats, the *Rayo*, *Ariete* and *Azor,* and three destroyers, the *Plutón*, *Furor* and *Terror*. At the Canaries Villaamil was directed to proceed 1,000 miles further southwest to the Cape Verde Islands with the understanding that Cuba would be his ultimate destination. *The Times* Special Correspondent at Havana reported that 'it raises the spirits of the Spaniards to know that they have these powerful instruments of war close at hand to assist them in their hour of need'.[28] Instructions were also given to hasten the refitting of the *Pelayo* and *Carlos V* so that the ships would be ready by mid-April. Despite Bermejo's professed desire for peace, the deliberate and well-publicized movement of ships expressly designed to attack armoured vessels only made war more likely.

26 Cervera to Bermejo, 9 March 1898, cited in ibid., vol. ii pp. 105–6.
27 Bermejo to Cervera, 13 March 1898, cited in ibid., vol. ii p. 106.
28 *The Times* (London), 14 April, 1898.

Cervera assumed that he would soon have to join Villaamil because the torpedo-boat flotilla could achieve very little on its own and would need the protection of armoured ships. But no specific instructions were forthcoming from Madrid. Bermejo explained that the cabinet was completely distracted by the crisis in diplomatic relations with the United States. A thoroughly frustrated Cervera telegraphed on 6 April:

> It is precisely on account of the general anxiety prevailing that it is very important to think of what is to be done, so that, if the case arises, we may act rapidly and with some chance of efficiency and not be groping about in the dark, or, like Don Quixote, go out to fight windmills and come back with broken heads. . . . If we are caught without a plan of war, there will be vacillations and doubts, and after defeat there may be some humiliation and shame.[29]

The telegram appeared to sting Bermejo into action. Instructions were sent to Cervera next day ordering him to proceed to the Cape Verde Islands with the two armoured cruisers, *Cristóbal Colón* and the *María Teresa*. As Cervera had predicted, the *Pelayo* and *Carlos V* were not ready for service. At the Cape Verdes he would link up with the torpedo-boat flotilla and the armoured cruisers *Vizcaya* and *Oquendo* which were on their way from Havana. The exact purpose of this rendezvous was not divulged, although it was evident that the squadron was being placed on a war-footing consistent with Bermejo's 'two centres of resistance' strategy. In fact, Cervera believed that his mission would be to defend Puerto Rico rather than Cuba, simply because the Americans were considered more likely to attack the smaller island than risk an assault upon the more strongly fortified Havana. The admiral, however, was more immediately concerned about the choice of the Cape Verdes for the rendezvous. Unlike the Canaries, the Cape Verde Islands were not a Spanish possession. Should war be declared between Spain and the United States, the Portuguese authorities would enforce the neutrality provisions and surely request that ships of these two nations leave the islands as soon as possible.

Faithfully following instructions, the *Cristóbal Colón* and *María Teresa* reached St Vincent in the Cape Verdes on 14 April.

29 Cervera to Bermejo, 6 April 1898, cited in Chadwick, *United States and Spain*, vol. ii p. 108.

Villaamil's flotilla of six vessels was already present. On 19 April the *Vizcaya* and *Oquendo* arrived. The squadron was duly assembled, but was hardly ready for battle. The flagship, *Cristóbal Colón*, had left Spain before her main armament of 10-inch guns could be fitted. On each of the four cruisers many of the guns could not work properly because of disrepair or shortage of ammunition. The squadron also lacked speed. The boilers of two of the torpedo-boats, *Rayo* and *Ariete*, had broken down so that both ships would need to be towed. The bottom of the *Vizcaya* was judged to be in urgent need of cleaning and repair. Moreover, all the ships had exhausted most of their coal on their respective voyages. Re-supply was found to be difficult and expensive because the local American consul had astutely bought up most of the available coal. Although the little that remained was purchased by Cervera, the quantity was only half of what his ships required. A frantic request was made to the Canaries for a collier to be urgently despatched.

With the knowledge that a declaration of war was imminent, Cervera summoned his senior officers on 20 April to a 'council of war' on board the *Cristóbal Colón*. Although everyone present affirmed their willingness to give their lives for Spain, the general mood was pessimistic. The main points of the conference were telegraphed to Madrid in what could only be described as a devastating indictment of the home government's naval strategy. First, the anticipated policy of concentrating on the defence of Puerto Rico was regarded as flawed so long as Cuba was denied naval protection. The removal of the *Vizcaya* and *Oquendo* from Havana meant that only a few gunboats and various small craft remained on duty in Cuban waters. However, should an important Cuban city be in danger of falling to the Americans, it was argued that public opinion in Spain would force the government to transfer ships from Puerto Rico to save Spanish lives and honour. Secondly, the officers expressed concern that the diversion of the major part of the Spanish fleet to the Caribbean would risk the danger of being outflanked by the Americans. Aware of the creation of the Flying Squadron, the Spaniards feared that Schley would seize control of the weakly defended Canaries and use those islands as a base for raids against the Spanish coastline. Such an eventuality would soon compel the recall of Spain's armoured ships from the Caribbean. Finally, the plan to send the squadron to the Caribbean was considered a strategic error simply because the American fleet was so powerful that any major engagement must inevitably result in disaster for Spain. The recommendation of the conference was that the fleet return to the Canaries where it could continue to refit and carry out repairs while also providing the most effective line of defence for the homeland.

On 22 April Bermejo telegraphed to Cervera official confirmation that war had been declared. He also stated that the Canaries were 'perfectly safe' and that the squadron should prepare to move north to Puerto Rico.[30] On the next day, conscious of the need to seek expert advice and approval, Bermejo convened a council of senior naval officers. Thirteen admirals and five captains attended. Cervera's recent telegram was read out. Its pessimistic assessment, however, was countered by a telegram just received from Captain General Blanco stating that public spirit in Havana was 'very high'. More pertinently, Blanco warned that the arrival of Cervera's squadron was expected daily and, if this did not materialize, 'disappointment will be great and an unpleasant reaction is possible'.[31] Public expectations of action fused with national pride. Like the vast majority of Spain's political and military leaders, the assembled naval officers were psychologically unwilling to abandon the 'ever-faithful isle'. Glossing over Cervera's warnings of disaster, the council decided that he should proceed immediately to the Caribbean with the primary purpose of defending Puerto Rico, though the exact strategy to be adopted would be governed by the exigencies of war and the admiral's own judgement and discretion. Underpinning the decision was Bermejo's belief which he had consistently held 'that the victory would be on the side of Spain, owing to the good qualities of her ships, the skill of those who commanded them, and the valour of the crews'.[32]

Once again Cervera was totally dumbfounded. 'It is impossible', he telegraphed Bermejo, 'for me to give you an idea of the surprise and consternation experienced by all on the receipt of the order to sail.'[33] Nevertheless, he and his fellow officers and men were determined to do their duty for Queen and country. After taking on additional supplies of coal and provisions, the squadron of four armoured cruisers and three destroyers – the unseaworthy torpedo-boats were left behind – set sail on 29 April for San Juan, Puerto Rico. In view of his many serious misgivings Cervera would have

---

30 Bermejo to Cervera, 22 April 1898, cited in ibid., vol. ii p. 120.
31 Blanco to Moret, 22 April 1898, cited in ibid., vol. ii p. 119.
32 Cited in ibid., vol. ii, p. 123.
33 Cervera to Bermejo, 25 April 1898, cited in Herbert H. Sargent, *The Campaign of Santiago de Cuba* (3 vols; Chicago, 1914), vol. i p. 64.

been amazed to know of the alarm which his squadron had unleashed in America. Despite their superior warships, equipment, training and logistical advantages, American naval commanders were extremely wary of meeting a squadron which was described by *The Times* as 'a real fighting force, fast, modern and formidable of its kind' [sic].[34]

34 *The Times* (London), 3 May 1898.

4 THE WAR AT SEA

THE BLOCKADE OF CUBA

While Spanish naval strategy fitfully evolved, the McKinley administration acted promptly. On the evening of 21 April the first stage of the War Plan was put into effect when orders were telegraphed directly from Long at the Navy Department in Washington to Sampson at Key West to institute an immediate blockade of the northern coastline of Cuba starting from the bay of Bahía Honda, west of Havana, and extending eastwards almost 150 miles to the port of Cárdenas. The United States government was exercising its legal right as a nation at war to establish a blockade of the enemy's ports and coastline. The purpose was essentially to cut off trade between Cuba and the rest of the world and thereby starve the Spanish garrison into surrender. Any enemy vessel encountered would be captured or destroyed. Merchant ships of neutral nations would be stopped and searched for contraband, a legal term which was broadly defined as goods possessing military value to the enemy. Any such items discovered would be confiscated. However, for a blockade to be binding on neutral nations, it had to be 'effective'. This meant in practice that all ships must find it difficult and dangerous to enter or leave the designated area. The qualification was significant because it prevented a belligerent power from simply proclaiming the existence of a blockade without providing adequate naval forces for enforcement. Consequently, the United States deliberately limited the area of blockade to that part of Cuba which was judged to be not only the most important militarily and economically but also was easily accessible to the North Atlantic Squadron. Moreover, the creation of the Flying Squadron meant that Sampson initially had only twenty-six ships under his command so that he clearly lacked the capability to enforce an effective blockade over the whole coastline of Cuba, which stretched for 2,000 miles. During the Civil War the Union had used more than 600 ships to maintain a blockade of the Confederacy!

On 22 April the North Atlantic Squadron steamed towards Havana. *En route* the light cruiser *Nashville* fired a gun – the first shot of the Spanish-American War – to intercept and board a Spanish merchant ship, the *Buenaventura*, which was carrying a cargo of timber to Holland. Arrangements were made to take the *Buenaventura* to Key West as a 'prize of war'. Reminiscent of the days when privateers roamed the Spanish Main, such ships and their cargoes came under the jurisdiction of 'prize courts' which were empowered to order the sale of contraband and to split the resulting 'prize money' equally between the federal government and the crew who captured the ship. The seizure of the *Buenaventura* was therefore greatly pleasing to her captors and also to the whole American fleet, which hoped that the ship's name – 'Good Luck' – was a positive omen for future battles and more prizes. In fact, five more enemy merchant vessels were seized during the first week of the war, though afterwards this high rate of success fell away sharply as Spanish ships either stayed in harbour or avoided entering the blockaded area.

By nightfall of 22 April the North Atlantic Squadron had taken up position outside Havana. The standing instructions to all ships were to adopt defensive tactics and not to risk damage by approaching within range of the land batteries or engaging the various enemy light cruisers and gunboats sheltering in the harbour. During the previous day Captain General Blanco had held a public meeting in Havana at which he had boasted of the strength of the city's fortifications. Noting that 'the enemy's fleet is almost at our doors', he defiantly predicted that 'we will hurl them back into the sea'.[1] But Blanco had no powerful warships under his control, so that any attempt to drive away the Americans was inconceivable until the arrival of Cervera's Atlantic Squadron. In the meantime, Sampson methodically stationed his smaller vessels close to the harbour while the squadron's flagship, the *New York*, and the battleships *Iowa* and *Indiana* stood off to form a line some miles from the shore. On 23 April individual cruisers were sent to blockade the ports of Mariel, Cabañas, Matanzas and Cárdenas. An attempt to widen the area of blockade was made on 26 April, when the *Marblehead* and *Nashville* were despatched to the important southern port of Cienfuegos. However, the local unavailability of coal convinced the captain of the *Marblehead* that an effective blockade was not

1 Speech dated 21 April, cited in *The Times* (London), 23 April 1898.

currently feasible and the ships returned to the main fleet on 29 April.

The availability of coal was crucial to the whole squadron because the efficient enforcement of the blockade required frequent movement to reconnoitre the coast and to intercept passing ships. Wherever possible coal stocks were provided at sea by colliers, but the latter were in short supply, and coaling was also often made difficult by inclement weather conditions. Consequently, a number of ships had to return to Key West for coaling and to take on supplies especially of fresh water. As the initial enthusiasm of going to war began to diminish and the opportunity for capturing prizes became more scarce, the task of blockading became monotonous. 'The appalling sameness of this pacing up and down before Havana works on the nerves of every one, from captain to cook's police,' complained the journalist Frederic Remington, who had joined the *Iowa* in search of adventure and journalistic scoops. After seven days he was glad to leave the ship. He reckoned that the only memorable incident to relieve the tedium had been the general excitement caused when the ship's black cat was lost overboard.[2]

Although Sampson's instructions were to keep his armoured warships away from the range of Havana's heavy guns, he did have the authority to engage light artillery whenever he thought this to be appropriate. On 27 April he learned that the Spaniards were erecting fortifications at Matanzas. In his flagship, the *New York*, Sampson sailed towards Matanzas where he joined the cruiser *Cincinnati* and the monitor *Puritan*. As the American ships approached the port they were fired upon by the land batteries. Although no direct hits were recorded, this was the first occasion of the war that American military personnel had actually come directly under enemy fire. Sampson ordered the *New York* to return the fire and later allowed the *Cincinnati* and *Puritan* to let loose a number of rounds aimed at the fortifications on shore. It was a brief and inconclusive engagement which represented more an American desire for gunnery practice rather than a determination to gain any strategic advantage or wreak destruction on the Spanish garrison.

No other combat actions occurred until 11 May, when two incidents took place on the same day. The first was close to Cienfuegos, where the *Marblehead* and *Nashville* had returned to

2 See Charles H. Brown, *The Correspondents' War: Journalists in the Spanish-American War* (New York, 1967), p. 164.

cut the underwater transatlantic cable which linked Cienfuegos and Santiago de Cuba by telegraphic communication with Spain. The cruisers provided covering fire as four small boats conveyed marines to the shallow waters of the bay. The marines successfully cut two cables, but came under increasingly heavy fire from Spanish riflemen on shore. Eventually they had to withdraw without being able to cut the third cable. Two marines were killed and six were seriously injured. The second incident took place on the northern coast at Cárdenas, when the torpedo-boat *Winslow* strayed too far into the harbour and came under bombardment from the shore batteries and a Spanish gunboat. In what turned out to be Spain's one and only naval 'victory' of the war, the *Winslow* was badly damaged and had to be towed from the harbour by the revenue cutter *Hudson*. Moreover, the incident claimed the lives of one American officer and four enlisted men. The actions at Cienfuegos and Cárdenas produced the first American combat fatalities of the war. Like the sudden death of Martí in 1895, they were a grim reminder of the realities of war and the lesson that enthusiasm was no substitute for military experience.

However tedious and uneventful, the American blockade made good strategic sense. So long as the American army was unprepared for overseas campaigning and the Spanish navy out of reach, Mahan considered that blockading Cuba 'was the one decisive measure, sure though slow in its working, which could be taken'.[3] Nevertheless, the American public was disappointed that so few tangible results were forthcoming. Sampson sought primarily to cut off Cuba's commercial contact with Europe, but rumours abounded of a brisk trade developing between the island's southern ports and ships from Jamaica and Mexico. 'It is difficult', remarked *The Times*, 'to see how a blockade on this scale can be rendered effective with the naval forces at the command of the American Government.'[4] However, later evidence from official Spanish sources disclosed that the blockade was extremely successful in securing compliance from neutral powers and reducing contraband trade to a trickle. During the period from late April to early August 1898, a mere two ships escaped from Havana while only eight ships were recorded as entering Cuban ports – four from Spain and the rest from France,

---

3   Alfred T. Mahan, *Lessons of the War With Spain, and Other Articles* (Boston, 1899), p. 105.

4   *The Times* (London), 25 April 1898.

England and Norway.[5] Despite the confident statements of General Blanco that local spirits were high, one American visitor, who was in the capital at the beginning of May, observed: 'The distress in Havana is already severe'.[6] An even greater blow was inflicted upon Spanish hopes when news arrived during the first week of May of a major naval battle occurring not in the Atlantic or the Caribbean but far away at Manila Bay in the Pacific Ocean.

THE BATTLE OF MANILA BAY

It might seem puzzling that the Philippines should be the scene of the first major battle of a war ostensibly fought over the future of an island in the Caribbean. One explanation for this untoward train of events has taken the form of a 'conspiracy theory' which argues that Theodore Roosevelt was primarily responsible for directing Commodore Dewey to Manila Bay. This was part of the evolving 'large' foreign policy in which Roosevelt, with the aid of his friend, Senator Henry Cabot Lodge of Massachusetts, and other like-minded 'expansionists', perceived the crisis with Spain as an opportunity of promoting the rise of the United States to its predestined status as a world imperial power. Certainly, the Assistant Secretary of the Navy had lobbied vigorously to secure the appointment of Dewey as the commander of the Asiatic Squadron in November 1897. He was also the sender of the celebrated telegram dated 25 February 1898 instructing Dewey to concentrate the squadron at Hong Kong and prepare for offensive measures against the Philippines. But Roosevelt was merely amplifying what had always been an element of the War Plan against Spain. The attack on the Philippines was not conceived as part of a grand design to establish an overseas American 'empire', but was one of several means of exerting military and economic pressure upon Spain to force the latter to make peace over Cuba.[7] The same strategic

5　See David F. Trask, *The War with Spain in 1898* (New York, 1981), pp. 110–11.

6　Charles Thrall, 'The Thrilling Adventures of a World Scout in Cuba', *New York World*, 8 May 1898.

7　The historical interpretation emphasizing the influence upon American foreign policy of Theodore Roosevelt and like-minded 'imperialists' was first presented in Julius W. Pratt, 'The "Large Policy" of 1898', *Mississippi Valley Historical Review* 19 (1932), pp. 219–42. More recent studies which stress the role of naval officers are John A. S. Grenville, 'American Naval Preparations for War with Spain, 1896–1898', *Journal of American Studies* 2 (1968), pp. 33–47; and Ronald Spector, 'Who Planned the Attack on Manila Bay?', *Mid-America* 53 (1971), pp. 94–102.

purpose, which had motivated Roosevelt's telegram in February, was accordingly stressed by Secretary of the Navy Long in conversation with McKinley on the day that war was declared. The President agreed that available naval resources in the Pacific should be used to strike at Spanish shipping and commerce. On Sunday 24 April he approved the recommendation that Dewey attack the Philippines.

Meanwhile, Dewey was in the process of transferring his squadron 30 miles east of Hong Kong to Mirs Bay on the coast of China. The move was a direct result of news that war had broken out between the United States and Spain. On 24 April, in accordance with his home government's declaration of neutrality, the British governor of Hong Kong had requested that American warships leave the port within 24 hours. In the absence of a similar notification from the Chinese government, Dewey chose to sail to Mirs Bay where he received the following orders from Washington on Monday 26 April:

War has commenced between the United States and Spain. Proceed at once to the Philippines. Commence operations against the Spanish squadron. You must capture or destroy. Use utmost endeavors.[8]

On the next day the American Consul at Manila, Oscar Williams, arrived to give Dewey up-to-date information about the state of Spanish defences in the Philippines. Although the archipelago consisted of more than 7,000 islands, the centre of Spain's power and wealth was the capital city of Manila on the island of Luzon. Williams reported that the Spanish fleet was prepared for battle and was most likely to position itself at Subic Bay to the north of Manila. But Dewey was confident of success. All his various sources of information pointed to the fact that the opposing Spanish ships were antiquated, slow and poorly armed. Only a few weeks earlier on 31 March he had written to Long that 'with the squadron under my command, the Spanish vessels could be taken and the defenses reduced in one day'.[9] At 2 p.m. on Wednesday, 27 April, the Asiatic Squadron set sail for Manila.

8   Long to Dewey, 24 April 1898, cited in French E. Chadwick, *The Relations of the United States and Spain: The Spanish American War* (3 vols; London, 1911), vol. ii p. 157.
9   Dewey to Long, 31 March 1898, cited in Ronald Spector, *Admiral of the New Empire: The Life and Career of George Dewey* (Baton Rouge, LA, 1974), p. 49.

Despite being at war, there was no attempt to maintain secrecy. Indeed, American intentions were publicly proclaimed. Even before Dewey had actually reached the Philippines, the American press ran headlines which predicted: 'Fighting to Begin at Manila'.[10] Nevertheless, Dewey was convinced that, whether forewarned or not, the Spaniards would not attempt to intercept him and force a battle on the high seas. He reckoned that the voyage of 600 miles to the Philippines would be fairly smooth and uneventful and that he would reach his destination on Saturday 30 April.

Ever since the beginning of 1898 the Spanish authorities in the Philippines had been only too well aware of Dewey's intention to adopt an offensive rather than a defensive strategy. However, their requests to Madrid for ships and supplies had elicited little tangible response. Captain General Basilio Augustín and Admiral Patricio Montojo y Pasarón had therefore to plan the defence of the islands with limited military resources at their disposal. Like Cervera at Cartagena, Admiral Montojo had nominally an impressive number of more than thirty vessels under his command. But the majority were old and unseaworthy gunboats. In fact, only seven ships were judged to be of any value for fighting purposes. Montojo therefore ruled out the strategy of directly confronting Dewey's more powerful squadron in a major naval battle. It was decided instead to prepare a defensive stronghold at Subic Bay, about 30 miles north of Manila Bay. The plan was eminently sensible in its underlying assumption that the American squadron would not dare to move on to Manila so long as Spanish warships were at Subic and could threaten to attack from the rear. Moreover, the Americans would be able to make little impression on the Spanish ships within Subic Bay, where the latter would be protected by land batteries and by mines placed across the relatively narrow entrance to the harbour. So far away from their bases and with diminishing supplies, the Americans would ultimately be forced to withdraw.

Learning of the outbreak of war, Montojo's squadron of seven ships left Manila for Subic Bay on Monday 25 April. Arriving the next day, the admiral was 'disgusted' to find no heavy guns had been mounted and that only five mines had been placed in the harbour.[11] Nor was there adequate time to remedy the deficiencies.

10 For example, the *Chicago Tribune*, cited in Brown, *Correspondents' War*, p. 182.

11 Montojo's 'Report', cited in Chadwick, *United States and Spain*, vol. ii pp. 167–8.

On Thursday 28 April news arrived that Dewey was on his way from Hong Kong. Montojo convened a council of war with his senior officers. It was agreed that Subic could not be defended against an attack by Dewey's more powerful fleet. Naval experts later wondered why Montojo did not try to offset his weakness in relation to the American squadron by scattering his ships. Such action would have caused considerable confusion and disruption to Dewey's battle plans.[12] What appeared uppermost in the Spanish naval mind, however, was the conviction that Dewey was heading straight for Manila and that it was the duty of the navy to defend Spanish *pundonor* by preventing the Americans from bombarding the capital. The decision pleased Captain General Augustín who, only a few days earlier on 23 April, had sought to bolster local morale by issuing a proclamation stating that 'the struggle will be short and decisive' and would result in a Spanish victory 'as brilliant and complete as the righteousness and justice of our cause demand'.[13]

However, Montojo was deeply pessimistic about the likely outcome of a battle with the Americans. He had even told General Augustín in March that his 'poor squadron would not be able to withstand the onslaught of the American ships, and that he was firmly convinced that it would be destroyed'.[14] Nevertheless, Montojo's defensive tactics were inherently less risky than the offensive strategy adopted by Dewey. In contrast to the invading Americans, the Spanish forces enjoyed the advantage of having a fixed home base. The task of preparing the defence of Manila was also facilitated by geographical factors. Manila Bay comprises a large area whose shape is often likened to a large pear. The entrance forms the stem of the pear and extends to a maximum width of around 10 miles. It was protected in 1898 by artillery batteries at Gorda Point on the high ground to the north and Restinga Point on the southern shore. The small islands of Corregidor and Caballo divide the entrance into the Boca Chica, a 2-mile wide northern channel, and the Boca Grande, a broader channel to the south around 4 miles in width. In order to impede the passage of hostile ships, heavy guns were mounted on Corregidor and Caballo and

---

12 See William R. Braisted, *The United States Navy in the Pacific, 1897–1909* (Austin, TX, 1958), p. 26. Dewey was very critical of Montojo's tactics. See George W. Dewey, *Autobiography of George Dewey, Admiral of the Navy* (New York, 1913), pp. 292–3.

13 23 April 1898, cited in Chadwick, *United States and Spain*, vol. ii p. 158, note 1.

14 Montojo's 'Report', cited in ibid., vol. ii p. 161.

also on El Fraile, a rock located midway between Caballo and Restinga Point. In addition, a number of mines and torpedoes were placed in the southern channel close to Caballo Island though their effectiveness was greatly limited by the depth of the water and frequent strong tides. Once inside the entrance, the city of Manila lay almost 30 miles to the northeast. The city was not heavily fortified, but it was protected by land batteries containing more than 200 guns and a thick wall stretching for a mile along the bay.

Montojo's strategy was basically to place his ships in as strong a defensive position as possible and await the arrival of Dewey. By locating close to Manila, the Spanish squadron would gain the advantage of support from the city's artillery. The disadvantage, however, was that, in any resulting naval battle, the Americans would inevitably bombard the city and cause damage and injury to residential areas and civilians. Partly for humanitarian reasons, therefore, Montojo decided to move his ships away from the capital and anchor them 6 miles to the south in the shallow waters of Cañacao Bay. The bay was protected to the west by a narrow land peninsula with guns placed on high ground at Sangley Point. Adjoining the bay to the south was the Cavite naval dockyard from which additional artillery covering fire, and also ammunition and supplies, would be available. By Friday 29 April the Spanish squadron was in position within Cañacao Bay. On the next day Montojo learned that Dewey had been sighted at Subic Bay and was on his way to Manila. Even though battle seemed imminent, the admiral and several of his officers faithfully attended a reception held in the city on the night of Saturday 30 April. It is not known whether this was an example of Spanish absence of mind or unquestioning obedience to social protocol. More likely, the Spaniards simply assumed that Dewey would not attempt to enter Manila Bay at night. If so, this was a grievous miscalculation.

Dewey's fixed intention was to do battle with the Spanish fleet at the earliest opportunity. During the afternoon of 30 April he reached Subic Bay and was relieved to learn that Montojo had withdrawn to the more open expanses of Manila Bay. The order was given to proceed south to Manila and for all ships to be prepared to pass through the Boca Grande channel under cover of night. The risks were high. Mines were known to have been placed in the entrance, but Dewey judged that the deep water of the channel made contact unlikely. Of more concern were the guns on Restinga Point and especially those mounted on the nearby islands of Caballo and Corregidor. The obvious fear was that the American ships might be damaged or even disabled while trying to enter the bay. 'If the guns commanding the entrance were well served', Dewey later noted in his *Autobiography*, 'there was danger of damage to my squadron before it engaged the enemy's squadron.'[15] Nevertheless, the Americans had the advantages of surprise, darkness and a determination to accomplish their mission. There was also the spirited example set by their commander, who insisted that he would personally lead the squadron into the bay.

At midnight on 30 April the Asiatic Squadron successfully entered Manila Bay in single file. No mines were encountered. The flashing of lights on Corregidor seemed to indicate that the Spaniards had observed the movement of the ships, but, to the surprise and delight of the American sailors, no shots were forthcoming from that direction. Just as the last two vessels, the *Concord* and *Boston*, were about to enter the bay, three single shots were fired from a Spanish gun on El Fraile. No damage resulted. Unscathed, the squadron proceeded steadily towards Manila in anticipation of the naval battle which Dewey was planning to initiate just as dawn was breaking.

The American battle fleet comprised the four protected cruisers, *Olympia*, *Baltimore*, *Raleigh* and *Boston*, the unprotected cruiser *Concord* and the gunboat *Petrel*. The cutter *McCulloch* and the two colliers were not to be involved in the fighting. The opposing Spanish squadron included Montojo's flagship, the unprotected cruiser *Reina Cristina* and an antiquated wooden cruiser, the *Castilla*, and five gunboats, the *Don Juan de Austria*, *Don Antonio de Ulloa*, *Isla de Cuba*, *Marqués del Duero* and *Isla de Luzon*. The best Spanish ship, the *Reina Cristina*, was equivalent to the *Concord*. The ships of the American fleet were considerably more modern in design and construction and displaced 19,098 tons against the Spanish figure of 11,328 tons. Moreover, the American warships boasted fifty-three heavy guns compared to the thirty-seven similar guns possessed by the Spanish squadron. However, the American superiority in firepower would be offset by the support which Montojo expected to receive from the land batteries on Sangley Point and the Cavite arsenal.[16]

Just after 5 in the morning of Sunday, 1 May, a column of six American ships each about 400 yards apart steamed directly towards the Spanish squadron in Cañacao Bay. Shots were fired from the

15 Dewey, *Autobiography*, p. 208.
16 For details of naval forces, see Chadwick, *United States and Spain*, vol. ii p. 169.

land batteries in Manila and on Sangley Point, but they all fell well wide of the mark. At the head of the column was Dewey in the *Olympia*. He carefully held fire until the *Olympia* was within a range of 5,500 yards of the enemy. Thereupon, at exactly 6.19 a.m., Dewey issued the celebrated order to his executive officer, Captain Charles Gridley: 'You may fire when ready, Gridley.'[17] Firing their guns directly at the enemy, the American squadron passed along the line of Spanish ships, then turned round for another attack. More than one hour of fighting ensued. Edwin Harden of the *New York World* observed:

> Five times our ships went up and down that line, each time with lessened distance, and all the time they kept up a steady, rapid fire upon the enemy. The Spaniards were not slow about returning the fire. There was an almost continuous roar of their guns from the time the *Olympia* opened until, after passing for the fifth time, our vessels turned away, and started slowly across the bay out of the range of fire. [18]

The apparent withdrawal of the American ships was the result of an order given by Dewey at 7.45 a.m. to break off the engagement with the enemy. Newspaper wags would later claim that Dewey wished to give his men time for the breakfast which they had missed earlier that morning. The chance to snatch breakfast was taken, but there was a much more serious explanation for Dewey's decision. Amid the confusion of battle he had been informed by Gridley that the *Olympia* was nearing the end of her ammunition. Firing was still continuing from the Spanish ships so there was no alternative but to withdraw and assess battle damage.

For the first time since leaving Mirs Bay Dewey confronted the prospect of failing to accomplish his mission. One newspaper correspondent recalled that 'the gloom on the bridge of the *Olympia* was thicker than a London fog in November'.[19] However, once clear of the noise and smoke of battle it was discovered that Gridley's alarmist report was wholly inaccurate. Moreover, despite the intensity of the fighting, no fatalities were reported nor had any American vessel suffered serious damage. On the other hand, a

17 Cited in Spector, *Life of Dewey*, p. 58.
18 Cited in Brown, *Correspondents' War*, p. 192.
19 The comments of Joseph L. Stickney, cited in Chadwick, *United States and Spain*, vol. ii p. 181.

glance across the bay revealed that the *Reina Cristina* was ablaze and that Montojo had transferred his flag to the *Isla de Cuba*. In fact, most of the Spanish ships were on fire and were attempting to use the respite in the fighting to retreat to the shelter of the Cavite dockyard. Soon the gunboat *Don Antonio de Ulloa* was the sole remaining Spanish ship in Cañacao Bay.

The refreshed and reinvigorated American sailors resumed battle at 10.45 a.m.. Spanish resistance was now virtually non-existent. The *Baltimore* steamed ahead and used her heavy guns to silence the batteries on Sangley Point. The rest of the squadron concentrated first on sinking the *Don Antonio de Ulloa* and then directing their fire at the ships which had retreated behind the Cavite dockyard. At about 12.15 p.m. a white flag of surrender appeared. Dewey responded by ordering an end to the American bombardment. Three Spanish ships had been sunk – the *Reina Cristina, Castilla* and *Don Antonio de Ulloa*. The rest were set on fire and destroyed so that not one Spanish warship remained by 12.50 p.m. Spanish casualties had also been heavy. During the battle 161 Spaniards had been killed and 210 were wounded. By contrast, American losses were amazingly light. Although every one of the American ships had been struck by Spanish shells, no significant damage was reported. In fact, no American fatalities had occurred. Only nine men had been wounded – eight on the *Baltimore* and one on the *Boston*. Dewey had truly won the Battle of Manila Bay 'before breakfast and without losing a man'.

While the fighting was coming to an end in Cañacao Bay, the land batteries in Manila City continued to fire intermittently at the American ships. Dewey informed the Captain General that he would bombard the city if this irritant to his ships continued. The Spanish authorities complied and stopped firing. However, they rejected a further request from Dewey that he use the cable to Hong Kong to telegraph news to the United States. In retaliation, Dewey ordered the cutting of the cable. This action was understandable, but it rebounded on Dewey by severing his own telegraphic communications with the rest of the world, including President McKinley and the Navy Department in Washington.

Dewey had achieved his objective of destroying the Spanish Pacific Squadron and he now awaited instructions on what to do next. In the meantime, the city of Manila was at his mercy. The sensible policy to pursue in the short term was to secure his position militarily and thereby reduce the risk of a possible Spanish counter-attack. Accordingly, marines were sent ashore on 2 May to take control of the Cavite arsenal. On the next day the guns at the entrance to the bay were disabled. However, Dewey showed no intention of occupying the city. Such an action was hardly practicable so long as he had little more than 1,700 men under his command. 'I control bay completely and can take city at any time', he wrote to Long, 'but I have not sufficient men to hold.'[20] The despatch was dated 4 May and was put aboard the *McCulloch* which set off the next day for the telegraph station at Hong Kong.

Prior to the cutting of the cable, the Captain General had informed Madrid of a fierce battle in which the Spanish squadron had performed 'in brilliant combat' and had inflicted heavy losses on the enemy.[21] Subsequent telegrams from Montojo gave a much more accurate account of events. By releasing to the press only extracts of the news from Manila, the Spanish government contributed to the growing public uncertainty not only in Spain but also in the United States as to the exact outcome of the battle. This did not prevent several New York newspapers from claiming on 2 May that Dewey had achieved a smashing victory. But nagging doubts were raised by the enforced silence from Manila. The remarkable scale of the American triumph was not finally confirmed until 7 May when the *McCulloch* reached Hong Kong and telegraphed Dewey's despatches to Washington. Two brief telegrams succinctly stated that the Spanish squadron had been engaged and destroyed. In response, the Navy Department prepared to send supplies and reinforcements from San Francisco. It would not be long before the Philippines became a major problem for American diplomacy and military policy, but for the moment any worries about the future were overshadowed by the outburst of public joy at news of the great naval victory. Dewey soon became known as the 'hero of Manila' and was lauded throughout the country. 'Every American is in your debt,' telegraphed Theodore Roosevelt.[22] President McKinley showed the nation's appreciation by promoting Dewey to the rank of rear-admiral, while Congress voted $10,000 to give him a gift in the form of a jewelled sword designed by Tiffany's. Bronze medals were also awarded to all the other ranks who took part in the battle. However gratifying and glorious, the action at Manila Bay was a sideshow which had damaged Spain, but was not enough to bring an end to the war. While praising Dewey's achievement, *The*

20 Dewey to Long, 4 May 1898, cited in ibid., vol. ii p. 212.
21 Telegram dated 1 May 1898, cited in ibid., vol. ii p. 208.
22 Roosevelt to Dewey, 7 May 1898, cited in Spector, *Life of Dewey*, p. 65.

Times also remarked upon Spain's deep attachment to military honour and predicted: 'The disaster in the Philippines will make her all the more eager to strike a blow, while the war lasts in the Atlantic or the Gulf of Mexico.'[23]

THE ELUSIVE SPANISH SQUADRON

On 29 April Cervera's squadron of four armoured cruisers and three destroyers left the Cape Verde Islands. The fact was reported quickly to the Navy Department in Washington and to the American public in the following day's New York press. Although the squadron was definitely sailing to the west, its exact destination was unknown. Indeed, Americans were not to learn the answer to this question for another whole month. In the meantime, speculation was rife. Some anxious American civilians continued to fear Spanish raids against their homes along the east coast. Government and military officials privately discounted this threat. They generally assumed that Cervera's mission was to bring military supplies to Havana and to use that port as a base for operations against the American navy. Moreover, it was confidently believed that Cervera did not have sufficient coal to complete a continuous voyage from the Cape Verdes to Havana. At some point he would have to make a stop for coaling and repairs. Puerto Rico was under Spanish control and was considered the most sensible and logical first port of call. Another possibility was the French island of Martinique, where the local authorities were regarded as sympathetic to Spain. The mixture of wartime tension and uncertainty prevailing in Washington even caused some officials to argue that Cervera was not primarily concerned about coal, but might be planning to strike a major psychological blow at American morale by intercepting the *Oregon* as she left Rio de Janeiro to complete the final leg of her celebrated voyage from San Francisco to Florida.

In fact, American naval strategy was already decided and was basically to wait patiently for Cervera's arrival. This was demonstrated by the positioning of the Flying Squadron at Hampton Roads and the employment of the rest of the North Atlantic Squadron to blockade the northern coast of Cuba. But the spectre of the Spanish squadron steadily moving closer from the other side of

23 *The Times* (London), 4 May 1898.

the Atlantic preyed on American nerves and soon prompted a controversial change of tactics. Though ships could not easily be spared from blockading duties, three light cruisers were despatched to scout the waters around Puerto Rico and the Windward Islands for signs of the enemy. On 4 May the blockading fleet was substantially depleted when Sampson suddenly sailed eastwards with a powerful squadron consisting of the three armoured warships, *Iowa, Indiana* and *New York*, two unprotected cruisers, two monitors and additional light vessels.

Reminiscent of Dewey's tactics in the Philippines, the North Atlantic Squadron was going on to the offensive. Sampson believed that Cervera was headed for Puerto Rico. Estimating that the fast Spanish squadron would arrive at San Juan on 8 May, Sampson intended to be there too and force a battle. However, by that day the American ships had only reached as far as the Windward Passage separating Cuba and Haiti. For a squadron to remain united, the overall speed has to be dictated by the slowest ship. Sampson's progress was accordingly hampered by delays caused by the battleship *Indiana*, whose boilers were leaking and required constant attention. Even more irritating and time-consuming were the two monitors, *Amphitrite* and *Terror*, both of which proved to be unsuitable on the high seas and had to be towed by the *Iowa* and *New York*. 'Never was a commander-in-chief more harassed by any ships under his command,' complained Sampson.[24]

Moving at only half its normal speed the American squadron eventually approached San Juan, Puerto Rico on 12 May, almost four days behind schedule. The voyage had been disappointing and personally embarrassing for Sampson because it had not produced the anticipated encounter with the enemy. Nor was there any sign of them in the harbour of San Juan. Sampson was aware, however, of a newspaper report suggesting that Cervera had been spotted on 7 May more than 500 miles to the south in the vicinity of Martinique. The American commander worried that he might somehow have missed the Spaniards. It was even conceivable that they had already passed through Puerto Rico and were presently on their way to Havana. If so, Sampson had badly miscalculated in leaving the blockade. The American squadron would therefore have to retrace its steps and return to Cuba in pursuit of the elusive Cervera. Nevertheless, having come so far, Sampson decided to implement the

24 William T. Sampson, 'The Atlantic Fleet in the Spanish War', *The Century Magazine* 57 (1899), p. 889.

plan which he had previously prepared for the contingency of confronting the Spanish squadron at San Juan. Beginning at dawn on 12 May his ships bombarded the harbour for three hours. The firing was conducted from a long distance so that only minor damage was inflicted on either side. However, one American was killed and seven wounded. Compared to the Battle of Manila Bay, the engagement at San Juan produced little glory. 'On our side, the value of the action lay not a little in the practice it gave the men under fire,' observed Sampson.[25] When the order was given to cease firing, the American ships swung around and headed back to Key West.

While the American ships had been lumbering towards Puerto Rico, Cervera's squadron had neared Martinique. On 10 May Captain Villaamil was sent ahead with the destroyers *Furor* and *Terror* to the port of Fort de France. His main purpose was to ascertain the availability of coal supplies. If Villaamil had arrived a day earlier he would have been spotted by the American cruiser *Harvard*. But the latter had departed in the belief that the Spanish squadron must have already passed through the Windward Islands. Like the North Atlantic Squadron, the practical performance of the Spanish ships had fallen a long way short of their rated speeds. The poor mechanical condition of the destroyers had caused particular difficulties and delays. As American officials had correctly predicted, the Spaniards now urgently required coal. But no relief was available at Fort de France. The French authorities declared their neutrality in the war and would not therefore permit the coaling of Spanish warships. Moreover, they stated that ships of belligerents which entered the harbour would be detained for the duration of the war. Villaamil was allowed to leave in the *Furor*, but the unseaworthy *Terror* had to remain behind. On 12 May Villaamil informed Cervera that coaling was ruled out in Martinique. He was also able to report the even gloomier news that the American navy had mounted a blockade of Havana and that Sampson was *en route* to Puerto Rico.

Desperate for coal, Cervera chose to press on eastwards to the Dutch island of Curaçao. If he could only acquire adequate stocks of fuel his latitude for manoeuvre would be enormously increased. Arriving at Curaçao on 14 May he found the Dutch authorities only slightly more sympathetic than their French counterparts in Martinique. They would allow him merely 600 tons of coal and

25 Ibid., p. 891.

insisted that all Spanish ships leave the port within 48 hours. Where should they go next – Puerto Rico or Cuba? Puerto Rico had been Cervera's original objective and, at 550 miles from Curaçao, was nearer than Cuba. But the reported presence of American warships in the vicinity of San Juan made Puerto Rico too dangerous. Of the leading Cuban ports, Havana was known to be blockaded and Cienfuegos was within close range of attack from the American fleet. This left Santiago de Cuba, a relatively small and isolated port which offered few naval facilities and supplies. On the other hand, the distance to Santiago from Curaçao was 300 miles less than to Cienfuegos and the risk of encountering American warships was believed to be slight. Moreover, the squadron had been at sea for weeks and was short of everything ranging from coal to fresh water and food. A spell in a safe harbour was urgently required, and proximity made Santiago de Cuba the obvious choice. The choice reflected expediency rather than strategic calculation. As Mahan later explained, the Spanish admiral was an 'opportunist, solely and simply'.[26] Leaving Curaçao on 15 May, Cervera arrived at Santiago de Cuba on 19 May. Remarkably, the squadron had taken more than two weeks to complete the journey from the Cape Verdes to Cuba and had not once come into contact with an American warship.

Nevertheless, the confirmed presence of the Spanish squadron in the Caribbean began the countdown for the long anticipated battle of the fleets. On 12 May the Navy Department learned of Villaamil's visit to Martinique. The next day Commodore Schley was instructed to move the Flying Squadron south to Charleston, South Carolina, and await orders. On 15 May, after receiving reports that the Spanish squadron had definitely been seen at Curaçao, the Navy Department directed Schley to Key West where he was to meet and discuss tactics with Sampson. Officials in Washington believed that Cervera would avoid Puerto Rico and aim for Cienfuegos primarily on account of that city's direct railroad connection with Havana. This facility would enable him to achieve his aim of delivering munitions and supplies to the capital. The United States would seek to disrupt Cervera's plans by sending the Flying Squadron to blockade Cienfuegos or, if necessary, meet and destroy the Spanish squadron in battle.

Sampson and Schley conferred at Key West on 18 May. They agreed that the Flying Squadron should go directly south to

26 Mahan, *Lessons of War With Spain*, p. 123.

Cienfuegos through the Yucatan Passage. The squadron was also significantly strengthened by the addition of the battleship *Iowa*. Should Cervera be heading for Havana, he would therefore be intercepted by a superior force of American armoured ships consisting of the *Iowa, Massachusetts, Texas* and *Brooklyn*. On 19 May Schley left for Cienfuegos. No sooner had this occurred than telegrams were received in Washington reporting that Cervera had put in not at Cienfuegos but Santiago de Cuba. This information reached Sampson in Key West on 20 May. Thus began a curious drama in which Schley, the man-on-the-spot, stubbornly held to the view that the Spanish squadron was at Cienfuegos. The confusion arose primarily because Cervera had done the unexpected. At first, Navy Department officials doubted the report. Sampson was also reluctant to accept that the Spaniards had chosen Santiago de Cuba, a remote place that was not only lacking in strategic value but was also virtually unknown to Americans. Consequently, on 20 May Sampson sent off a despatch merely informing Schley of the rumour that Cervera was in Santiago and requesting him to remain at Cienfuegos. It was not possible to communicate by telegraph with ships at sea so that messages were carried back and forth by small vessels, usually converted steam-liners. Sampson's despatch, therefore, was not received by Schley until shortly after the latter arrived off Cienfuegos on 22 May. In the meantime, Sampson had become more inclined to believe that Cervera was probably in Santiago de Cuba. New instructions were sent to Schley on 22 May directing him to go and investigate what was happening at Santiago. If the Spanish squadron was in port, a blockade must be immediately established. Schley received this message on 23 May.

At sea Schley considered that he exercised an independent command which gave him full authority over the Flying Squadron. He was most reluctant to leave Cienfuegos because, in his opinion, all the signs pointed to the fact that he had actually found Cervera. On approaching Cienfuegos, Schley later recalled that he had heard the noise of guns and interpreted this as the firing of a salute to welcome the arrival of the Spanish squadron. Not wishing to risk fire from the shore batteries, Schley remained some distance from the harbour. It was therefore impossible for him to make out what enemy ships were actually present, but a number of ships' masts were perceived from the crow's nest. Schley decided, therefore, to comply with Sampson's instructions dated 20 May and to remain on station at Cienfuegos. He did not obey the second despatch and leave for Santiago de Cuba until 24 May and only after receiving reports from Cuban insurgents on shore that Cervera was definitely not in the harbour.

On 26 May, at a distance of around 30 miles from Santiago de Cuba, Schley encountered three American scout light cruisers which stated that they had no knowledge of the whereabouts of the Spanish squadron. Rather than approach closer to the port and investigate for himself, Schley astounded his junior officers by stating that shortage of coal necessitated an immediate return to Key West. *En route* he received a despatch from the Navy Department at Washington requesting him to remain at Santiago. Convinced that Cervera was in that port, American officials realized that the opportunity had finally arisen to trap and destroy the elusive Spanish squadron. Speedy and resolute action by Schley would give the American navy command of the seas. But the Commodore sent back a totally unexpected reply: 'Much to be regretted, cannot obey orders of Department. Have striven earnestly; forced to proceed for coal to Key West by way of Yucatan passage. Cannot ascertain anything positive respecting enemy.'[27] The despatch brought intense gloom to the Navy Department and also to the White House on 28 May. Secretary of the Navy Long remarked:

> It was the most anxious day in the naval history of the war and was the only instance in which the Department had to whistle to keep its courage up. ... The feeling that the Spanish fleet might leave the harbor of Santiago was a heavy weight upon the President's mind. To deal with it was not difficult when its whereabouts were known, but to feel that it might leave the Cuban coast, that its movements might be lost track of, and that it might appear at any time on the coast of the United States, was depressing beyond measure.[28]

Meanwhile, Schley had halted his squadron in mid-voyage, perhaps to ponder the wisdom of his recent actions. Without divulging his reasoning, he decided on 28 May to return to Santiago de Cuba and reconnoitre the harbour. Early in the morning of 29 May the *Cristóbal Colón* was positively sighted and it was soon confirmed that the rest of the squadron was in the bay. For those present the jubilation of the moment was tempered with the

27 Cited in Walter Millis, *The Martial Spirit* (Boston, 1931), p. 234.
28 Cited in G.J.A. O'Toole, *The Spanish War: An American Epic* (New York, 1984), p. 220.

awareness that Schley's conduct during the past week would now be seen as unwise, if not foolish. Indeed, he would later be severely criticized for his days of aimless wandering about the Caribbean. Such behaviour had only increased the anxiety in Washington that Cervera would escape and the pursuit would have to begin all over again. That this did not occur was due to particular circumstances prevailing at Santiago de Cuba rather than the skill or vigour of the American navy.

Necessity had brought Cervera to Santiago de Cuba. As he expected, the city provided disappointingly little in the way of coal, food and supplies. 'It is to be regretted', he wrote to the Spanish commander, General Arsenio Linares Pomba, 'that bad luck brought me to this harbour, which is so short of everything we need.'[29] Acutely conscious of the movement of the Flying Squadron towards Cienfuegos, Cervera intended to depart from Santiago as soon as practicable. But the voyage across the Atlantic had been long and exhausting. The ships were in poor condition and the crews needed rest. Moreover, a mood of defeatism was fast taking hold. This was hardly surprising since Cervera and his senior officers had been resolute critics of the original decision to leave the Cape Verdes. Now that they were in the Caribbean, there seemed no obvious avenue of escape. If the squadron left Santiago, it would be pursued by the Americans. Whichever port the Spaniards entered, the Americans would soon establish a blockade. Unaware that Schley's dithering had presented a golden opportunity to leave, the whole question became redundant on 28 May when it was learned that the Flying Squadron was approaching Santiago de Cuba.

The news that Cervera was definitely in Santiago de Cuba was a relief for Sampson. In fact, a pincer movement to trap the Spanish squadron had already been put into effect. Leaving behind some light cruisers to maintain the blockade of Havana, Sampson had set out eastwards from Key West on 28 May. His flagship, the *New York*, was notably accompanied by the first-class battleship *Oregon* which had only recently docked in Florida after successfully completing her journey from the Pacific Ocean. Sampson arrived off Santiago de Cuba early in the morning of 1 June and assumed command. Despite their outward civility, relations between Sampson and Schley were awkward and strained. Nevertheless, Sampson avoided personal recriminations and concentrated on the military

---

29 Cervera to Linares, 25 May 1898, cited in Chadwick, *United States and Spain*, vol. ii p. 314.

task in hand. The blockading fleet assembled under his command comprised three first-class battleships, the *Iowa, Massachusetts* and *Oregon*, the second-class battleship *Texas*, two armoured cruisers, the *Brooklyn* and *New York*, the protected cruiser *New Orleans*, the unprotected cruiser *Marblehead*, and several smaller vessels. The much smaller Spanish squadron consisted of the four armoured cruisers, *María Teresa, Oquendo, Vizcaya* and *Cristóbal Colón*, and the two destroyers, *Furor* and *Plutón*.

Despite the powerful warships under his command, Sampson was not tempted either to emulate the feat of Captain Morgan in 1662 and storm Santiago de Cuba or to adopt the aggressive tactics of Commodore Dewey and attack the Spanish fleet at its moorings in the harbour at Manila Bay. In contrast to Havana, Sampson had no personal experience of Santiago de Cuba and possessed few details of its defences. At first sight, the topography and fortifications appeared quite formidable. The interior bay and harbour were approached along a narrow and winding channel stretching for almost a mile long and ranging in width from 300 to no more than 400 feet. On either side of the entrance were steep bluffs containing artillery batteries to the east at the Morro Castle and to the west at La Socapa. Not only would invading ships present virtual sitting targets to the batteries above, but they would also face the danger of electrical mines which were known to have been placed in the channel. The military risks were therefore much greater than those faced by Dewey at Manila Bay.

Although the narrow entrance was an obvious obstacle to hostile ships, it provided a similar impediment to vessels trying to leave. Sampson, therefore, approved the ingenious scheme proposed by Lieutenant Richmond Pearson Hobson to trap the Spanish ships within the harbour by sinking the collier *Merrimac* just inside the entrance. The plan was to pack the *Merrimac* with explosives and to enter the channel under cover of darkness. Once inside the entrance the collier would be run aground and blown up so that its length of 333 feet and large structure weighing 7,000 tons would effectively block the channel just like a cork in a bottle. The mission, however, was highly risky. Lieutenant Hobson asked for six volunteers to accompany him on what was, in reality, a floating bomb. Patriotic fervour was such that there was no shortage of volunteers. Indeed, the captains of the battleships were forced to state that only one man could be released per ship.

The operation commenced at 3 a.m. on 3 June. The *Merrimac* actually entered the channel without interference, but was then sighted and fired upon by the shore batteries. Within fifteen minutes she was sunk, but ended up sideways and too far from the centre of the channel to inconvenience shipping. It was reported later that Hobson and all seven of his men – the extra was a stowaway – were captured by the Spaniards. Amazingly, however, they had not been injured in spite of the heavy firing and multiple explosions. Initially, it was believed that the *Merrimac* had actually succeeded in blocking the channel. To the American press, the incident was treated therefore as the greatest event to occur since the Battle of Manila Bay. The young lieutenant quickly became a national hero. 'The name of Hobson', enthused the *New York Journal*, 'has gone on the list of American heroes, with Lawrence, Paul Jones, Perry, Cushing, and the rest.'[30]

Despite the undoubted bravery of Hobson and his men, the mission had failed. To prevent the Spanish ships from escaping, Sampson established a close blockade. Throughout each day a semicircle of ships patrolled at a distance of 4 to 6 miles from the Morro Castle. At night they came to within 3 miles and used searchlights to illuminate the entrance. Mindful of his standing instructions not to risk damage to his armoured ships, Sampson avoided bringing the battleships too close to the shore. Occasionally, however, he ordered them to bombard the land batteries. This first occurred on 6 June, when 2,000 rounds of ammunition were fired for three hours at a range of 3 to 4 miles. The action was repeated on 16 June. Sampson placed little emphasis on naval bombardment because he was convinced that shelling from a long distance had limited impact upon fixed fortifications. He also believed that the effective destruction of the batteries on the Morro and La Socapa required the landing of a substantial military force and was therefore a task for the army. In his opinion, the arrival of the Expeditionary Force was vitally important. 'If 10,000 men were here', he telegraphed to Long on 6 June, 'city and fleet would be ours within forty-eight hours.'[31]

In fact, Sampson had a number of soldiers under his command in the form of a marine battalion. On 10 June, 650 men from this unit were put ashore to take possession of the hills overlooking the eastern side of Guantánamo Bay. Around 40 miles east of Santiago de Cuba, the bay was considered a very suitable harbour for

---

30 Cited in Brown, *Correspondents' War*, p. 294.
31 Sampson to Long, 6 June 1898, cited in Russell A. Alger, *The Spanish-American War* (New York, 1901), p. 71.

bringing in supplies and allowing ships to coal in calm waters. After an uneventful landing the marines later came under attack from Spanish troops sent from the local garrison in the town of Guantánamo at the other end of the bay. With the aid of Cuban insurgents and covering artillery fire from American ships offshore, the marines successfully forced the Spaniards to withdraw, though six Americans were killed in the fighting. The engagement attracted little attention from the press, but, in reality, it marked the beginning of the American 'invasion' of Cuba.

The action at Guantánamo Bay was merely a prelude to the arrival off Santiago de Cuba of the American Expeditionary Force and the launching of major operations on land. By locating and blockading Cervera's squadron, the American navy had removed the major impediment to the safe transport of American troops to Cuba. But time was of the essence because the blockade was stretching American naval resources to the limit. 'Before the Spanish war', Sampson noted later, 'it was an axiom of naval strategy that a whole fleet could not be completely blockaded.'[32] The most feared contingency was that Spanish ships would attempt to break the blockade either singly or in pairs. Nor did Cervera necessarily have to fight his way out. There was always the chance that unpredictable factors such as bad weather, poor visibility, a collision at sea or an error of judgement by an American captain might present the Spaniards with an opportunity to escape. Moreover, the hurricane season was not far away. In the case of a fierce tropical storm striking, the American ships would have to disperse and thereby lift the blockade. There was also the possibility that warships might eventually be sent from Spain to attack, or more likely, to detach ships from the American squadron. The maintenance of the blockade was therefore both vital and difficult. 'No more onerous and important duty than the guard off Santiago fell upon any officer of the United States during the hostilities,' remarked Mahan in praise of Sampson.[33] Nevertheless, Sampson was relieved to learn that troop transports had left Tampa on 14 June. This meant that the city of Santiago de Cuba would soon be under attack from both land and sea.

American fears of a Spanish naval counter-attack were not entirely groundless. All sorts of rumours emanated from Madrid during May. In reality, Spanish political and military leaders were

32 Sampson, 'Atlantic Fleet', p. 913.
33 Mahan, *Lessons of War with Spain*, p. 182.

shocked and dismayed by the disastrous news from the Philippines. Growing public disquiet and talk of a military *coup* to overthrow the monarchy prompted the declaration of martial law within the city of Madrid on 3 May. The firm attitude of the government was further demonstrated by Sagasta's dismissal of suggestions to enter into peace negotiations with the United States. None the less, despite the public statements that vigorous action against the Americans would soon be forthcoming, government policy was clearly in disarray. For example, the Ministry of the Marine issued instructions on 8 May to expedite the refitting of the *Pelayo* and *Carlos V*. It was suggested that Admiral Manuel de la Cámara would shortly take the ships to the Philippines to restore Spanish honour by doing battle with Dewey. Almost simultaneously, Minister of the Marine Bermejo sent a despatch to Cervera on 12 May giving the admiral permission to return to Spain if he so wished. Soon afterwards, a major government reshuffle took place in which Bermejo was replaced by Captain Ramón Auñón y Villalón, who immediately instructed Cervera to remain in the Caribbean. In fact, the change of minister merely underlined the shortcomings long inherent in Spanish naval policy. Auñón's ideas were just as unrealistic as those of his predecessor. His first days in office were marked by the reaffirmation of the strategy which entailed sending the *Carlos V* and some light cruisers to the Caribbean to help Cervera's squadron accomplish its mission of harassing American merchant shipping and raiding ports along the east coast of the United States.

The McKinley administration had always anticipated that Spain would eventually send the *Pelayo* and *Carlos V* to the Caribbean. The prospect was alarming, because the arrival of those two armoured warships would decisively alter the balance of naval power between the respective fleets. The Office of Naval Intelligence of the Navy Department was given the task of closely observing Spanish naval developments. For this purpose an elaborate network of attachés and spies was set up to report information acquired in the Canaries, Cádiz, Madrid, Paris and London. The emerging 'intelligence service' also had other uses. To put the Spaniards off-guard and on the defensive, American officials in Europe were instructed to disseminate reports that, as soon as Cervera's squadron was destroyed, the American navy intended to mount a massive attack upon Cádiz.

The programme of disinformation proved highly successful. Indeed, the reports were taken so seriously in Madrid that they provided the Spanish government with a compelling reason to maintain most of its remaining naval strength in home waters. Similarly, rather than send the *Pelayo* and *Carlos V* to combat the powerful American battleships in the Caribbean or the Atlantic, the Ministry of the Marine preferred the much less risky alternative of despatching the ships to the Pacific Ocean. Accordingly, on 16 June a squadron under the command of Admiral de la Cámara and consisting of the *Pelayo*, *Carlos V*, two cruisers, three destroyers, two troop transports carrying 4,000 troops, and four colliers left Cádiz for the Philippines. The voyage was to be made via the Suez Canal so as to avoid coming into contact with American warships. The Spanish government had evidently decided that its priority was to attempt to regain control of the Philippines. No ships or reinforcements were to be sent to the Caribbean. The news was extremely depressing for Captain General Blanco in Havana and Admiral Cervera in Santiago de Cuba. After having endured the American naval blockade for several weeks, they now faced the disturbing prospect of the arrival of the American Expeditionary Force.

5 THE AMERICAN EXPEDITIONARY FORCE

CREATING AN ARMY

Ever since the sinking of the *Maine* in February 1898 thousands of Americans had enthusiastically declared their willingness to volunteer and fight for their country against what they perceived to be the treachery of Spain. However, the assimilation of so much patriotic zeal into an organized military force was by no means a straightforward task for President McKinley and his officials at the War Department. The first issue to resolve was the optimum size of the federal army. Even before war with Spain was actually declared, American political and military leaders were in no doubt that the army must be considerably increased from its prescribed peacetime strength of 25,000 enlisted men.[1] Both the Secretary of War, Russell Alger, and the Commander of the Army, General Nelson A. Miles, thought that the requirements of an overseas campaign could be accomplished with a total federal army of around 100,000 regular soldiers. But expansion required congressional approval. A bill to enact the figure recommended by Alger and Miles came to Congress for debate in early April. A favourable response was anticipated.

The measure, however, proved highly controversial. It was not surprising that a number of Congressmen should voice the traditional American distrust of powerful standing armies as a threat to liberty. A suspicion also existed that federal officials were seeking to use the crisis with Spain to foist a permanently large and expensive military establishment upon the people. More unexpected, however, was the vigorous political lobbying against the bill undertaken by the National Guard. Alger and Miles believed that the burden of fighting the Spaniards would be properly undertaken by regular soldiers. The projected increase of the regular army to 100,000 men would be met by volunteers, some of whom would be ex-regulars, but most would inevitably be drawn from the state

---

1 The authorized Congressional limit did not include officers.

militias, forming the National Guard. Volunteers would be trained by regulars and assigned to regiments in the army. Alger and Miles were generally dismissive of the fighting qualities of the state militias and regarded the latter as primarily a police force that would be best allocated to coastal defence duties during wartime. They greatly underestimated, however, the strength of local feeling and especially the political influence of the state militias. Each militia was headed by the governor of the state and was an important source of political patronage and prestige. An inglorious defensive role was hardly what the governors had in mind for the men of their particular states. Moreover, if guardsmen were simply allowed to be absorbed into a federal volunteer army, local militia regiments would be seriously depleted in strength and the whole structure of the state militia would soon be in danger of collapse. Domestic political considerations suddenly loomed large as the National Guard, the collective body representing the state militias, sensed a threat to its very existence. What had started as a reasonable proposal to expand the size of the regular army was transformed into a controversy over federal encroachment upon the constitutional right of the states to maintain their own militias.

While Congress debated McKinley's War Resolution, earnest discussions were simultaneously taking place between Congressmen and officials of the War Department over the size and composition of the federal army. No one disputed that war with Spain would require an army in excess of 100,000 men. This was not so much a reflection of strategic necessity as a concession to the extraordinary popular demand of many thousands of Americans to participate personally in the actual fighting. The really contentious issue was how many of these soldiers would be under direct federal control. A compromise was eventually reached by which the federal army would be allowed to recruit up to a total maximum strength of just over 65,000 for a period of two years. This became law on 26 April, and was contingent upon the passage four days earlier on 22 April of a bill providing substantial concessions to the National Guard. This bill stipulated that a presidential call for volunteers would be issued to meet the large number of additional soldiers which would still be required above the ceiling of 65,000. Volunteers must be between the ages of eighteen and forty-five and should serve for the duration of the war but no more than two years. Although the President was given special authority to form three separate cavalry regiments each containing 1,000 men with special cavalry qualifications – one regiment became the celebrated 'Rough Riders'

– only members of the National Guard were generally eligible to volunteer.

The ability of the National Guard to highlight state participation in the war effort was further underlined by the establishment of quotas of volunteers for each state based upon population. Moreover, volunteers were expected to join not as individuals but collectively as complete state regiments serving under their own officers. Although under the overall direction of federal commanders, a separate volunteer army was essentially being created alongside the regular army. This development mollified the concern of the National Guard that guardsmen might lose their local identity and, even worse, be placed under the command of out-of-state 'West Pointers'. Indeed, the question of officers remained highly sensitive. The right to nominate officers of state regiments was a vital source of local political patronage and one which state governors would not willingly abandon even during time of war. McKinley bowed to political expediency and agreed that volunteer officers would be chosen only from recommendations made by the state governors.

On 23 April President McKinley issued a call for 125,000 volunteers. The actual number was more than had been expected by Alger and Miles. The White House let it be known to the press that the President wished to avoid repeating Lincoln's mistake in 1861 of asking for only 75,000, a figure which had soon turned out to be inadequate. None the less, a combined army of almost 200,000 regulars and volunteers seemed more than sufficient for war against Spain. Perhaps, the President also sought to impress upon the Spanish government the futility of fighting so powerful a nation as the United States. However, the fact that 125,000 virtually equalled the estimated strength of the National Guard suggested the primacy of domestic political factors. In effect, the whole of the National Guard could be transferred directly into the volunteer army. The National Guard had therefore triumphed over Alger and Miles, but the result was a decentralized system of recruiting, confusion over mustering and training, and simply too many men chasing too little equipment, weapons and accommodation. Ironically, Alger and his officials at the War Department would later bear the brunt of criticism for the nation's scandalous lack of military preparation. It was, however, not by their choice that the United States had determined at short notice to put into the field a mass volunteer army.

On 25 April Secretary of War Alger telegraphed official requests to each state to call up its quota of volunteers. During the following month men travelled to their local state assembly points where they were given physical examinations. The large majority, who were passed as fit for duty, were sworn into the federal army and supplied with whatever uniforms and weapons were available. General Miles had recommended that the volunteers receive several weeks' basic training in their home states. This was ruled out, however, not only by the lack of equipment and facilities but also by the acute shortage of officers and instructors. Consequently, the volunteers were speedily mustered into their regimental units and put on trains destined mainly for the large federal army base at Chickamauga Park, or the new military camp established in Virginia close to Washington and named Camp Alger.

Most of the 125,000 volunteers had been called up by the end of May. In the meantime, however, McKinley's decision to extend army operations to include the Philippines and Puerto Rico had resulted in a perceived need for even more troops. Consequently, on 25 May the President issued a second call for volunteers, on this occasion requesting an additional 75,000 men. A total of 8,970 officers and 173,717 enlisted men joined the army as a result of the two calls. In addition, 763 officers and 16,992 men with special qualifications such as engineers and cavalrymen were recruited separately as United States Volunteers. The number of volunteers was therefore 200,442, two-thirds of whom remained in the United States and never saw service overseas. The recruitment of soldiers into the regular army also continued throughout the war. It was not until August 1898, however, that the federal army reached its permitted ceiling of 65,000 men.

No major difficulties were encountered during the war in obtaining sufficient personnel for the army. Volunteers came forward from all social classes, large cities and small towns in every state of the Union. In fact, Alger estimated that at least 1 million men responded to McKinley's first call for volunteers. 'It was the apotheosis of patriotism,' he noted.[2] There were so many public

2 Russell A. Alger, *The Spanish-American War* (New York, 1901), p. 7. Not all Americans welcomed the coming of war with Spain. The dilemma which the war posed to ethnic, religious and political groups within the United States is explored in: William B. Gatewood, Jr, *Black Americans and the White Man's Burden* (Urbana, IL, 1975), pp. 22–40; Graeme S. Mount, 'Nuevo Mexicanos and the War of 1898', *New Mexico Historical Review* 58 (1983), pp. 381–96; D. Michael Quinn, 'The Mormon Church and the Spanish-American War: An End to Selective Pacifism', *Pacific Historical Review* 43 (1974), pp. 342–66, and Howard H. Quint, 'American Socialists and the Spanish-American War', *American Quarterly* 10 (1958), pp. 131–41.

demonstrations to wave 'the boys' goodbye that the production of American flags and bunting could not keep pace with demand. So widespread was the popular enthusiasm that the war was regarded as a welcome means of affirming national unity and finally reconciling the sectional divisions between the North and the South which had been inflamed by the Civil War and the period of Reconstruction during the 1860s. The shelling of the *Winslow* at Cárdenas on 12 May, which resulted in the death in action of Ensign Worth Bagley of North Carolina, caused the *New York Tribune* to comment: 'The South furnishes the first sacrifice of this war. . . . There is no north and no south after that, we are all Worth Bagley's countrymen.'[3] Southern blacks as well as whites responded eagerly to McKinley's patriotic appeal. The approval of the West and Midwest for the war was demonstrated by William Jennings Bryan's acceptance of a commission in the Third Nebraska Volunteers. During his campaign for the presidency only two years earlier, Bryan had condemned McKinley as a creature of eastern capitalist interests.

The most celebrated example of national togetherness was provided by the First United States Volunteer Cavalry regiment. Commanded by Colonel Leonard Wood, an army surgeon who had formerly been McKinley's personal physician, it included the larger-than-life figure of Theodore Roosevelt. As soon as war had been declared, Roosevelt announced his intention to resign as Assistant Secretary of the Navy and to volunteer for the army. With somewhat uncharacteristic modesty, he turned down the offer to command a regiment and chose to serve as a lieutenant colonel under his friend, Leonard Wood. Like Roosevelt, a number of the young men who joined the First United States Volunteer Cavalry were also from wealthy Ivy League backgrounds. However, the majority of volunteers, who assembled at the mustering point in San Antonio, Texas, were westerners from nearby New Mexico, Arizona and Oklahoma. On first meeting them, Roosevelt enthusiastically remarked:

> They were a splendid set of men, these Southwesterners – tall and sinewy, with resolute weather-beaten faces, and eyes that looked a man straight in the face without flinching. They included in their ranks men of every occupation; but the three

3 Cited in Richard E. Wood, 'The South and Reunion, 1898', *The Historian* 31 (1969), p. 427.

types were those of cowboy, the hunter and the mining prospector – the man who wandered hither and thither, killing game for a living, and spending his life in the quest for metal wealth.[4]

The evocative image of western cowboys riding to do battle for freedom exerted a powerful spell on the press and public. The First United States Volunteer Cavalry regiment soon acquired a separate identity, initially as the 'Rustler Regiment' and 'Teddy's Terrors' and later more popularly as the 'Rough Riders'.

The granting of army commissions to Wood and Roosevelt was a tiny part of an enormous administrative burden inflicted by the war upon McKinley and Alger. Although the state governors essentially made most of the appointments to the volunteer regiments, McKinley and Alger were still directly inundated with thousands of requests from civilians for commissions. The Secretary of War described his own particular predicament:

> The life of the Secretary of War was not a happy one in those days of active military operations. With over a quarter of a million men in the army, it seemed as if there was hardly a family in the United States that did not have a friend or relative in the service, and that for one reason or another some member from each of these found it necessary to write to, or personally visit, the War Office.[5]

During the first month of the war an estimated 25,000 applications for commissions were received at the White House, of which McKinley personally approved around 1,000. Although the pervasive pressure of 'spoils politics' could not be entirely ignored, the choice of senior officers reflected the President's concern to select men of proven merit and military experience gained either during the Civil War or from service in the regular army. Notable volunteers who received appointment as generals were James H. Wilson and especially the former Confederate officers, Fitzhugh Lee and Joseph 'Fighting Joe' Wheeler.

Ever since the middle of April most of the regular army had steadily been concentrated in the southeast of the United States. During May they were joined by increasing hordes of volunteers. A

4 Theodore Roosevelt, *The Rough Riders* (New York, 1902), p. 15.
5 Alger, *Spanish-American War*, p. 29.

relatively small number of volunteers drawn from the western states were directed instead to California in preparation for service in the Philippines. For organizational purposes the army was divided into seven separate corps. Each corps was intended to contain up to 30,000 men and would be commanded by a major-general. Most of the volunteer regiments were organized into the First and Third Corps, which were stationed at Chickamauga Park. Provision was made for a Sixth Corps at the same camp though this particular unit never actually materialized. The Second Corps was based at Camp Alger and the Fourth Corps at Mobile, Alabama. The Expeditionary Force, which was being prepared at Tampa, consisted of the Fifth and Seventh Corps. The Fifth Corps contained mainly regular soldiers and was regarded as the most professional of the army units. During June the Eighth Corps was created at San Francisco to comprise the troops destined for campaigning in the Philippines. In addition to the army corps were several smaller units of specialized personnel such as cavalry, engineers and signalmen, and the ten regiments of 'immune' infantry consisting of men who were believed to be resistant to tropical disease. Black regular soldiers made up four of these regiments. These 'buffalo soldiers' had proved their fighting qualities in a series of campaigns against the Indians in the West and were considered to be well suited for campaigning in Cuba.

The organization of thousands of men into a vast army was an enormous undertaking. As Commander-in-Chief of the army and navy, President McKinley possessed the ultimate authority in deciding how American forces would fight the war. Although McKinley worked hard and conscientiously, the process of decision-making tended to be inefficient because no specific war plans had been formulated and no general staff existed to implement policy. The inherent difficulties of directing a massive military operation were made even worse by growing personal friction between Alger and Miles. McKinley soon lost confidence in both men and came to rely more and more upon Alger's own chief of staff, Henry C. Corbin, a skilled administrator who held the office of Adjutant-General in the War Department. The divisions at the top were often replicated throughout the whole of the War Department and the army, as a result not so much of longstanding inter-service rivalries but of the serious shortage of experienced officials and staff officers to deal with the ever-increasing pressure of work. Though it was hardly their fault, the Quartermaster, Ordnance and Commissary departments of the War Department were clearly unprepared. Existing stocks of food, supplies, weapons and ammunition were understandably based on the needs of a small peacetime army. Forward planning to remedy anticipated inadequacies had been virtually made impossible by the uncertainty as to the exact size of the volunteer army and the particular military strategy which it was likely to adopt. As soon as war was declared, Congress voted large appropriations, but just about everything was in short supply. 'Improvisation' was the magic word as the American economy geared itself to the demands of war. Government officials bought whatever was available and placed orders for more. Tons of equipment and supplies were soon being transported night and day along the railway tracks, rivers, canals and roads leading to the army bases. The variety and quantity of goods was staggering. This was illustrated by a list which Alger later presented of items which the Quartermaster's Department had either manufactured or purchased during the period from May to August 1898. Among the examples included were: 546,338 blankets, 523,203 trousers, 476,705 campaign hats, 153,167 canvas field uniforms, 782,303 shoes, 622,211 dark-blue flannel shirts, 38,963 axes, 34,344 camp-kettles, 64,980 tents, 16,618 horses, 20,182 mules, and 5,179 wagons.[6]

Administrative shortcomings and general unpreparedness were vividly highlighted in the camps. Consignments of supplies arrived every day, but the contents were not usually listed on the crates and boxes. Even if the contents could be identified, the facilities for efficient loading and distribution rarely existed. Consequently, the thousands of men in the camps suffered from poor accommodation and shortages of basic necessities. Unpalatable food was a particularly common complaint. Irritation and boredom also set in as it was realized that, so long as the army favoured despatching regular troops to Cuba, volunteers were personally most unlikely to be sent overseas. As the summer progressed the incidence of disease, especially typhoid, rose alarmingly. The problem was greatly compounded by the fact that the camps lacked adequate sanitation and health-care facilities primarily because they had been originally conceived as temporary transit points rather than permanent encampments. By 30 September 1898 disease had claimed the lives of 425 soldiers at Chickamauga and 107 at Camp Thomas.[7]

6 Ibid., pp. 24–5.
7 Walter Millis, *The Martial Spirit* (Boston, 1931), p. 366.

Showing more concern about the progress of the Expeditionary Force in Cuba, the press and public initially paid little attention to the deplorable living conditions in the camps. However, they gradually came to public notice and prompted an official investigation after the end of the war. Criticism was concentrated especially on Secretary of War Alger, who was accused of callous insensitivity and administrative incompetence. The remote location of some of the camps aroused sensational allegations that he had been personally involved in secret deals with landowners and railway interests. Although these charges were never substantiated, the general condemnation of Alger was scarcely diminished. For thousands of young Americans life in the camps was a squalid and disheartening experience. Alger and his officials at the War Department could not escape their share of the blame for this, but they had struggled sincerely and conscientiously to attempt to fulfil the unrealistic expectation of the American people that a huge army could be created within a short space of time.

PRELIMINARY PLANS TO INVADE CUBA

Despite being overwhelmed by the task of organizing an army of more than 100,000 volunteers, officials at the War Department could not ignore the increasing demands not only of the press and public but also of Congress and especially President McKinley for some kind of overt action by the American army against the Spaniards in Cuba. The most immediately feasible option was to send relatively small units of regular troops to the island where they could join forces with the insurgents and attack vulnerable Spanish garrisons. General Miles was very much in favour of this approach and, as early as 9 April, had approved a secret mission in which Lieutenant Andrew S. Rowan travelled to Oriente to seek out and establish personal contact with the rebel leaders. Rowan was successful in locating Calixto García, but he did not return to the United States until 11 May.

In the meantime, Miles and the War Department had devised a modest scheme to demonstrate that the army could play just as active a part in the fighting as the navy. The operation would be carried out by regular units of the Fifth Army Corps under the command of Major-General William Rufus Shafter. Shafter was a Civil War veteran who, like many of the regular officers, had spent much of his military career fighting the Indians in the West. More than sixty years old and weighing over 300 pounds, Shafter would find service in the tropics particularly onerous. His appointment to command the Fifth Corps was explained by a combination of seniority and the fact that he hailed from Alger's home state of Michigan and was a friend of the Adjutant-General, Henry Corbin. On 29 April Shafter received orders from Miles to assemble 5,000 troops at Tampa. These men were to be transported as soon as possible to Cape Tunas, a remote landing point on the southern coast of Cuba about 70 miles east of Cienfuegos. Once ashore they were to move inland and deliver supplies and weapons to the insurgent forces led by Máximo Gómez. No extensive campaigning was envisaged, though American troops would be allowed to cooperate with the insurgents in joint attacks upon the Spaniards. The American forces would leave after a few days and, if practicable, repeat the same operation in the northwest of Cuba. After accomplishing this, they were to return immediately to the United States. Miles described the mission as a 'reconnaissance in force'.[8] While it sought to serve certain tangible military purposes, the operation was mostly inspired by a desire of the army to be seen to be doing something and thereby promote a positive image among American public opinion.

Miles's plan was sound in theory, but left a lot of questions unanswered concerning its execution. For example, it was simply assumed that adequate transport vessels would be available at Tampa. Nor had provision been made for prior consultation with either Admiral Sampson or the Cuban insurgents. A great burden of responsibility was consequently placed directly upon Shafter, who had actually only arrived to take up his command in Tampa on 29 April. 'In conducting this enterprise', Miles ingenuously informed the general, 'great confidence is placed in your zeal, judicious management, and good judgement.'[9] Indeed, it was perhaps fortunate for Shafter and all concerned that external factors intervened to cancel the operation. The despatch of orders from Miles to Shafter coincided with the receipt of news in Washington that Admiral Cervera and the Spanish squadron of fast armoured warships had left the Cape Verdes. This meant that safe transportation from Tampa to Cuba could not be guaranteed

8 See Corbin to Shafter, 29 April 1898, cited in Alger, *Spanish-American War*, p. 44.
9 Ibid.

because it was now impossible for Sampson to release warships for convoy duty. Shafter simply remained in Tampa, desperately trying to familiarize himself with his new command while waiting for orders from Washington.

Notwithstanding the anxiety over the whereabouts of the Spanish naval squadron, the political and public pressure for immediate offensive action in Cuba remained as powerful as ever. On 2 May McKinley brought Alger, Miles, Long and Admiral Sicard to the White House to discuss the various military options. It was decided to make Havana the principal target of a new and much larger expedition. Havana was regarded as the symbol of Spanish power whose capture would most likely bring the war to a rapid close. The proximity of the naval base at Key West and the warships of the North Atlantic Squadron also made military operations against the northern coast of Cuba much safer than in the more distant Caribbean. The plan which emerged from the meeting at the White House was for a force of several thousand regular troops to establish a beachhead at Mariel, about 25 miles west of Havana. The navy would send in supplies of food, ammunition and especially reinforcements, so that the army would build up a powerful military presence amounting to around 50,000 men. Dates were imprecise, but it was assumed that this force would make a successful land assault on Havana within weeks and, it was hoped, by the end of May. In essence, the plan was virtually identical to the one floated at the meeting of army and navy officers on 4 April. One notable difference, however, was the omission of a combat role for the Cuban insurgents. American soldiers were to do the fighting in what was evidently conceived as a purely United States military operation.

Although Shafter confirmed that he was able to attack Mariel at short notice, Alger was uncertain whether the follow-up stage could be successfully accomplished simply because sufficient numbers of trained and equipped reinforcements were not yet available for overseas duty. Inter-service rivalries came to the surface at a cabinet meeting on 6 May when Long pointedly criticized Alger for prevaricating. According to the Secretary of the Navy, the army had only to land 50,000 men on Cuban soil and the war would come to an end. Instead of a military operation in Cuba, the result was a Washington merry-go-round. Goaded by Long's comments, Alger ordered Miles on 8 May to assemble a force of 70,000 men and prepare for a direct frontal assault on Havana. Miles was taken aback. He had actually dissented from the more modest plan made only four days earlier at the White House. Rather than discuss the matter with Alger, the general characteristically went directly to McKinley. Arguing that the President had been misinformed about 'the real military conditions', Miles stated that not only were the Spanish defences at Havana much stronger than was believed, but also that there was not even enough ammunition currently available in the United States to supply an army of 70,000 men. McKinley agreed to withdraw Alger's order of 8 May and, according to Miles, 'thereby saved many thousands of lives, and possibly a national disaster'.[10]

Nevertheless, the scheme to establish a beachhead at Mariel as a prelude to attacking Havana was still extant. On 9 May Alger ordered Shafter to implement the plan as soon as possible. No doubt, to Alger's satisfaction and Long's embarrassment, this proved impracticable because the Navy Department was still unable to provide protective cover for a troop convoy. The resulting delay of a few days seemed likely to become of much longer duration when it was learned that Cervera was definitely in the vicinity of Cuba. The Mariel operation was postponed until such time as the American navy had located and destroyed the Spanish squadron. This allowed Shafter at least two additional weeks to build up the Expeditionary Force at Tampa. For War Department officials the postponement similarly provided more precious time to proceed with their even bigger task of organizing the thousands of volunteers who continued to arrive daily at the army camps.

An 'expedition' was, however, actually sent to Mariel. Since the declaration of war the army had become directly involved in assisting a small number of ships to sail from Florida to Cuba loaded with supplies, ammunition and recruits intended for the insurgent forces. For example, Captain Joseph Dorst of the United States Cavalry had landed close to Mariel on 3 May, but had been driven off by Spanish gunfire. Dorst prepared a bigger expedition, including more than 100 American infantrymen, to leave from Tampa on 10 May in the side-wheel riverboat steamer *Gussie*. Accompanied by several American journalists, the progress of the *Gussie* was so visible and well-publicized that a thousand Spanish troops were waiting for her arrival at Mariel on 12 May. A brief landing was effected further down the coast near Cabañas – the first time in the war that a detachment of American troops had been put ashore on Cuban soil. The approach of Spanish troops from the

10 Nelson A. Miles, *Serving the Republic: Memoirs of the Civil and Military Life of Nelson A. Miles* (New York, 1911), pp. 272–3.

local garrison resulted in desultory fighting, though no American casualties were reported. Eventually the American soldiers returned to the *Gussie*, which sailed away without being able to make contact with the insurgents. However, two weeks later, on 26 May, Dorst was conspicuously successful when he safely entered the port of Banes in Oriente and was able to unload from the steamer *Florida* a substantial cargo, including 7,500 Springfield rifles, 1,300,000 rounds of ammunition, various amounts of clothing and equipment plus about 100 horses and mules. A small number of similar landings involving American army personnel were made during May and June, though none was as successful as Dorst's achievement in the *Florida*.

The despatch of supplies to the insurgents received official approval, but was neither a systematic nor strategically significant policy. In fact, by its refusal to grant diplomatic recognition to the provisional government formed by the Cuban rebels, the McKinley administration ensured that there would be no formal alliance between American military leaders and the insurgent generals. There was, therefore, no suggestion of the Cubans being directly incorporated within the American army or command structure. Where contact was established between American junior officers and insurgents, it was unofficial and informal. Any suspicions that Cubans might harbour of American intentions towards them were overcome by their pressing need for weapons and supplies and their general delight that the government of the United States had finally pledged itself to support *Cuba libre*. Once war was declared, however, less and less attention in Washington was given to consideration of the military contribution which the insurgents might make to winning the war. The implicit assumption which emerged was that victory would be secured principally, if not solely, by the efforts of the American army and navy.

General Miles was unusual among American political and military leaders in emphasizing the fighting abilities of the Cuban insurgents. Until the United States had recruited and trained a large invasion force, he argued that the insurgents should assume the major combat role in land operations. But this view received scant support from his colleagues, who regarded the insurgents not as an organized army but as disparate factions of irregulars roaming the mountains and countryside. The possible exception was the large force commanded by Calixto García which was known to be operating on virtually equal terms with the Spanish army in Oriente. Even Miles deliberately bypassed Máximo Gómez, the commander of the Cuban Liberating Army, and preferred instead to open communications with Calixto García. Following orders from Miles, Lieutenant Andrew S. Rowan located Calixto García's headquarters in Oriente on 1 May and returned to the United States a short time later accompanied by three senior members of García's staff. These officers met with Miles and Alger in Washington and imparted valuable information about military conditions in Oriente. The link with Calixto García acquired vital importance when it was learned that Cervera's naval squadron was in Santiago de Cuba.

The report that Cervera was in Santiago de Cuba prompted an urgent reappraisal of American strategy. The subject was first discussed at a council of war held at the White House on 26 May. Alger, Miles and Long were among those present at the meeting. They agreed that southeastern Cuba had suddenly become the critical area of military concern. It was decided therefore to postpone the assault on Havana until later in the year so that the Expeditionary Force could be sent instead to Santiago de Cuba. Provision was also made for a separate attack upon Puerto Rico after the fall of Santiago. Miles was delighted by the switch of emphasis from a frontal attack on Havana to the outflanking manoeuvres which he had always recommended. Over the next few days he submitted operational plans to McKinley and Alger, advocating, first, the capture of Santiago de Cuba, secondly, the seizure of Puerto Rico to complete the isolation of Cuba by preventing the arrival of Spanish naval reinforcements, and, finally, a progressive advance westwards by American forces from Santiago de Cuba to Havana.

Essential to Miles's thinking was his desire to minimize the exposure of American soldiers to the disease-ridden rainy season. But a lengthy campaign extending into 1899 and, much of it conducted in the mountainous region of Oriente, raised major problems of supply and transportation. Alger grasped the opportunity to strike a blow at his rival's reputation. 'Many of the general's proposals were obviously impracticable, and not infrequently absolutely impossible,' summed up the Secretary of War.[11] On this occasion, McKinley sided with Alger. As soon as it was confirmed that Cervera was definitely in Santiago de Cuba, the President favoured the immediate despatch of the Expeditionary Force to that city. After Santiago de Cuba was captured and the Spanish squadron destroyed, an attack would be made on Puerto

11 Alger, *Spanish-American War*, p. 57.

Rico. However, instead of Miles's 'movement to the west',[12] the President reaffirmed his clear personal preference for the more direct alternative offered by the Mariel scheme. He directed the War Department to organize additional volunteer regiments in preparation for a major assault on Havana.

For some weeks Shafter had waited at Tampa. On 26 May the following instructions arrived from Miles: 'Be prepared to load on transports 25,000 men, including infantry, four batteries light artillery, eight siege guns, including siege mortars, and one squadron cavalry.'[13] A few days later Miles indicated that the destination of the expedition was Santiago de Cuba. The orders were confirmed by Alger on 31 May. Shafter and the Fifth Corps were to proceed in naval convoy to Santiago de Cuba, make a landing at a suitable point and 'cooperate most earnestly ' with the navy to destroy the Spanish fleet in the harbour. The despatch ended with the question: 'When will you sail?'[14] On the same day Miles left Washington for Tampa, presumably to assume charge of the operation. It was clear to Shafter that the time for action had now arrived and that his superiors in Washington expected the speedy departure of the Expeditionary Force for Santiago de Cuba.

EMBARKATION FROM TAMPA

From the vantage point of officials in Washington, Tampa, Florida, appeared to be the ideal embarkation point for small-scale army expeditions to Cuba. In 1898 Tampa was a little-known city of 26,000 inhabitants, but it was reputed to possess a fine deep-water bay and suitable docking facilities. Although it was much smaller than Charleston, South Carolina, or Gulf ports such as Mobile and New Orleans, this was more than compensated for by its closer proximity to Cuba. Indeed, before the war steamships had regularly plied the route between Tampa and Havana. Moreover, Tampa Bay's location on the west coast of Florida gave protection from the weather and presented a difficult target for a Spanish naval raid. In retrospect, however, the choice of Tampa was flawed. This was not the particular fault of War Department officials. Any site along the whole length of the Atlantic and Gulf coasts would have similarly

---

12 Miles to Alger, 27 May 1898, cited in ibid., p. 51.
13 Miles to Shafter, 26 May 1898, cited in ibid., p. 63.
14 See Corbin to Shafter, 31 May 1898, cited in ibid., pp. 64–5.

found it virtually impossible, first to accommodate, and then despatch, a large expeditionary force at short notice. But the task was made even more difficult by the fact that the state of Florida was relatively economically undeveloped and possessed limited railway connections with the rest of the United States. The advantage of proximity to Cuba was therefore outweighed by remoteness from the nation's major factories and supply depots. Nor did the problem of communications end at Tampa. The docks at Port Tampa were 9 miles distant from the city and were connected by a single railway line. Within a short space of time the track was jammed with railway trucks while trains destined for Tampa formed a line extending for miles outside the city. 'Unquestionably', Alger later summed up, 'Tampa was not adapted to the concentration and the effective handling of the vast quantities of supplies necessary for an army of 25,000 men.'[15]

For the large numbers of troops who arrived daily in Tampa from late April onwards, the immediate impression was of heat and an abundance of sand. The journalist, George Kennan, recalled his previous travels to remote parts of Russia and unkindly likened the place to Semipalatinsk, a Siberian city which Russian army officers nicknamed 'the Devil's Sand-box'.[16] The problems of adjusting to the climate and environment were made worse by the evident inexperience of army staff officers in organizing large numbers of men into an expeditionary force. The result was confusion frequently bordering on chaos. The basic problem was one of supply. Quite simply, men were coming in faster than the food and equipment to sustain them could be unloaded and distributed. Feelings of irritation were moderated by a strong sense of patriotism and by the fact that the majority of soldiers were regulars and therefore accustomed to the privations of military life. The poorly equipped volunteer regiments did not arrive until late May and stayed only a short time in Tampa. Nevertheless, signs of discontent were present and were aggravated by a combination of the climate, the poor living conditions, the incompetence of many officers and, most of all, the frustrating delay in joining battle against the Spaniards. The latent tensions at Tampa received minimal publicity until the journalist Poultney Bigelow published a scathing indictment of military shortcomings in *Harper's Weekly* on 28 May. In sharp contrast to the idealized and stirring stories to which the public had

---

15 Alger, *Spanish-American War*, p. 65.
16 George Kennan, *Campaigning in Cuba* (Port Washington, NY, 1971), pp. 2–3.

become accustomed, Bigelow stressed the misery of daily life in the camp: 'Down here we are sweltering day and night with the thermometer ninety-eight in the shade. Nobody dares complain for fear of appearing unpatriotic. . . . Here we are thirty days after the declaration of war, and not one regiment is yet equipped with uniforms suitable for hot weather.'[17]

In addition to the difficulties of housing, feeding and equipping thousands of troops, War Department officials and army staff officers faced the problem of organizing their embarkation. The army had no professional experience of major overseas campaigning and did not possess transport ships or landing craft. It was a handicap which could not be made up in a few days. Nevertheless, the orders given to Shafter on 29 April for an immediate expedition to southern Cuba presumed that adequate shipping was available. In fact, there was an acute scarcity of suitable ships. In April when War Department officials sought to acquire transports, they discovered that the vast majority of seaworthy vessels were already in the possession of the navy. Quartermaster General Marshall I. Ludington eventually purchased or hired twenty-nine transports plus various light vessels for use at Tampa. However, the vast majority were antiquated steam freighters used in the coastal trade and never intended to be troop transports. They could carry bulk cargoes, but needed considerable refitting to accommodate passengers. Time was available only for the most limited changes and repairs.

Shafter's immediate task had finally become crystal clear on 31 May: he was to load a fully equipped army of 25,000 and proceed without delay to Santiago de Cuba. In a frantic effort to implement these orders, thousands of men and their supplies were rushed to the railway terminal at Tampa and put aboard transports at a wharf which could handle a maximum of no more than nine ships at any one time. 'On arriving at Tampa', observed General Miles on 1 June, 'I found great confusion and the place crowded with an indiscriminate accumulation of supplies and war materials.'[18] It was hoped, however, that the embarkation could take place on Saturday 4 June. 'Men are working night and day,' Miles telegraphed to Alger.[19] But the deadline was missed. To general dismay it was

---

17 *Harper's Weekly* (New York), 28 May 1898, cited in Charles H. Brown, *The Correspondents' War: Journalists in the Spanish-American War* (New York, 1967), p. 231.

18 Miles, *Serving the Republic*, p. 275.

19 Miles to Alger, 1 June 1898, cited in Alger, *Spanish-American War*, p. 67.

discovered that the available fleet of transports had the capacity to accommodate not 25,000 men and their supplies but only around 18,000 to 20,000 at the most. Even with this reduction in size, Shafter admitted that embarkation could not take place before Tuesday, 7 June. Early that day the Navy Department at Washington received a telegram from Sampson reporting his bombardment of Santiago de Cuba, and adding: 'If 10,000 men were here, city and fleet would be ours within forty-eight hours. Every consideration demands immediate army movement. If delayed, city will be defended more strongly by guns taken from fleet.'[20] Unless urgent action was taken, it appeared that a golden military opportunity would be lost. It was a moment which called for the exercise of decisive presidential leadership. A personal telegram was accordingly sent from McKinley to Shafter: 'Information from Sampson says he has practically reduced fortifications, and only waits your arrival to occupy Santiago. Time is the essence of the situation. Early departure of first importance.'[21] The cable arrived as desperate efforts were being made at Tampa to load men and supplies, including artillery and livestock. Shafter himself was spending most of the daylight hours of every day supervising loading operations at the wharf of Port Tampa. In reply to the President, he telegraphed to Alger at 10.15 p.m. on 7 June: 'I expect to have 834 officers, 16,154 men on transports by daylight, and will sail at that hour.'[22]

The almost indecent haste to leave Tampa resulted in disorder and chaos. Attempts by staff officers to organize the loading of ships in an efficient and methodical manner were abandoned due to pressure of time and the awareness that there would not be sufficient space for every regiment. In effect, most commanders were not told until the evening of 7 June that the expedition intended to depart early the following morning. In fact, no official announcement was actually made. The news was carried by word of mouth. Theodore Roosevelt understood the implication perfectly: 'We had no intention of getting left, and prepared at once for the scramble which was about to take place'.[23] Amid scenes of confusion, Roosevelt and Colonel Wood gave up waiting for a

20 Sampson to Long, 6 June 1898, cited in ibid., p. 71.

21 McKinley to Shafter, 7 June 1898, cited in ibid.

22 Shafter to Alger, 7 June 1898, cited in David F. Trask, *The War with Spain in 1898* (New York, 1981), p. 180.

23 Roosevelt, *Rough Riders*, p. 57.

passenger train and unceremoniously packed their men and equipment aboard a coal-train which took them to Port Tampa. At the dock they learned that their regiment was to travel in the *Yucatan*. The same ship, however, had also been assigned to the Second Infantry and the Seventy-first New York Volunteers. An administrative error had obviously been made because the *Yucatan* was capable of taking only half the combined numbers of the three regiments. There was no time for bureaucratic niceties. Instead, Roosevelt decisively resolved the issue by taking possession of the *Yucatan* for the Rough Riders and preventing anyone else from coming aboard. 'There was a good deal of expostulation, but we had possession,' he jubilantly remarked.[24]

By fair means or foul, the loading of the transports continued throughout the night. On the morning of 8 June Shafter was finally able to report to the War Department that the Expeditionary Force was ready to sail for Cuba. Curiously, Miles had chosen not to take command of the mission and preferred to remain behind in Tampa. He later blamed Alger for not clarifying his exact role in the operation. Whatever the truth of the allegation, Miles was, perhaps, fortunate to be spared the many discomforts and frustrations experienced by those who had been so eager to board the transports. Their suffering commenced while the Expeditionary Force was still within sight of Tampa. In fact, as the convoy was in the process of leaving the harbour, Shafter received a briefly worded cable from Alger instructing him to bring everything to a halt. The order was genuine even though it flatly contradicted the days of remorseless pressure exerted on Shafter by the government at Washington to expedite the embarkation from Tampa. It all seemed so reminiscent of the recently aborted Tunas and Mariel operations.

The reason for the dramatic change of orders arose from telegrams, which had reached the Navy Department at Washington earlier that morning, stating that an American scout ship had sighted two Spanish ships, possibly an armoured cruiser and a torpedo-boat, in the Nicholas Channel off the northern coast of Cuba. The spectre of powerful, fast Spanish warships prowling the waters off Cuba had suddenly re-emerged. Moreover, the report was particularly worrying to officials in Washington because the bulk of the North Atlantic Squadron was on duty in the Caribbean. Consequently, it was considered too dangerous for the expedition to proceed. For

24 Ibid., p. 60.

their own protection the transports moved back to Tampa Bay, but did not return all the way to the docks because they might be required to leave at any moment. In fact, the unwelcome interruption dragged on for five days. 'The heat, the steaming discomfort, and the confinement, together with the forced inaction were very irksome,' noted Roosevelt, but he added that patriotism and thoughts of imminent action meant that 'there was little or no grumbling'.[25] When it was confirmed that the sighting of the Spanish warships had been mistaken, the expedition eventually departed from Tampa on the morning of 14 June.

The convoy constituted the largest expeditionary force ever to leave the United States and would not be surpassed in size until World War I. On board the 29 transports and 6 supply vessels were 819 officers and 16,058 enlisted men, 30 civilian clerks, 272 teamsters and packers, 107 stevedores and more than 100 accompanying journalists and foreign military observers. In addition, there were 959 horses and 1,336 pack and draft mules and tons of equipment ranging from heavy artillery to cooking utensils.[26] The navy provided a protective escort including the battleship *Indiana*, the unprotected cruisers *Detroit* and *Castine* and a variety of smaller ships. The ships attempted to keep together and maintain formation, but navigational skills and speeds varied so much that stragglers gradually fell miles behind the main convoy. Fortunately, the weather was calm and the Spaniards refrained from launching any attacks. The chosen route was eastwards along the northern coast of Cuba to the Windward Passage. The total distance covered was almost 1,000 miles. Cuba itself was often in sight by day, prompting a British journalist to recall: 'It is notable that so large a fleet should have been brought without injury, either from attack by the enemy or from collision among its own vessels . . . Perhaps no nation but Spain would have allowed us a passage unmolested.'[27] No lives were lost, and none of the transports experienced any significant damage during the voyage. In fact, one of the most dangerous moments had probably occurred in Tampa Bay just as the expedition set sail when the *Yucatan* veered almost out of control and, in Roosevelt's words,

25 Ibid., p. 62.
26 This information is taken from Alger, *Spanish-American War*, pp. 75–79 and French E. Chadwick, *The Relations of the United States and Spain: The Spanish American War* (3 vols; London, 1911), vol. iii p. 19.
27 John Black Atkins, *The War in Cuba: The Experiences of an Englishman with the United States Army* (London, 1899), pp. 79–80. Atkins was the correspondent of the *Manchester Guardian*.

came 'within an ace of a bad collision' with another freighter, the *Mattewan*.[28] It would not be the last occasion on which the Rough Riders came perilously close to disaster.

On the morning of 20 June, six days after leaving Tampa, the Expeditionary Force approached Guantánamo Bay. For the men aboard the convoy it was the realization of their wishes; their delight was moderated not by apprehension of the dangers which lay ahead but by the awareness that many thousands of their less-fortunate compatriots had to remain behind in the United States. In contrast to the American navy, the American army had been slow to become actively involved in the war. However, Alger and his officials at the War Department had started with few of the advantages enjoyed by their counterparts at the Navy Department. They faced the mammoth task of transforming a tiny peacetime force into a massive citizen-army capable of fighting a major overseas campaign. None the less, in the space of two months an army of almost 200,000 men had come into being and an American Expeditionary Force had been organized and put to sea. As the American soldiers gazed at the Cuban coastline, the confusion and disorder of Tampa receded into past memory. From the point of view of a relieved Secretary of War, a most difficult job had been accomplished and the wishes of the President had been fulfilled. 'The expedition from Tampa', summed up Alger, 'was a success and unmarred by loss of life or treasure.'[29]

28 Roosevelt, *Rough Riders*, p. 64.
29 Alger, *Spanish-American War*, p. 82.

6 THE BATTLE FOR SANTIAGO DE CUBA

DISEMBARKATION

The firing of guns and cheering from their naval colleagues greeted the arrival of the American Expeditionary Force in the waters off Santiago de Cuba on 20 June. For Admiral Sampson it was the end of two weeks of frustrating delay and uncertainty. The assault on the city would now shortly take place. However, Sampson was well aware that he had no authority over the Expeditionary Force, which, to underline that it was part of the army, would be more commonly referred to as the 'Fifth [Army] Corps'. In effect, Sampson could only offer General Shafter advice on what military strategy to pursue. Accordingly, he sent his chief of staff, Captain French Ensor Chadwick, to the *Seguranca*, a converted steamer which served as the general's flagship and headquarters. Chadwick acquainted Shafter with Sampson's recommendation that the priority of any land operation should be the destruction of the batteries on the Morro and La Socapa. Once this objective was achieved, the navy would be able to clear the mines from the channel and thereby enable its powerful armoured ships to emulate the exploits of Dewey by entering the harbour and destroying the Spanish squadron. Despite later denials from Shafter, Chadwick came away from the meeting with the understanding that the general concurred with Sampson's plan. This was only the first in a series of crossed communications between the army and navy.

Sampson had no fixed opinion on the other important question of where the army should disembark. He did, however, envisage an important role for the insurgents and had already established direct contact with them on this matter. This followed up an initiative taken by General Miles on 2 June when Miles had sent a message from Tampa to General Calixto García asking for an increase in military activity by the insurgents against the Spaniards in the region of Santiago de Cuba. Within a week García replied from his base near Bayamo that his forces would actively assist the landing of the American army and that he regarded Miles's 'wishes and suggestions as orders'.[1] No formal agreement had been proposed or was ever entered into between Miles and García, but the latter's response implied that he was voluntarily placing himself and his troops under American direction and control. Shortly afterwards, García began the difficult journey from Bayamo across the Sierra Maestra to a point on the coast west of Santiago de Cuba where he would be able to meet both Sampson and Shafter. On 19 June he came on board Sampson's flagship, the *New York*, but seasickness compelled his return to land. A conference of the three commanders was arranged for the next day at the village of Aserradero, where García had established his temporary headquarters and assembly point for local insurgent forces.

Meanwhile, General Shafter had been using the voyage from Tampa to learn all he could about Santiago de Cuba. After so many changes in his orders from Washington he was, no doubt, relieved finally to be given a definite mission. Up until the last days of May he had been preparing the Fifth Corps for a landing at Mariel, to be followed by an advance on Havana across relatively flat and open countryside. The tactics in such a campaign would not be greatly different from those he had experienced during the Civil War and operations against the Indians in the southwest of the United States. But the topography and fortifications of Santiago de Cuba posed quite a different prospect. Moreover, the lessons of military history were not encouraging. In 1741 a British army of 5,000 men had landed at Guantánamo only to be decimated by fever and disease on its march to Santiago de Cuba. Shafter was convinced that, once ashore, the Fifth Corps must act quickly and decisively before the rigours of the tropical climate began to be felt.

The immediate question, however, was where to disembark. The same high cliffs and bluffs, which ruled against a direct assault on the harbour of Santiago de Cuba, extended for several miles both to the east and west. The most suitable place for landing a large army was Guantánamo Bay. Not only did Guantánamo possess a fine harbour but also a strong detachment of American marines was already on shore. However, Guantánamo was more than 40 miles distant from Santiago de Cuba, and Shafter had no intention of repeating what all the military manuals regarded as a disastrous

---

1 Sampson to Long, 6 June 1898, cited in Nelson A. Miles, *Serving the Republic: Memoirs of the Civil and Military Life of Nelson A. Miles* (New York, 1911), p. 278.

decision made by the British in 1741. Among other alternatives was the small harbour of Cabañas, which was only 2 miles west of La Socapa. In approaching Santiago de Cuba from the west, however, troops would come within range of the heavy guns of the Spanish warships in the harbour. A similar consideration applied to Fort Aguadores, which was east of the city and about 3 miles from the Morro. A few miles further to the east and safely out of Spanish artillery range were the villages of Siboney and Daiquirí. Siboney appeared the better choice because it possessed a larger beach and was connected by a single-track railway line to a wharf in Santiago Bay. It also lay astride the Camino Real (the Royal Highway), the largely unpaved and only local 'road' which led to Santiago de Cuba. The Camino Real continued from Siboney for about 7 miles to the tiny mining village of Daiquirí. The latter was known to possess docking facilities in the form of an iron pier and a wooden dock formerly used by ships carrying iron ore for the American-owned Juragua Mining Company. In reality, both sites were basically strips of sandy beach. Whichever one was selected, the disembarkation of thousands of men and their equipment would be a major operation. Moreover, moving large numbers of troops inland would also be extremely difficult. The countryside which lay between Santiago de Cuba and Siboney and Daiquirí was hilly and covered by trees, brush and thick jungle vegetation. The main thoroughfare, the Camino Real, was poorly maintained and frequently deteriorated into a muddy trail during the rainy season.

On 20 June Shafter was able to view the coastline at first hand as he travelled from Guantánamo to Santiago de Cuba, where Sampson joined him on board the *Seguranca*, and on to Aserradero for the meeting with Calixto García. Later that same day the three commanders came together to discuss military strategy. A vital consideration was the strength of the local Spanish defences. García recommended Daiquirí as the best landing point, primarily because the local Spanish garrison numbered no more than 300 men. He believed that a larger force of 600 Spaniards was stationed at Siboney. Shafter approved the choice of initially landing at Daiquirí and then moving on to Siboney. The date for disembarkation was scheduled for 22 June. 'General Shafter', remarked Sampson, 'impressed me as a man who could decide a question like a master of his business, and who would make quick work of the campaign.'[2]

2 William T. Sampson, 'The Atlantic Fleet in the Spanish War', *The Century Magazine* 57 (1899), p. 904.

Establishing a beachhead on hostile territory is always an extremely risky enterprise. At Daiquirí it was expected that the Spaniards would entrench themselves in strong defensive positions on the cliffs overlooking the beach. 'Five hundred resolute men', Roosevelt later acknowledged, 'could have prevented the disembarkation at very little cost to themselves.'[3] However, the likelihood of serious Spanish resistance was greatly reduced by García's extremely cooperative attitude. He stated that local insurgent forces under General Demetrio Castillo Duany would attack the Spanish garrison at Daiquirí. Castillo's troops would also provide a protective cordon for the disembarking Americans. In addition, the three commanders formulated a plan to confuse the Spaniards as to the exact location of the landing. While the Americans were coming ashore at Daiquirí, an insurgent force under General Jesús Rabí would make a diversionary raid at Cabañas to the west of Santiago de Cuba. Americans warships would contribute to the feint by briefly bombarding Cabañas and would also further confuse the Spaniards by shelling the Morro, Siboney and Daiquirí. In the meantime, García would assemble an estimated force of 3,000 men at Aserradero. On 24 June these troops would be transported by American ships to the beachhead established at Daiquirí where they would join with the American forces in the battle for Santiago de Cuba.

Shortly after 9 a.m. on 22 June the ships of Sampson's squadron commenced their planned bombardment of Spanish positions from Cabañas to Daiquirí. The shelling of Daiquirí began at 9.40 a.m. and was halted after only 20 minutes. The alarm raised by the sight of armed Cubans coming on to the beach after the end of the naval bombardment turned out to be misplaced. They were not Spanish soldiers but insurgents under the command of General Castillo. In fact, it was later learned that the Spanish garrison had withdrawn some hours earlier. To Shafter's great relief, therefore, the disembarkation was unopposed. Sampson could only describe the absence of prepared Spanish defensive positions as 'a mystery'.[4] 'It was great luck for us, but it was not war', observed George Kennan.[5]

Despite the military incompetence of the Spaniards, the landing was an arduous and time-consuming operation which evoked

---

3 Theodore Roosevelt, *The Rough Riders* (New York, 1902), p. 75.

4 William T. Sampson, 'Atlantic Fleet', p. 905.

5 George Kennan, *Campaigning in Cuba* (Port Washington, NY, 1971), p. 80.

comparisons with the disorderly embarkation from Tampa. 'We did the landing as we had done everything else', caustically remarked Roosevelt, 'that is, in a scramble, each commander shifting for himself.'[6] One reason for the general disorganization was that Shafter and his officers had no experience of conducting amphibious operations. This deficiency was addressed by the seconding of naval personnel from the blockading squadron. Shafter later praised the contribution of the naval officers. 'Without them I could not have landed in ten days, and perhaps not at all,' he noted.[7] The masters of the transports, however, were civilians employed under contract to the army. Reluctant to enter uncharted coastal waters and to become directly involved in what they anticipated would be fierce fighting, they preferred instead to remain a long distance from the shore. This meant that, in some cases, boats had to be conveyed up to 5 miles from the transports to the dock. The efficiency and speed of the operation were also seriously impeded by the inadequate number of steam launches to tow the various assortment of vessels such as cutters, lifeboats and rowing-boats which were packed with soldiers and their equipment. Moreover, not only were the pier and dock in a state of disrepair, but also docking was made difficult and often dangerous by a strong southeasterly wind which produced a heavy surf. Although a number of injuries occurred, the only fatalities were two black cavalrymen who fell overboard from their landing boat and were drowned.

At 10 a.m. Midshipman Halligan of the *Brooklyn* was the first American to step ashore at Daiquirí. He was followed by regiments of General Lawton's Second Infantry Division. By 6 p.m. some 6,000 men had landed and the beachhead had been successfully established. On the following day most of the landing vessels were diverted to the calmer waters of Siboney after it was learned that the Spaniards had also abandoned that location. The disembarkation of the troops took longer than expected and was not completed until 26 June. Throughout this period Shafter remained on the *Seguranca*. For him and his staff officers, the problem of landing men on the beaches was replaced by the even bigger task of supplying a fighting army. The inability of ships to anchor off the beaches at Siboney and Daiquirí meant that all equipment and goods had to be put into small boats and then brought ashore for unloading. Priority was

6 Roosevelt, *Rough Riders*, p. 70.

7 Shafter to Corbin, 23 June 1898, cited in Russell A. Alger, *The Spanish-American War* (New York, 1901), p. 101.

given to ammunition, food rations and medical supplies. These items were despatched to the front as quickly as possible, though the acute shortage of wagons and mules combined with the deplorable condition of the one 'road' in the vicinity meant that movement was laboriously slow. Equipment such as the heavy artillery brought specifically for the purpose of attacking the fortifications at Santiago de Cuba was left behind on the beach. The particular dilemma of how to transport the hundreds of mules and horses brought from Tampa was summarily resolved by pushing them overboard into the sea with the hope that they would swim to the beach.

From 22 to 26 June about 17,000 Americans were landed. There were two infantry divisions each numbering 5,000 troops, the large majority of whom were regular soldiers. Brigadier-General J. Ford Kent commanded the First Infantry Division consisting of regular units under Brigadier-General Hamilton S. Hawkins and Colonel Charles Wikoff and volunteer regiments under Colonel Edward P. Pearson. Brigadier-General Henry W. Lawton headed the Second Infantry Division. His senior officers were Brigadier-General Adna Chaffee, Brigadier-General William Ludlow and Colonel Evan Miles. In command of the Cavalry Division of 2,700 men was Major-General Joseph Wheeler. Brigadier-General Samuel S. Sumner headed the regular cavalry units, while Brigadier-General Samuel Young was in charge of the volunteer cavalry regiments. With the exception of a few senior officers, cavalrymen were without horses and fought as infantry or 'dismounted cavalry' throughout the whole campaign. In addition to the three main divisions, an Independent Brigade of about 1,100 regular infantry under General John C. Bates acted as a reserve unit. The arrival at Siboney on 27 June of a transport containing 2,500 Michigan Volunteers led to the creation of a brigade of volunteer infantry commanded by Brigadier-General Henry Duffield. There were also separate units of engineers, signal corps, medical personnel and a battalion of light artillery with the capacity to deploy sixteen 3.2-inch field guns and four Gatling machine-guns.

As the beachhead was being established at Daiquirí, Shafter ordered General Lawton to take two regiments of the Second Infantry Division and advance along the Camino Real to Siboney. Unless he met resistance from the Spaniards, Lawton's specific instructions were to secure control of the village 'go into camp, intrench, and remain there'.[8] Lawton began the 7-mile march late in

8 McClernand to Lawton, 22 June 1898, cited in ibid., p. 102.

the afternoon of 22 June. The Americans quickly found that the dense tropical undergrowth prevented them from spreading out and forced them to keep in single file or no more than two abreast along the narrow 'road'. Even with the assistance of Cuban scouts, progress was so slow that Lawton decided to halt and rest his men during the night. The march recommenced at daybreak on 23 June. Except for a few shots fired by snipers at his advance guard, Lawton reached Siboney without mishap at 9.20 a.m. The Spanish garrison had repeated the example of their colleagues at Daiquirí and had withdrawn to the north as the Americans approached. During their retreat they were pursued, however, by a group of about 100 insurgents under General Castillo, who had accompanied Lawton from Daiquirí.

From his headquarters on the *Seguranca*, Shafter sent similar instructions to the other generals at Daiquirí to move their units to the vicinity of Siboney. Fearing a possible counter-attack from the large Spanish army in Santiago de Cuba, Shafter's intention was evidently to build up a strong defensive position at Siboney until the disembarkation was successfully accomplished. This cautious approach was sensible, but clashed with the eagerness of his men to spring into combat with the enemy. It was, perhaps, fitting that 'Fighting Joe' Wheeler, the general with the most bellicose reputation gained from the Civil War, should be instrumental in striking the first blow at the Spaniards. While proceeding with his cavalry regiments towards Siboney on 23 June, Wheeler learned from Castillo that the local Spanish forces, numbering about 1,500, had regrouped at Las Guásimas, a stopping-place on the Camino Real about 3 miles to the northwest. True to his reputation, Wheeler believed that prompt action must be taken to remove this threat to the American position at Siboney. Everything pointed to an easy victory and glory both for himself and the men of the United States Cavalry. Indeed, Castillo predicted that the Spaniards would fall back towards Santiago de Cuba rather than confront a large American force. Citing the fact that Shafter's initial orders had been addressed either to Lawton or the 'Senior Officer at the Front', Major-General Wheeler pulled rank over Brigadier-General Lawton. He assumed command and instructed General Samuel Young to prepare the Cavalry Division for a 'reconnaissance in force' against the enemy.[9]

9 See ibid., p. 103.

Young divided his force of almost 1,000 men into two roughly equal columns. Accompanied by Wheeler, Young planned to take the first group along the Camino Real which led directly to Las Guásimas and the nearby hamlet of Sevilla. The Rough Riders under Colonel Wood formed the second group. Their orders were to detach themselves from the main body and make their own way to Las Guásimas by following a separate trail about a mile to the west of the Camino Real. General Castillo agreed to mobilize his force of 800 insurgents to support the American advance from the rear.

The cavalrymen began their march at daybreak on 24 June. The distance was relatively short, but, as always, the dense jungle ensured that progress was agonizingly slow. Previously there had been no resistance from the Spaniards but, on this occasion, they decided to test the mettle of the Americans. Most of the 1,500 Spanish troops under the command of General Antero Rubín had positioned themselves behind stone fortifications on the top of a ridge, but a number concealed themselves in the woods where they sniped at the approaching Americans. Colonel Theodore Roosevelt was initially delighted by his first sight of the tropical forest in all its splendour, but he was soon disconcerted by the particular dangers of jungle warfare:

> The air seemed full of the rustling sound of the Mauser bullets, for the Spaniards knew the trails by which we were advancing, and opened heavily on our position. Moreover, as we advanced we were, of course, exposed, and they could see us and fire. But they themselves were entirely invisible.[10]

Fighting began in earnest at 8 a.m. when both the American columns came within sight of the Spanish defensive position on top of the ridge. The Americans charged forward and thereby sparked off a battle that raged for more than two hours. It was not only a fierce baptism of fire but also a rude awakening to reality for American troops who had become accustomed to believe that the Spaniards lacked the will to fight. Wheeler was taken aback by the sheer amount of rifle fire and reckoned that it was more intense than any he had experienced during the Civil War. The explanation was simple. The Spaniards were using rifles equipped with magazines which enabled them to fire bullets much more rapidly than the muskets of thirty years previously. The results were

10 Roosevelt, *Rough Riders*, p. 89.

gruesome for the advancing Americans. The mounting list of casualties compelled Wheeler to send back a message to Lawton asking urgently for reinforcements. Just after 10 a.m., however, the firing decreased as the Spanish troops began to pull back towards Santiago de Cuba. Wheeler was jubilant and, with his thoughts set on another time and place, reportedly cried out: 'We've got the damn Yankees on the run.'[11] Young's troops took control of the ridge and were quickly joined by the Rough Riders.

Next day, the American press proclaimed a great victory for the United States cavalry and gave special mention to the bravery of Theodore Roosevelt and the Rough Riders. The McKinley administration was delighted. 'An unseen enemy, with a much superior force, in his own country, and intrenched in the position of his choice', remarked Alger, 'had been driven from his rocky fastnesses, completely routed, and forced back to his principal works of defence before Santiago.'[12] The Spaniards responded by asserting that they had made a tactical withdrawal to stronger defensive positions after inflicting heavy losses on the Americans. The claim was not totally without foundation. In terms of casualties sixteen Americans died and fifty-two were wounded, while Spanish losses were ten killed and twenty-five wounded.

Save for its boost to American morale, the skirmish at Las Guásimas possessed no great lasting military significance. For General Wheeler, however, the outcome demonstrated that nothing succeeds like success. Not only had he deliberately flouted the intent of Shafter's orders, but he had also risked the lives of his men in a frontal assault against an enemy entrenched in prepared defensive positions. On the other hand, the Spaniards had been routed and the road to Santiago de Cuba now lay open. 'Your news is excellent,' Shafter wrote personally to Wheeler.[13] To preserve and consolidate the gains of the victory at Las Guásimas, Shafter ordered the speedy despatch of reinforcements of men and artillery. In the process the American military front was decisively shifted inland and a strong forward base was built up around the hamlet of Sevilla. Much to the annoyance of Admiral Sampson, it became evident that Shafter had unilaterally rejected the navy's scheme of attacking the forts at the entrance to the harbour in favour of an inland advance on the city. In effect, Wheeler's unauthorized initiative actually presented Shafter

11 Cited in Walter Millis, *The Martial Spirit* (Boston, 1931), p. 274.
12 Alger, *Spanish-American War*, p. 112.
13 Shafter to Wheeler, 25 June 1898, cited in ibid., p. 117.

with a justification to adopt a strategy which emphasized the role of the army while significantly diminishing the military contribution of the navy. Sampson was not therefore to have the opportunity to repeat Dewey's action at Manila Bay.

The events at Las Guásimas not only strained relations between Shafter and Sampson but also highlighted a growing friction between the members of the Fifth Corps and the insurgents. The initial contacts between Shafter and Calixto García had been extremely cordial and constructive. In fact, the insurgents had contributed significantly to the successful landing of the Expeditionary Force. They had provided military cover at Daiquirí and had carried out the diversionary feint at Cabañas. In addition, the mere presence of local insurgent forces acted as a powerful constraint upon the movement of Spanish troops throughout the military division of Santiago de Cuba. Nevertheless, the American soldiers soon developed an attitude of contempt for their nominal allies. There was particular criticism of the peripheral role assumed by General Castillo and his troops at Las Guásimas. But Americans were mistaken in believing that the Cubans were unwilling to fight. In effect, the insurgents were pursuing their customary guerrilla tactics and could not understand the impetuous desire of the Americans to engage the enemy in a pitched battle.

American perceptions of the Cubans were also strongly influenced by racial prejudice. The 'yellow' press had been successful in portraying the insurgents as an organized army of patriots who were in most respects just like the Americans themselves. But American journalists wrote exclusively about Havana and the western provinces. None had personal experience of Oriente, which was not only the poorest region of Cuba but also the most racially mixed. American troops landing at Daiquirí were therefore surprised and shocked to be confronted by insurgents who visibly failed to meet the idealistic expectations built up in the United States. George Kennan expressed the most common American reaction, when he observed that 'fully four-fifths' of the insurgents were mulattos or blacks. 'If their rifles and cartridge-belts had been taken away from them', he added, 'they would have looked like a horde of dirty Cuban beggars and ragamuffins on the tramp.'[14]

The military value of the insurgents was also soon brought into question. 'It was evident, at a glance', remarked Theodore Roosevelt, 'that they would be no use in serious fighting, but it was

---

14 Kennan, *Campaigning in Cuba*, p. 92.

hoped that they might be of service in scouting.'[15] This was the view held by the American military command, who quickly dropped the idea of the Cubans taking on a major combat role, preferring instead to assign them to defensive duties and especially routine tasks as scouts, messengers, sentries, porters, and trench diggers. General García was greatly offended, and later protested that his men should be regarded as soldiers and not labourers. His protests were ignored. General Shafter was careful to stress that the insurgents were not under his formal command. He considered their services to be voluntary, in return for which he would provide rations and supplies. As the battle for Santiago de Cuba evolved, it became clear that the American–Cuban military relationship was not intended to be an equal one.

BATTLES OF EL CANEY AND SAN JUAN HILL

Prior to the outbreak of war with the United States, Spanish military leaders in Cuba had actually considered the possibility of an American attack on the island's second largest city, Santiago de Cuba. However, no tangible steps were taken to prepare for its defence. Priority was given instead to concentrating troops and artillery batteries around Havana, which was understandably regarded as the most likely American target. This policy was maintained throughout the duration of the war. General Arsenio Linares Pomba, the commander of the military division of Santiago de Cuba, appreciated only too well that promised reinforcements would not be forthcoming either from Havana or from Spain. He would have to make the best of his own dwindling military resources.

In June 1898 the city of Santiago de Cuba was defended by a garrison numbering more than 10,000, including 319 officers, 9,111 enlisted men and 1,000 sailors seconded from Cervera's naval squadron. Within a radius of less than 100 miles were an additional 20,000 soldiers located in garrisons scattered across Oriente, the most important of which were Manzanillo in the west, Holguín in the northwest, Baracoa in the northeast and Guantánamo on the southern coast. An obvious step would have been to transfer these troops to Santiago de Cuba and thereby give Linares superiority in numbers over the American Expeditionary Force. Such a policy does

15 Roosevelt, *Rough Riders*, p. 75.

not appear to have been actively considered by the defensively minded Spanish commander. In any event, it was effectively ruled out by the sheer difficulty of moving large numbers of men and their equipment during the rainy season and, in contrast to Havana and the western provinces, the absence of railway links between the cities. In fact, the greatest obstacle to the redeployment of Spanish troops was the military power of the insurgents. The Spaniards were confined to garrisons in the towns and cities precisely because they could not move freely about the countryside. If the garrisons were evacuated, the insurgents would surely take over the centres of civilian population. These negative considerations, however, did not deter Colonel Federico Escario, the commander of the garrison at Manzanillo, who, on learning that the Americans had landed, resolved on 22 June to march 200 miles with 3,700 men to relieve Santiago de Cuba. Escario's positive example was not shared by the commanders of the other Spanish garrisons in Oriente.

For three years the Spanish army in Oriente had fought what had become a losing battle against the insurgents. By June 1898, therefore, Linares and his soldiers in Santiago de Cuba faced an extremely precarious future. Neither the government in Madrid nor Captain General Blanco in Havana could offer any real prospect of salvation. Their apparent indifference was underlined by the fact that soldiers' pay was in arrears by more than a year. Living conditions in Santiago de Cuba were steadily deteriorating. The onset of the rainy season brought its usual quota of sickness and death. Rations were increasingly inadequate. The local economy had been so ravaged by the war against the insurgents that most of the army's provisions had to be imported. The last ship to bring in supplies had docked at Santiago de Cuba on 25 April. The pressure on existing stocks of food was intensified by the unexpected arrival of Cervera's squadron on 19 May and the establishment of the American naval blockade on 1 June. A further blow to morale was the news in mid-June that the American Expeditionary Force had sailed from Tampa and would shortly be approaching the city. Linares and his army had no alternative but to wait and prepare for battle against the invading Americans. The presence of the powerful American squadron only a few miles from the coast and the insurgents in the countryside effectively removed the option of military evacuation either by sea or land.

In organizing the defence of Santiago de Cuba, Linares concentrated most of his troops and heavy artillery around the entrance to the harbour, which he considered the most likely point of attack by the Americans. During May and June extra guns were mounted on the Morro and La Socapa, including four 6.3-inch guns removed from the antiquated cruiser *Reina Mercedes*. Powerful guns were therefore in position to fire out to sea and at any ships which managed to enter the channel. Enemy vessels would also face destruction from two rows of electrical torpedo mines which had been placed in the channel. Like Admiral Sampson, Linares regarded the control of the Morro and La Socapa as crucial. The strategic importance of their artillery batteries was underlined by that fact that almost 4,000 troops were deployed to resist the anticipated American land attack.

The threat of insurgent raids meant that well-established lines of defence were already in place around the outskirts of Santiago de Cuba. In June 1898 the city was surrounded by a virtual *trocha* consisting of several rows of trenches and rifle-pits protected by barbed wire. At a distance varying from 1 to 3 miles forward of the trenches ran another more flexible line of defence which consisted mainly of strategically located blockhouses and fortified positions. This was effectively the city's first line of defence. It stretched for more than 8 miles from north to south, and guarded the Camino Real and the various trails which approached the city from the north and east. Advancing enemy forces would also come under fire from the city's light artillery batteries and the heavy guns of Cervera's naval squadron. Finally, the defensive perimeter extended to Siboney, Daiquirí and Guantánamo whose garrisons essentially made up what amounted to an outer line of defence.

The strategy adopted by Linares assumed that the Americans would launch their main attack upon the entrance to Santiago Bay. If they were deterred from doing this, Linares expected that a landing would be attempted on the southern coast at either Guantánamo, Daiquirí or Siboney. The Spanish commander showed no desire to rush reinforcements of men and artillery to his outer line of defence in order to prevent or even frustrate the American disembarkation. No attempt was even made to combine the garrisons at the coast so that they might confront the Americans with a powerful show of force. Linares was evidently reconciled to the fact that the interposition of insurgent forces had cut off his contact with the Spanish garrison at Guantánamo. Without substantial reinforcements, the relatively small detachments of Spanish troops at Daiquirí and Siboney could not be expected to hold their positions for very long against an American advance. Perhaps Linares believed that these units would fight the Americans as they landed on the beaches, but his own basic strategy assumed that they would eventually fall back to the first defensive line. In effect, this is what occurred at Daiquirí, Siboney and Las Guásimas.

Linares used the days following the skirmish at Las Guásimas to reinforce the first defensive line. Additional troops were assigned to defend the hamlet of El Caney and to man the fortified positions on San Juan Hill and Kettle Hill, two prominent ridges on the San Juan Heights about half a mile to the east of the second defensive line.[16] Just over 500 Spaniards were stationed at El Caney, while a similar number defended the San Juan Heights. The numerical strength of both these garrisons remained relatively weak because Linares still believed that the main American attack would be at the entrance to the bay. Consequently, more sailors from Cervera's squadron were brought on shore to reinforce the garrisons at the Morro and La Socapa. In effect, Linares was spreading his military resources too unevenly over too wide an area. The news that Escario's relief column from Manzanillo would soon reach Santiago de Cuba provided a welcome boost to Spanish morale. However, this was little compensation for the damaging consequences arising from a flawed strategy which, by emphasizing defence, not only allowed the Americans to land unopposed but also gave them invaluable time to manoeuvre their forces into position for a massive attack upon Santiago de Cuba.

Linares's passivity effectively handed the military initiative to General Shafter. It was a heavy responsibility for the American general, who had no previous experience of conducting a major military campaign. The result was a strategy which preferred caution to taking risks. 'It is my intention to proceed from Daiquirí to Santiago as rapidly as I can,' Shafter had written to Sampson on 22 June.[17] Two days later the American victory at Las Guásimas appeared to open the way for an immediate attack on Santiago de Cuba. Although Shafter genuinely wished to capture the city as soon as possible, he told Wheeler not to undertake another 'reconnaissance in force'.[18] Caution prevailed. Time was needed to

---

16 Kettle Hill was the name coined by American soldiers. On top of the hill was a large iron cauldron used in sugar refining. From a distance the cauldron resembled a kettle.

17 Shafter to Sampson, 22 June 1898, cited in French E. Chadwick, *The Relations of the United States and Spain: The Spanish American War* (3 vols; London, 1911), vol. iii p. 48.

18 Shafter actually instructed Wheeler, 'do not try any forward movement until further orders'. See Shafter to Wheeler, 25 June 1898, cited in Alger, *Spanish-American War*, p. 118.

complete the disembarkation and to establish a system of command and supply on land. Troops and equipment were despatched to reinforce Wheeler, but their exact deployment for offensive operations awaited the gathering of detailed information about the local terrain and the strength of the Spanish defences. Part of Shafter's preparations also included a personal examination of conditions at the front. The general landed at Siboney on 27 June and travelled to El Pozo, a hill west of Sevilla from which it was possible to survey the land approach to Santiago de Cuba.

During the week following the skirmish at Las Guásimas the Camino Real was choked with men and equipment on the move from Siboney and Daiquirí to the front at Sevilla. Frequent tropical showers turned the road into mud. The most dependable means of transportation were wagons drawn by teams of mules. Heavy equipment could be moved only with great difficulty. Most notably, the siege guns, which had been brought for the specific purpose of bombarding the city, were left behind. However, the inefficient unloading of equipment and provisions at Daiquirí and Siboney meant that virtually everything was in short supply. 'There was nothing like enough transportation with the army, whether in the way of wagons or mule-trains; exactly as there had been no sufficient number of landing-boats with the transports,' summed up Theodore Roosevelt.[19] Consequently, the chaos of Tampa was soon replicated in Sevilla. For the American troops the psychological pressure of being at the front line was increased by inadequate rations and poor living conditions. In their winter-weight uniforms they also had to endure the full impact of tropical summer weather in which the days were steamy and hot, the rains came every afternoon and the nights were cool. Cases of sickness and fever soon began to occur. In addition, the soldiers suffered from the unwelcome attentions of masses of insects, including mosquitoes, tarantulas, scorpions and, most feared of all, the large land-crabs which emerged in their hundreds at night to scavenge. The journalist George Kennan had no particular liking of tarantulas, rattlesnakes and lizards, but he found these creatures preferable to the Cuban land-crab which he described as 'the most disgusting and repellent of all created things'.[20]

On Sunday, 26 June, Shafter informed Sampson that he would soon have ready 15,000 Americans and 4,000 insurgents to advance

19 Roosevelt, *Rough Riders*, p. 110.
20 Kennan, *Campaigning in Cuba*, p. 101.

on Santiago de Cuba. Having acquired the information that the main Spanish forces were located at the entrance to the harbour, Shafter intended to strike at the less well-defended area around El Caney to the northwest of the city. He hoped to break right through the Spanish defensive line and compel Linares to surrender. In a separate despatch to Alger sent two days later, Shafter predicted victory, although he acknowledged that attacking armies invariably suffered heavy casualties. For this reason he was delaying the assault until the maximum number of troops were available. 'There is no necessity for haste', he argued, 'as we are growing stronger and they weaker each day.'[21]

The receipt of a report on 28 June that Escario's relief column, erroneously described as under the command of General Pando, was within a few days' march of Santiago de Cuba created concern at Shafter's headquarters. The Spaniards were estimated to number at least 8,000 men, with plentiful supplies of weapons, ammunition and provisions. Should this force successfully reach Santiago de Cuba, it would dramatically transform the military balance in favour of Linares. Shafter appreciated the need for urgent action. Calixto García's army of 3,000 insurgents which had been transported from Aserradero was asked to move to a position north of the city where it could block the passage of the relief column. At the same time Shafter finalised his plans for the attack on the Spanish defensive line, which was now scheduled for Friday 1 July. The immediate objective was to gain control of the San Juan Heights, a series of hills and ridges which lay directly between the army at Sevilla and Santiago de Cuba. But Shafter's plans still retained an attack on El Caney. In fact, the location of this position about 5 miles to the north meant that it could be used as a base by the Spaniards to outflank the American troops engaged in attacking the San Juan Heights. Even though it would mean dividing his forces, Shafter judged that the capture of El Caney was an essential preliminary to the advance on the San Juan Heights.

The task of attacking El Caney was assigned to Lawton's Second Infantry Division with support from a light artillery battery commanded by Captain Allyn Capron. The troops moved out on the afternoon of 30 June ready to attack the Spaniards at daybreak the next day. The Spanish garrison was estimated to number around 500 men. Influenced by the recent example of Las Guásimas in

---

21 Shafter to Alger, 28 June 1898, cited in David F. Trask, *The War with Spain in 1898* (New York, 1981), p. 227.

which 1,500 Spaniards had been forced into retreat by less than 1,000 American cavalrymen, Lawton confidently predicted that El Caney would fall in two hours. He would then swing south to join Kent's First Infantry Division and Wheeler's Cavalry Division which would have already positioned themselves for the main assault on the San Juan Heights. Shafter's plan of battle also included a diversionary raid against Fort Aguadores to the east of the Morro. This would be carried out by the Michigan Volunteers under General Duffield and would be supported by naval bombardment from American warships. The intention was to divert Linares's attention away from the San Juan Heights by leading him to believe that a major attack was about to be launched by the Americans at the harbour entrance.

Perhaps, to counter criticism that he had stayed too long on the *Seguranca*, Shafter established his headquarters a mile east of El Pozo with the intention of personally directing the battle. However, suffering from a combination of heat exhaustion and gout, he was confined to his tent and forced to rely upon his aides, Colonel Edward McClernand and Lieutenant John Miley, to maintain communications with the generals at the front. McClernand took up an observation position on El Pozo and remained in contact with Shafter by field telephone. Miley joined the advance on the San Juan Heights and communicated with McClernand by couriers. It was hardly an efficient method of conducting complicated military operations, especially among officers who had minimal experience of actual combat and of commanding large numbers of troops. In this respect, Shafter was not helped by his own persistent infirmity and the illness suffered by his senior cavalry commanders, General Wheeler and General Young. Both were struck down by fever on 30 June. General Sumner replaced Wheeler, while Colonel Wood took over from Young. Wood was promoted to the rank of Brigadier-General. His elevation resulted in Colonel Roosevelt assuming command of the Rough Riders.

The one operation that proceeded exactly according to plan was the feint along the coast. At daybreak on 1 July the Michigan Volunteers under General Duffield marched from Siboney towards Aguadores. Ahead of their advance Admiral Sampson ordered a brief bombardment of the fort. In the afternoon Duffield returned to Siboney without having engaged the enemy. Meanwhile, more dramatic events were taking place further to the north. Overnight Lawton had approached El Caney with more than 5,000 men of the Second Infantry Division. Captain Allyn Capron's artillery battery of four 3.2-inch guns was also in place. Shortly after 6.30 a.m. on 1 July the guns opened fire at a range of just over 1 mile. At 7 a.m. several brigades of Lawton's infantry began their advance across the open ground in front of the Spanish positions. They were halted in their tracks by a hail of rifle fire and forced to withdraw. Evidently the American artillery had neither frightened the Spaniards into flight nor caused much damage to the wooden blockhouses and the stone fort known as El Viso which served as the Spanish command post. For once, the Americans had seriously underestimated their enemy. Though heavily outnumbered and lacking artillery, the Spanish riflemen took full advantage of their well-prepared defensive positions. A fierce battle ensued. Captain Arthur Lee, a British officer who accompanied the attack as an observer, recalled the 'deadly effect' of the Spanish fire. He added: 'They knew every range perfectly and picked off our men with distressing accuracy if they showed as much as a head.'[22]

The setback experienced at El Caney meant that Lawton was unable to support the attack on the San Juan Heights. Shafter's initial response was to reinforce Lawton with 1,000 men from Bates's Independent Brigade. At 2 p.m. Shafter ordered Lawton to break away from El Caney and join the main assault against the San Juan Heights. 'I would not bother with little block-houses; they cannot harm us,' he remarked.[23] The dismissal of El Caney as strategically insignificant appeared strange after Shafter had already committed one-third of his army to its capture. More immediately pertinent was Lawton's dismay at receiving Shafter's instructions. Withdrawal would signify defeat. In fact, his troops were so actively engaged in combat that it was not feasible to pull them back. Lawton requested permission to continue the assault, but the issue became academic at around 3 p.m. when Capron's artillery struck a number of direct hits on El Viso. The remaining Spanish forces soon began to retreat and El Caney fell under American control at 4.15 p.m. Of the original Spanish garrison of 520 men, 235 had been killed or wounded and 120 taken prisoner. Among the fatalities was the Spanish commander, General Joaquín Vara del Rey. American casualties were listed at 81 dead and 360 wounded. The American commanders were at a loss to explain how 520 Spaniards could resist 5,400 Americans for more than nine hours. They could only

---

22 Cited in G.J.A. O'Toole, *The Spanish War: An American Epic* (New York, 1984), p. 305.

23 Shafter to Lawton, 1 July 1898, cited in Alger, *Spanish-American War*, p. 143.

believe that the Spaniards fought so bravely out of the conviction that they would be slaughtered without mercy if they surrendered. In effect, the Americans had tasted their first experience of trench warfare and the carnage that resulted from attempting a frontal assault across open and difficult terrain against a well-entrenched and resolute enemy. But El Caney was not a unique experience. A similar infantry battle was taking place just a few miles to the south at the San Juan Heights.

At dawn on 1 July, 8,000 American troops were assembled at El Pozo. To the west, less than 2 miles away, lay the San Juan Heights defended by a little more than 500 Spaniards. Despite their superiority in numbers, the Americans faced a daunting task. The hills were well fortified with a combination of trenches and rifle-pits protected by barbed wire. The projected attack would also involve two American divisions having to make their way on foot for more than a mile along a narrow road with dense jungle on either side concealing Spanish snipers. After fording the San Juan River, which in reality was a stream rather than a river, the Americans would then advance in the open across a meadow more than 400 yards in length before storming the principal Spanish defensive positions on San Juan Hill and Kettle Hill. For much of the advance the attacking forces would also be exposed to fire from an enemy enjoying the advantage of holding the higher ground. It was perhaps fortunate that the American soldiers knew little of the formidable obstacles that lay ahead. While acknowledging that the Spaniards enjoyed a commanding territorial advantage, they took comfort in the conviction that the enemy's marksmanship and fighting spirit was poor. A mood of 'uneasy excitement' pervaded the American ranks. 'We did not talk much', recalled Roosevelt, 'for though we were in ignorance as to precisely what the day would bring forth, we knew we should see fighting.'[24]

The sound of guns firing to the north indicated that the assault at El Caney had taken place on schedule. At 7 a.m. Sumner's cavalry division set off. Their instructions were to continue along the road until an opportunity came to move towards the right in order to mount an attack upon Kettle Hill. Kent's infantry division followed behind the cavalrymen. They would seek to branch to the left and aim for San Juan Hill, which was the larger ridge located about 200 yards to the west of Kettle Hill. Progress was painfully slow as thousands of fully equipped soldiers simultaneously groped their

24 Roosevelt, *Rough Riders*, p.115.

way along the congested Camino Real. As planned, the advance received artillery support. Just after 8 a.m. Captain George Grimes's battery of four 3.2-inch guns mounted near El Pozo began firing on the Spanish positions. After a lull of some minutes the Spanish artillery replied. The shrapnel shells fell close to Grimes's battery and inflicted a number of casualties. The deadly accuracy of the Spanish gunners resulted from their knowledge of the local terrain and also the fact that they could pinpoint the position of their opponents by the smoke from the black powder ammunition used by the American guns. By contrast, Grimes could not locate the Spanish guns because the latter used smokeless powder.[25] Consequently, the American guns soon fell silent. It was one more example of the relative ineffectiveness of American artillery demonstrated throughout the war. In terms of the battle for the San Juan Heights, this was a factor which placed the attacking troops at a serious disadvantage to the well-entrenched defenders.

Shafter's desire for a rapid advance meant that adequate reconnaissance had not been undertaken. The American 'can-do' spirit sought to remedy this deficiency by using an observation balloon. The balloon, containing Lieutenant-Colonels George McC. Derby and Joseph Maxfield, floated high above the trees and was carried along by men of the Signals Corps holding the guy ropes on the ground. The reconnaissance value of the balloon was evidently demonstrated when Derby discovered a separate trail running to the left and leading towards San Juan Hill. The trail was narrow and tortuous, but it appeared to present a means of outflanking the Spanish positions and also reducing the congestion on the Camino Real. Kent was therefore ordered to divert his men along this route. However, the balloon was directly above the advancing Americans and consequently revealed their position to the Spaniards, who simply fired in that direction and caused many casualties. 'It was a beautiful range marker for the Spanish artillery and infantry, and they promptly used it as such,' lamented one American infantryman.[26] The balloon was quickly shot down by Spanish fire. Both Derby and Maxfield escaped unhurt. It was a curious episode which reflected little credit on Shafter's generalship.

The Seventy-first New York Volunteers were the first unit to take the trail identified by Derby. The guardsmen were, however,

25 The use of the outdated Springfield rifle caused a similar problem for the American volunteer soldiers.

26 Charles J. Post, *The Little War of Private Post* (Boston, 1960), p. 170.

totally unprepared for their first experience of intensive combat action. Mauser bullets came at them from seemingly every direction. A Spanish artillery shell scored a direct hit and instantly killed twelve men. The guardsmen panicked and were only prevented from rushing into headlong retreat by the admonitions of their officers and the fact that it was impossible to fall back against the mass of men moving forward. In retrospect, this proved fortunate, because Shafter had prepared no contingency plans for a retreat, whether tactical or enforced. The journalist Richard Harding Davis graphically described the infantrymen as having entered a 'chute of death'. He explained:

> The situation was desperate. Our troops could not retreat, as the trail for two miles behind them was wedged with men. They could not remain where they were for they were being shot to pieces. There was only one thing they could do – go forward and take the San Juan hills by assault'.[27]

Despite suffering heavy casualties, including the loss of Colonel Wikoff, the American forces slowly but surely reached the meadow. At 1 p.m., realizing that the only realistic option was to go forward, Lieutenant Miley took the responsibility to order a direct attack on the Heights. As the men of the First Infantry Division surged across the meadow they were supported by four Gatling machine-guns which a detachment commanded by Second Lieutenant John Parker had managed to drag to the front. Each gun sprayed 900 rounds per minute at the Spaniards on San Juan Hill. There was only enough ammunition for 8 minutes, but that proved long enough to unnerve the majority of the defenders, who abandoned their positions and fled towards Santiago de Cuba. San Juan Hill was in American hands. The achievement was vividly evoked in the eye-witness report by Richard Harding Davis:

> It was a miracle of self-sacrifice, a triumph of bull-dog courage, which one watched breathless with wonder. The fire of the Spanish riflemen, who still stuck bravely to their posts, doubled and trebled in fierceness, the crests of the hills crackled and burst in amazed roars, and rippled with waves of tiny flame. But

27 Richard Harding Davis, *The Cuban and Porto Rican Campaigns* (New York, 1898), pp. 213–14. The 'chute of death' was more commonly called 'the bloody angle' by those officers and soldiers who took part in the battle.

the blue line crept steadily up and on, and then, near the top, the broken fragments gathered together with a sudden burst of speed, the Spaniards appeared for a moment outlined against the sky and poised for instant flight, fired a last/ volley and fled before the swift moving wave that leaped and sprang up after them.[28]

The charge up the hill was undoubtedly a brave and heroic action, though Davis omitted to point out the numerical superiority of the Americans. He also exaggerated the degree of resistance offered by the Spaniards. The Spanish trenches and rifle-pits were dug into the top of the hill so that rifle fire could be directed into the distance at troops in the valley below. It was much more difficult to fire upon an enemy advancing up the hill. This factor, plus the shock given to the Spaniards of suddenly receiving a hail of bullets from the Gatling guns, allowed the American troops to rush the Spanish positions without suffering many casualties. Ironically, the most serious danger to American troops reaching the summit of San Juan Hill was from 'friendly fire' resulting from the sudden decision by Captain Grimes to recommence firing at the hill. Although the shelling was soon halted, it had demonstrated the dangers arising from the lack of coordination among the American commanders.

As Kent's infantry were storming San Juan Hill, Sumner's cavalrymen similarly charged up Kettle Hill. The black troopers of the Ninth Cavalry were conspicuous in the vanguard, though the press later gave the credit for leading the attack to Theodore Roosevelt. Certainly, Roosevelt enthusiastically led the Rough Riders into battle and was among the first group of Americans to reach the summit of Kettle Hill.[29] As at San Juan Hill, the Americans suffered only light casualties as the surviving Spaniards chose to fall back to Santiago de Cuba rather than defend their positions to the death.

Having captured the San Juan Heights, the American attack came to a stop. An advance on Santiago de Cuba was tempting to the front-line troops, but was hardly feasible. After more than 7 hours of continuous marching and fighting the men were hungry and tired. Moreover, the next line of Spanish defences was no more than half a mile away and appeared quite formidable. In fact, the capture of the Heights represented only a partial success because the

---

28 Ibid., p. 220.

29 It is often mistakenly assumed that Roosevelt led the attack upon San Juan Hill.

Spanish army had yet to be defeated. 'It was a victory, but a doubtful victory,' reported the British journalist John Black Atkins.[30] Instead of launching an assault on the city, American officers were more immediately concerned about the possibility of an enemy counter-attack, and instructed their troops to dig trenches and establish fortified positions on the hill. Another necessary task was to remove the dead and tend the wounded prior to carrying them back to the field hospital which had been established close to El Pozo.

The hard fighting had certainly won the Spaniards a new respect from their opponents. 'On this day', remarked Roosevelt, 'they showed themselves to be brave foes, worthy of honor for their gallantry.'[31] Indeed, the Spaniards had inflicted heavy casualties upon the American army. Shafter had initially believed that American losses were limited to 400 and was dismayed to learn later that they numbered 1,385, more than three times the first estimate. Altogether 205 Americans were killed and 1,180 wounded. At El Caney 81 were killed and 360 wounded. Kent's infantry division listed 89 killed and 489 wounded in the attack on San Juan Hill, while Sumner's cavalry division recorded 35 killed and 328 wounded at Kettle Hill. Spanish casualties were 593, consisting of 215 killed, 376 wounded, and 2 taken prisoner.[32] The statistics demonstrated that mass frontal assaults on well-established defensive positions would result in heavy losses for the attacking forces especially if adequate reconnaissance and effective artillery support were also lacking. In the particular case of the infantry battles of 1 July, American bravery and numerical superiority had made the crucial difference between victory and defeat.

During the evening of 1 July the Spaniards maintained a steady stream of artillery and rifle fire at the Americans on the hills. But no counter-attack was forthcoming. On the following days the firing from the Spanish side noticeably diminished. Despite suffering relatively fewer casualties than the Americans on 1 July, the Spaniards had lost two of their principal commanders. Even though he was directing operations some distance behind San Juan Hill, General Linares had been seriously wounded and had been evacuated to hospital in Santiago de Cuba. General Vara del Rey

30 John Black Atkins, *The War in Cuba: The Experiences of an Englishman with the United States Army* (London, 1899), p. 136.

31 Roosevelt, *Rough Riders*, p. 156.

32 See Chadwick, *The United States and Spain*, vol. iii pp. 101–2.

had been killed at El Caney. General José Toral y Vázquez assumed command in most inauspicious circumstances. His troops had fought bravely, but were disheartened not only by military defeat but also by acute shortages of food and ammunition. By capturing El Caney, the Americans could prevent the flow of piped water into the city. Moreover, now that the Americans controlled the San Juan Heights they had the advantage of overlooking the Spanish defensive line. Toral naturally assumed that Shafter would soon move up his heavy siege guns and threaten to bombard the city and Cervera's squadron in the harbour. The depressing news was relayed by telegraph to Captain General Blanco in Havana and to the Ministry of the Marine in Madrid. Toral awaited their response.

Despite receiving numerous reports that the Spaniards were desperately short of food and supplies, Shafter had consistently overestimated the strength and resources of his enemy. He simply could not eliminate the possibility that Linares[33] would use the estimated 12,000 regulars under his command to launch a counter-attack against the vulnerable American position on the San Juan Heights or an outflanking movement against the thin American defensive line which now stretched from Aguadores to El Caney. The chances of a vigorous Spanish response would also be increased by the imminent arrival of Escario's relief column from Manzanillo. There were also rumours of another Spanish relief force being prepared at Holguín. Conversely, Shafter was pessimistic about the prospects of his own front-line troops. He was particularly dismayed by the heavy losses suffered in capturing the Heights. The American position was strengthened on 2 July by the arrival from El Caney of Lawton's infantry division and Bates's Independent Brigade. However, the difficulties of providing the front with adequate supplies were enormous. This negative thinking resulted in Shafter summoning a meeting of his generals at 7 p.m. on 2 July to consider the advisability of falling back to a more easily defensible position. The prevailing view of his senior officers was that the American forces should stay put. Shafter agreed, but stated that the policy would be reviewed after 24 hours. One day had seen the elation of victory dramatically transformed into a mood of despondency bordering on despair. Like many officers, Roosevelt was privately critical of Shafter. On 3 July he sent an urgent appeal to Senator Lodge:

---

33 At this time Shafter was unaware of the injury to Linares and that Toral had assumed command of the Spanish garrison.

Tell the President for heaven's sake to send us every regiment and above all every battery possible. We have won so far at a heavy cost; but the Spaniards fight very hard and we are within measurable distance of a terrible military disaster; we must have help – thousands of men, batteries, and food and ammunition.'[34]

Meanwhile, a tense mood also prevailed in the United States, where information about events in Cuba was sparse and incomplete. The unopposed landing of the Expeditionary Force had been well received, but the unexpectedly high American casualties arising from the skirmish at Las Guásimas had exerted a sobering impact. The outcome of Shafter's advance on 1 July was awaited with great apprehension by officials in Washington. Anxiety was heightened by the general's telegraphic communications, which were not only infrequent but also invariably brief and ambiguous in content. Indeed, it was not until after 10 p.m. on 1 July that the White House received a cable from Shafter stating that the 'outer works' of Santiago de Cuba had been captured and that an ultimately successful engagement had been fought at El Caney for most of the day.[35] This pleasing news appeared to be contradicted a few hours later by another cable reporting that the scale of American casualties was far heavier than had first been thought. A full day passed without any further word from Shafter. The press was full of rumours about the outcome of the fighting and the state of Shafter's mental and physical health. The pressure on the White House and the War Department for information was intense. McKinley and Alger, however, were reluctant to disturb the general so long as events were at such a critical juncture. But their patience could not hold out for ever. Finally, at 1 a.m. on Sunday, 3 July, Alger telegraphed from the White House: 'We are awaiting with intense anxiety tidings of yesterday.'[36]

Shafter remained silent because the question of whether he should hold the Heights or withdraw was still basically undecided. Before conferring with his generals during the evening of 2 July he had turned somewhat belatedly to Sampson for assistance. Since the meeting at Aserradero on 20 July, the general had treated the

---

34 Roosevelt to Lodge, 3 July 1898, cited in Elting E. Morison, ed., *The Letters of Theodore Roosevelt* (8 vols; Cambridge, MA, 1951), vol. ii p. 846.

35 Shafter to Alger, 1 July 1898, cited in Alger, *Spanish-American War*, p. 172.

36 Alger to Shafter, 3 July 1898, cited in ibid., p. 173.

admiral more as a junior executive officer rather than an equal partner. Without warning on 2 July Shafter asked Sampson to launch a naval attack immediately against the Morro and La Socapa. The aim was to reduce the likelihood of a Spanish counter-attack by diverting Linares's attention away from the San Juan Heights. Sampson refused on the grounds that such an attack would inevitably result in 'a great loss of life'. Shafter responded with undisguised irritation: 'I am at a loss to see why the Navy can not work under a destructive fire as well as the Army.'[37] Fully appreciating the fragile state of their relationship, Sampson sought a personal meeting with Shafter on 3 July. Shafter readily invited the admiral to come to his headquarters close to Sevilla. In the meantime, the general tried another stratagem. At 8.30 a.m. on 3 July an ultimatum was sent to Linares stating that, unless Santiago de Cuba was surrendered, the city would be bombarded. Such decisive action was uncharacteristic of Shafter and contrasted sharply with the mood of uncertainty and gloom prevailing at his headquarters. The most likely explanation was that Shafter was simply taking up a suggestion made to him that morning by his aide, Colonel McClernand. Whatever the reason for the ultimatum, the general's policy appeared to be in disarray. In the circumstances it was not surprising that he held off communicating with Washington.

While McKinley and Alger waited for news from Shafter, the general similarly awaited a response from the Spanish commander. It was not until almost noon and, only after receiving another cable from Alger sent at 11 a.m., that Shafter eventually replied, stating that the defences of Santiago de Cuba were so strong that he was 'seriously considering withdrawing'.[38] Washington's worst fears appeared to be confirmed. 'Sunday, the 3rd of July', remarked Alger, 'was the darkest day of the war.'[39] But American resilience quickly asserted itself. McKinley and his advisers were convinced that retreat would have disastrous consequences. Although some consideration was given to replacing Shafter with General Miles, it was recognized that the sensible and proper policy was to give their full backing to the general in command. Alger telegraphed within half an hour promising to send reinforcements immediately and firmly advising Shafter to hold the San Juan Heights because 'the effect upon the

---

37 Shafter to Sampson, 2 July 1898, cited in Trask, *War with Spain*, p. 253.
38 Shafter to Alger, 3 July 1898, cited in Alger, *Spanish-American War*, pp. 174–5.
39 Ibid., p. 172.

country would be much better than falling back'.[40] Not for the first time in the war, however, a dramatic naval battle was to take place which significantly affected the course of events.

THE NAVAL BATTLE OF SANTIAGO DE CUBA

Admiral Cervera's decision to take his squadron to Santiago de Cuba had turned a previously remote place into the focal point of wartime military attention. The subsequent establishment of the American naval blockade and despatch of the Expeditionary Force were intended not so much to seize the city as to capture or destroy the Spanish warships in the harbour. So long as the squadron existed, it posed a naval threat to the commerce and territory of the United States. But to be effective it had to leave Santiago Bay. However, acutely conscious of the superiority of the opposing American fleet and the poor condition and armament of his own ships, Cervera responded negatively to the promptings of the Ministry of the Marine in Madrid and Captain General Blanco in Havana that he attempt to run the American naval blockade. Such an enterprise was regarded by Cervera as too risky. In fact, much to Sampson's relief, the Spanish admiral was not even prepared to test the blockade by sending out one or two ships either at night or during a period of bad weather and poor visibility. Consequently, the squadron remained passively in the harbour while the American Expeditionary Force landed at Daiquirí and Siboney. On the other hand, Cervera did directly assist General Linares by sending ashore almost two-thirds of the squadron's total crew to help man the city's defences. Moreover, even inactivity had a beneficial aspect in that, so long as the squadron remained in the harbour, the most powerful ships in the American navy were restricted to monotonous blockade duty.

As the American army began its advance towards Santiago de Cuba, the Ministry of the Marine urged Cervera on 23 June to escape from the harbour at the earliest opportunity. The government at Madrid considered that the loss of the fleet would be not only an unmitigated military disaster but also a national humiliation. On 24 June Cervera convened a meeting with his senior officers at which they agreed that a sortie was still too hazardous. Their

---

40 Alger to Shafter, 3 July 1898, cited in Alger, *Spanish-American War*, p. 177.

recommendation was to join the army in resisting the anticipated American assault on the city and, if the worst came to the worst, scuttle the ships to prevent them falling into the hands of the enemy. But Captain General Blanco was strongly opposed to what he regarded as a defeatist attitude. He informed Cervera via a telegram sent to Linares on 26 June that two Spanish merchant ships had recently evaded the American blockade at Havana by sailing under cover of darkness. He urged that Cervera should adopt the same tactic. The consequences of doing nothing would be disastrous. 'If your cruisers are in some manner captured in Santiago harbour', warned Blanco, 'the effect in the whole world will be disastrous and the war may be considered terminated in favour of the enemy.'[41]

Cervera, however, was as despondent as ever. 'I have considered the squadron lost ever since it left Cape Verde', he wrote to Linares on 25 June, 'for to think anything else seems madness to me in view of the enormous disparity which exists between our own forces and those of the enemy.' Aware that the Ministry of the Marine had placed him directly under Blanco's authority, the admiral was content to express his professional opinion and await orders from Havana. 'It is therefore for him [Blanco] to decide', concluded Cervera, 'whether I am to go out to suicide, dragging along with me those 2,000 sons of Spain.'[42] Blanco's response was to repeat the instructions that a sortie should be made whenever Cervera deemed feasible. Early in the morning on 2 July, following receipt of news that the Americans had captured the San Juan Heights and were poised to attack the entrance to the harbour, Blanco amended his orders and told Cervera to leave Santiago de Cuba as soon as possible.

On 2 July Cervera accordingly re-embarked his men from their defensive duties on shore and prepared the ships for departure on the morning of Sunday, 3 July. The admiral was unwilling to move at night because the Americans illuminated the harbour entrance with a powerful searchlight and positioned their ships closer to the shore than during the day. The plan drawn up by Cervera called instead for the sortie to commence at around 9 a.m. The ships were

---

41 Blanco to Linares, 26 June 1898, cited in Chadwick, *United States and Spain*, vol. iii, pp. 118–19. One historian has argued that Cervera's commanders believed that the Spanish government cynically wanted the destruction of the squadron in order to bring an early end to the war. See José Varela Ortega, 'Aftermath of Splendid Disaster: Spanish Politics before and after the Spanish American War of 1898', *Journal of Contemporary History* 15 (1980), p. 325.

42 Cervera to Linares, 25 June, 1898, cited in Chadwick, *United States and Spain*, vol iii, pp. 116–17.

to proceed in single file along the narrow channel led by the admiral's flagship, the *María Teresa*, and followed at 600-yard intervals respectively by the *Vizcaya*, *Cristóbal Colón* and *Oquendo*. The *Plutón* and *Furor* would take up the rear at 1,000-yard intervals. The only other warship in the harbour, the antiquated cruiser *Reina Mercedes*, was considered too unseaworthy to join the sortie. On reaching the open sea the ships were to steam due west at full speed for Cienfuegos. American ships that were within range would be fired upon. The object, however, was not to fight a naval battle but to out-run the enemy. Cervera knew the disposition of the American squadron, and reckoned that the first ship to come into contact with the Spanish column would be the *Brooklyn*. If this occurred, the *María Teresa* would seek to ram the *Brooklyn* in order to deprive the American fleet of its fastest warship and clear the way to Cienfuegos for the rest of the Spanish squadron.

There appears to be no particular reason why Cervera chose 3 July for the sortie except to implement Blanco's orders as soon as practicable. He was evidently not concerned about waiting for bad weather because the day was fine and the sea was calm. Perhaps the Spanish admiral thought that the Americans might be distracted by Sunday morning prayers. Whatever the reasoning, Cervera was determined to carry out his orders even though he personally considered that his fleet courted certain disaster. However, a ray of hope presented itself prior to departure when his scouts reported that fewer American warships than usual were at their blockading stations. In fact, the battleship *Massachusetts* and two cruisers, the *New Orleans* and *Newark*, had gone to Guantánamo Bay for coaling. Moreover, just before 9 a.m. the armoured cruiser *New York* had left the blockade to take Admiral Sampson to Siboney for his pre-arranged meeting onshore with General Shafter. Consequently, only seven American ships were stationed in the semicircle extending for about 8 miles around the harbour entrance. From east to west they comprised the converted yacht *Gloucester*, the battleships *Indiana*, *Oregon*, *Iowa* and *Texas*, the armoured cruiser *Brooklyn* and the converted yacht *Vixen*. The Spanish ships had superior rated speeds, but four armoured cruisers and two destroyers were no match in firepower against four battleships, one armoured cruiser and two converted yachts. In reality, the Spaniards were at an even greater disadvantage because they were short of ammunition and many of their guns were not in working order.

The sight of an increasing number of small clouds of smoke alerted the American sailors watching the harbour entrance that unusual activity was taking place. At 9.35 a.m. the *María Teresa* dramatically appeared and turned towards the west. The five other ships followed one by one and had all cleared the channel by 10.10 a.m. On spotting the *María Teresa*, the *Iowa* had immediately hoisted flags to signal '250' which, encoded, meant that 'the enemy is attempting to escape'. Even though the officers and men of the blockading squadron had been waiting weeks for this moment, they were temporarily caught by surprise. Most notably, the American commander was absent. In May, Sampson had sparked off controversy by sailing from Havana to Puerto Rico in search of Cervera. Subsequently, he had spent a month waiting at Santiago de Cuba for his enemy to appear. On the morning of 3 July Sampson suddenly heard the noise of battle, but found that he was going in the opposite direction to Siboney. He described his first thought: 'Oh, that we had wings.'[43] The *New York* was immediately turned around. However, despite reaching a speed of 17 knots, she proved unable to join the battle. In Sampson's absence, Commodore Schley assumed command.

As the American ships frantically built up steam and sought to converge on the harbour entrance, they fired their first shots at the closest target, which initially was the *María Teresa*. Sighting the *Brooklyn*, the *María Teresa* sought to carry out Cervera's plan by ramming the American warship. Schley took evasive action by ordering the *Brooklyn* to steer to the starboard. The manoeuvre was successful in avoiding the *María Teresa*, but brought the *Brooklyn* into the path of the *Texas*. It was the moment of greatest danger that American ships would face during the whole battle. Collision was averted only because the *Texas* abruptly shut down her engines and came to a stop. The resulting confusion gave the Spanish ships an additional few minutes to effect their exit from the harbour, and provided additional grounds for the later criticism of Schley's naval competence. Nevertheless, the *Brooklyn* and *Texas* remained intact and joined the other American warships in pursuit of the Spaniards. In fact, the *María Teresa* had already suffered a number of direct hits from the American guns. Like all the Spanish vessels, her wooden deck was a potential firetrap. The ship was therefore soon ablaze and incapable of fighting. In order to avoid becoming an enemy prize, the *María Teresa* headed for the shore and ran aground at 10.35 a.m. about 5 miles from the harbour entrance. The

---

43 Sampson, 'The Atlantic Fleet', p. 907.

survivors swam to the beach, including Cervera, who was the last man to leave the ship.

The sacrifice of the *María Teresa* proved to have been in vain. The American armoured ships switched their fire to the *Oquendo* which, after receiving more than fifty hits, imitated the flagship and turned to the shore. At 10.40 a.m. the *Oquendo* ran aground and split apart just a short distance west of the *María Teresa*. The *Plutón* and *Furor* did not even proceed as far as the *María Teresa* and *Oquendo*. As the last in line of the Spanish column, they encountered a hail of fire as soon as they exited the harbour. Within minutes both ships were ablaze after receiving direct hits from the *Gloucester*. At 10.45 a.m. the *Plutón* struck a reef and broke up. A short time later the *Furor* exploded and sank.

At 11 a.m. only two Spanish ships, the *Vizcaya* and *Cristóbal Colón*, remained afloat largely because they had stayed closer to the shore so that the *María Teresa* and the *Oquendo* would draw the American fire away from them. However, the *Vizcaya* soon suffered heavy punishment and was run aground at 11.15 a.m. close to Aserradero. It was later revealed that the *Vizcaya* had been struck twenty-nine times. This left only the *Cristóbal Colón*. Faster than any of the American warships, the *Cristóbal Colón* opened up a gap of 6 miles between her and the *Brooklyn*, *Texas* and *Oregon*. But the distance began to shorten after noon as the *Cristóbal Colón* ran out of the good quality coal which she had brought from Cádiz. Once her speed began to slacken, she came within range of the *Oregon*'s big guns. Rather than see his ship and crew destroyed, Captain Paredes hauled down his flag at 1.15 p.m., turned to the shore and ran the *Cristóbal Colón* aground about 50 miles west of Santiago de Cuba.

In a telegram to Washington Sampson triumphantly described the outcome of the battle as 'a Fourth of July present' for the American people.[44] In less than 4 hours Cervera's squadron had been completely destroyed. Damage to the American fleet was slight and limited to the *Brooklyn*, *Texas* and *Iowa*. Amazingly, only 1 American seaman had been killed and 2 wounded. By contrast, 323 Spaniards were reported dead and 151 wounded. In addition, 1,720

---

44 Sampson to Long, 3 July 1898, cited in Trask, *War with Spain*, p. 266. Sampson misleadingly implied that the victory had been achieved under his personal command. The deliberate omission of any reference to Schley reflected the depth of personal antagonism in their relationship. Unfortunately, the dispute blighted the reputations of both officers.

officers and men had been taken prisoner. Among the latter was Admiral Cervera, who had been rescued from the beach by the *Gloucester* and later transferred to the *Iowa*. The Americans showed great respect and sympathy for the Spaniards whom they regarded as having fought with honour and courage. Captain Robley Evans recalled how Cervera was welcomed aboard the *Iowa*: 'As the brave old admiral came over the side . . . without shirt or hat, yet an admiral every inch of him, the officers saluted and the marines presented arms, and the buglers sounded the salute for an officer of his rank.'[45]

Cervera's prediction of disaster had been proved correct. Throughout his period of command he had been required to fulfil expectations which proved quite unrealistic given the inadequacy of his ships and naval resources. Nevertheless, Cervera contributed to the disastrous chain of events on 3 July by his unwillingness to run the blockade at an earlier date. Cervera also chose to confront the American fleet on a day when the sea was calm and the visibility was extremely good. Moreover, to Sampson's surprise, all the Spanish ships went in the same direction. If one or two ships had turned to the east, the American admiral believed that this would have confused the blockading squadron and prevented it from concentrating its fire on the enemy. Consequently, the other Spanish ships would have been given a better chance of effecting their escape westwards. But Cervera's faulty tactics were Sampson's gain. The anticipated battle of the fleets had eventually taken place and had ended in a complete triumph for the United States and more glory for the American navy. Although the war had not yet come to an end, American command of the seas meant that victory over Spain could not be long delayed.

CAPITULATION OF SANTIAGO DE CUBA

The destruction of Cervera's squadron greatly boosted the morale of the American troops surrounding Santiago de Cuba. 'The good news has inspired everybody,' Shafter gratifyingly reported.[46] None the less, the American naval victory did not materially affect the balance of military forces facing each other in the trenches. In fact, by

45 Robley D. Evans, *A Sailor's Log: Recollections of Forty Years of Naval Life* (New York, 1901), p. 456.

46 Shafter to Alger, 3 July 1898, cited in Alger, *Spanish-American War*, p. 181.

removing the original purpose for sending the Expeditionary Force to Santiago de Cuba, Cervera's disastrous sortie actually strengthened the case for a tactical American withdrawal from the San Juan Heights. In contrast to Havana, Santiago de Cuba possessed no significant strategic value and its capture would not necessarily bring the war in Cuba to an end. What appeared certain, however, was than an American assault against the well-established Spanish defensive line would result in heavy casualties. In Washington, General Miles suggested that troops be transferred from Santiago de Cuba to join his forthcoming expedition to Puerto Rico. He had always considered the latter to be a more important target.

Miles's proposal was ignored because the McKinley administration had already resolved to lay siege to Santiago de Cuba. This had been evident in Alger's telegram on 3 July urging Shafter not to pull back from the San Juan Heights and promising the immediate despatch of reinforcements. Indeed, a volunteer regiment of infantry and six artillery batteries sailed from Tampa for Siboney on 3 July. Just after midnight Alger was greatly relieved to receive news not only of the navy's triumph but also Shafter's one-sentence telegram stating: 'I shall hold my present position.'[47] The Secretary of War eagerly anticipated the speedy capture of the city.

On hearing of the American naval victory, Shafter had repeated his ultimatum to Toral to surrender the city. Like so many of his colleagues during the war, the Spanish commander faced seemingly inevitable military defeat. Even the arrival late on 3 July of Escario's relief column of more than 3,500 men was a mixed blessing. Escario's achievement was valuable for propaganda purposes, but the new arrivals only placed extra demands on the limited supplies of food available to the beleaguered garrison. While Toral was only too conscious of the desperate condition of his army, he also recognized that surrender was not for him personally an immediately available option. Such an act would be regarded as dishonourable and would almost certainly result in his imprisonment, court martial and, perhaps, execution when he returned to Spain. Moreover, he did not possess the authority to surrender the city. The decision rested with the Captain General in Havana and the Spanish government in Madrid. While he waited for definite instructions from his superiors, Toral sought to prolong his discussions with Shafter in the hope that a successful 'war of words' might lead to

47 Ibid., p. 180.

better terms. Late in the afternoon of 3 July he firmly rejected Shafter's ultimatum and coupled this with a statement that the resident foreign consuls would be informed of the American threat to bombard the city.

As Toral anticipated, the resident foreign consuls in Santiago de Cuba requested Shafter to postpone the bombardment for humanitarian reasons. Shafter agreed to suspend military operations until 5 July. In the meantime he envisaged that there would be an orderly evacuation from Santiago de Cuba to El Caney of foreign nationals and non-combatants such as women, children, the elderly and infirm. However, late at night on 4 July the antiquated iron cruiser *Reina Mercedes* appeared in the channel at the entrance of the harbour. Toral's intention was apparently to imitate the *Merrimac* action and sink the *Reina Mercedes* so as to block the entry of American ships into the harbour. The Spanish vessel was fired on by the *Texas* and *Massachusetts*. Fearing that the threatened American bombardment has started, droves of civilians began to leave the city. On 5 July an estimated 20,000 refugees fled to El Caney. The movement of so many civilians actually reduced the pressure on Toral's supplies of food while saddling the American army with the new and heavy burden of feeding, clothing and providing shelter and medical care for thousands of refugees. Roosevelt sympathetically described the refugees as 'wretched creatures'. 'As we had barely enough food for our own men', he observed, 'the rations for the refugees were scanty indeed and their sufferings great.'[48]

Shafter was a willing accomplice in the 'war of words' with Toral. Feeling unwell and still shocked by the scale of the casualties incurred on 1 July, the American general had no desire to precipitate another full-scale infantry battle. A state of virtual truce served his purposes very well because it afforded time to reinforce and strengthen the army's defensive line. In this respect Shafter was also strongly influenced by what can only be described as his persistent overestimation of the enemy's strength throughout the whole campaign. He was extremely displeased to learn that Escario's relief column had reached the city and blamed this on the 'negligence' of Calixto García.[49] In fact, Shafter erroneously believed that the reinforcements numbered 5,000. 'This puts a different aspect upon

---

48 Roosevelt, *Rough Riders*, p. 197.
49 Shafter to Sampson, 4 July 1898, cited in Herbert H. Sargent, *The Campaign of Santiago de Cuba* (3 vols; Chicago, 1914), vol iii p. 11.

affairs,' he told Alger, and asked for additional reinforcements from the United States.[50] Another concern was the report that Toral was moving troops from the harbour entrance to defensive positions in the city. To counter this manoeuvre Shafter revived his proposal that Sampson attack the forts on the Morro and La Socapa. 'If you will force your way into the harbour', Shafter wrote to Sampson on 4 July, 'the town will surrender without any further sacrifice of life.'[51]

In Washington inter-service rivalries emerged once more when Alger implied that Sampson was reluctant to assist Shafter. This only provoked Long into criticizing the lethargy of the army. McKinley intervened by telegraphing instructions on 5 July to both commanders to confer and organize a joint operation to capture Santiago de Cuba. Shafter and Sampson could not ignore the President's directive and agreed to meet at the general's headquarters on 6 July. But Sampson did not attend. Pleading illness, he sent Captain Chadwick as his representative. Uppermost in Sampson's mind, perhaps, was not so much personal annoyance with Shafter but the bitter memory that his journey to a similar meeting had resulted in his absence from the naval battle on 3 July. There was, however, no mention of personal differences at the conference on 6 July. Both Shafter and Chadwick knew that the President expected them to produce a plan for a combined operation. An arrangement was concluded in which it was agreed that the army would issue another demand for Toral to surrender and, if he refused, the navy would bombard the city on 9 July.

The note was communicated to Toral on 6 July. The Spanish reply was received on 9 July and contained an unexpected counter-proposal in which Toral offered to evacuate the city in exchange for a safe passage to Holguín for his troops with all their equipment and weapons. It was an astute initiative which, if accepted, would give up the city and would also permit Toral to extricate himself and his army intact and with no loss of *pundonor*. Moreover, it would vindicate Shafter's strategy of capturing the city by negotiation rather than armed assault. The American general suspended the threat of bombardment and telegraphed the substance of Toral's proposal to Washington. A curt and uncompromising reply was forthcoming: 'You will accept nothing but an

50 Shafter to Alger, 4 July 1898, cited in Alger, *Spanish-American War*, p. 187.
51 Shafter to Sampson, 4 July 1898, cited in Sargent, *Campaign of Santiago de Cuba*, vol. iii p. 11.

unconditional surrender, and should take extra precautions to prevent the enemy's escape.'[52]

A few hours later Shafter sent another telegram, in which he presented several cogent reasons in favour of accepting Toral's proposal. The evacuation of the Spanish army would hand over control of the harbour, avoid loss of life and destruction of property, and allow refugees to return to their homes. A swift end to hostilities was also advisable, because three cases of suspected yellow fever had recently been reported among American troops at Siboney. The only disadvantage evident to Shafter was the loss of 'some prisoners we do not want and the arms they carry'. However, Shafter's superiors in Washington viewed matters very differently. Their desire to achieve a resounding military victory would be undermined by granting what were considered to be 'too lenient terms'.[53] President McKinley has deliberately left the conduct of military operations in the field to his generals and admirals, but he now personally drafted a direct instruction to Shafter: 'The Secretary of War orders, when you are strong enough to destroy the enemy and take Santiago, that you do it.' In effect, the note was a stinging rebuke. Shafter was disappointed, but he had no intention of challenging the chain of command. 'The instructions of the War Department will be carried out to the letter,' he obediently answered.[54]

A sequence of event ensued which was largely designed to satisfy officials in Washington and Madrid. Late on 9 July, Shafter informed Toral that his Government had rejected the evacuation proposal and, unless the Spanish forces surrendered unconditionally, the city would be bombarded at 4 p.m. on 10 July. Toral refused the demand, with the result that active hostilities resumed on 10 July for the first time since 3 July. At the San Juan Heights, there was some desultory firing of rifles and light artillery, but no serious attempt was made to advance from defensive positions. Acceding to the arrangement made on 6 July between Shafter and Chadwick, Sampson ordered the *Brooklyn* and *Indiana* to shell the city for 1 hour. But no sign of surrender was forthcoming from the Spanish defenders. A heavier bombardment was therefore instituted next day, in which Sampson's flagship, the *New York*, joined the

---

52 Alger to Shafter, 9 July 1898, cited in Alger, *Spanish-American War*, p. 194.

53 Charles G. Dawes, *A Journal of the McKinley Years* (Chicago, 1950), p. 164.

54 Shafter to Alger, 9 July 1898 and Alger to Shafter, 9 July 1898, cited in Alger, *Spanish-American War*, p. 194.

Brooklyn and *Indiana* in shelling the city from 9.27 a.m. until 1 p.m. Shafter then announced a cease-fire and proceeded to renew his efforts to persuade Toral to surrender. The American general was privately slighting of the efforts of his naval colleagues. He believed that the impact of the bombardment had been minimal. This was hardly surprising in view of the fact that the warships had stayed 2 miles offshore and aimed at a target 5 miles inland. 'This was our first experience in firing at such long range at an invisible target,' disarmingly explained Sampson.[55]

The military stalemate was broken on 11 July by a diplomatic breakthrough emerging from a surprising quarter. Officials in Washington were so confident of victory that they had already started discussing arrangements for dealing with Spanish prisoners of war. It was envisaged that a prison camp would be set up in Galveston, Texas. However, Alger ingeniously proposed that prisoners be repatriated to Spain at the expense of the United States government. The cost would be no more than bringing them to Galveston and the offer would be good public relations. According to Alger, it might even 'demoralise those Spanish soldiers remaining in Cuba, some of whom had been campaigning there three years, and were anxious to return to their homes'.[56] Alger's proposal was approved and communicated to Toral via Shafter on 11 July. For once Toral did not issue an outright rejection, but replied that he would refer the matter to Captain General Blanco. This was interpreted as a sign that negotiations were finally making progress.

On the same day General Miles arrived at Siboney and proceeded inland to Shafter's headquarters on 12 July. Miles's intention was to continue on to Puerto Rico, but he was instructed by McKinley to stop in Cuba and assist the capture of Santiago de Cuba. Though technically superior in rank to Shafter, Miles did not assume command. Nevertheless, the presence of the Commanding General of the Army was useful in providing Shafter with a plausible reason to suggest a personal meeting with Toral. The latter readily agreed. Consequently, the three generals met on 13 July at a point in no man's land between the opposing lines. The conversations lasted for 90 minutes. The American generals repeated the demand for unconditional surrender. Toral stated that he must defend the city 'to the bitter end' unless his government instructed otherwise.[57]

---

55 Sampson, 'The Atlantic Fleet', p. 906.
56 Alger, *Spanish-American War*, p. 198.
57 Memorandum of Conference held on 12 July 1898, cited in ibid., p. 207.

Neither side, however, wanted a bloodbath. Shafter consented to continue the truce until noon on 14 July to allow Toral time to consult with his superiors in Madrid and Havana. The concession aroused misgivings in Washington, where past experience had conditioned American officials to distrust Spanish political and military leaders. Concern was expressed that Toral was not negotiating in good faith. Despite the growing pressure on him to take the offensive, Shafter remained confident that the fall of Santiago de Cuba could be best achieved by negotiation rather than by fighting.[58]

In fact, Shafter's optimism was supported by developments in Spain, where the Spanish government was bracing itself to seek a negotiated end to the war. Prime Minister Sagasta recognized that the destruction of Cervera's fleet represented the extinction of Spain's last hope to reverse the sequence of military disasters. However, no major Cuban city had yet fallen to the Americans. The continued defence of Santiago de Cuba appeared futile, but to surrender the city would split the cabinet and, perhaps, provoke popular demonstrations which might lead to a military *coup* and the overthrow of the monarchy. As always, the army was the major obstacle to opening peace negotiations. For reasons of patriotism and *pundonor*, senior army officers were adamant that the war must go on. One of their most prominent supporters was Captain General Blanco, who had consistently stressed that the Spanish army in Cuba would not abandon the island. 'Surrender is impossible,' he had publicly stated in Havana on 6 July, and added: 'We must die rather than do so.'[59]

Blanco's bravado, however, was not shared by the civilian population of the capital. More than two months of naval blockade had reduced them to starvation. The Special Correspondent of *The Times* observed on 5 July that 'the people are in an angry mood and are losing confidence in their rulers'.[60] This was confirmed a few days later in Blanco's private report to Madrid in which he stated that the creoles now wished for an American victory. Even more disturbing was the revelation that he could no longer count upon the

---

58 Miles had arrived at Siboney with 1,500 troops and had made arrangements with Sampson to use these units in an attack at the harbour entrance should Toral not agree to unconditional surrender.

59 See *The Times* (London), 8 July 1898.

60 Ibid., 2 August 1898. The report of the Special Correspondent at Havana was dated 5 July.

peninsulares remaining loyal to the mother country.[61] Although Blanco was confident that Spanish soldiers at Havana would fight to the last man, he recognized that the garrison in Santiago de Cuba faced a desperate plight. The bitter reality was underlined by the wounded ex-commander of the city, General Linares, who, from his sick-bed, had dictated a letter which was telegraphed to Madrid on 12 July. 'The situation is fatal, surrender inevitable', lamented Linares, 'we are only prolonging the agony; the sacrifice is useless.'[62] In what was effectively an admission that *Cuba española* had become a doomed cause, Blanco reluctantly accepted on 13 July that Santiago de Cuba could not be held for much longer. Permission was given to Toral to continue his talks with Shafter on the basis of securing the repatriation of the garrison in exchange for 'capitulation'. [63] Throughout the ensuing negotiations the Spaniards would insist on using 'capitulation' instead of the more pejorative 'surrender'. This was accepted without dissent by the Americans as a mark of respect for their 'brave and chivalrous' opponents.[64]

At a brief meeting with Shafter and Miles on 14 July, Toral proposed that both sides appoint commissioners to settle the details of the capitulation. Federico Escario, now promoted to Brigadier-General, and Lieutenant-Colonel Ventura Fontán were selected to represent Spain. The American commissioners were General Wheeler, General Lawton and Lieutenant Miley. Although he kept Sampson informed of developments, Shafter ensured that army officers monopolized the negotiations. This was the opportunity for the army to gain its deserved share of glory. Indeed, Miles gratifyingly informed Alger by cable that Toral had 'formally surrendered'.[65] Contrary to American expectations, however, the meeting of the commissioners on the afternoon of 14 July did not result in a conclusive agreement. The Spaniards explained that everything had to be formally approved by the government in Madrid. An additional conference had therefore to be scheduled. The news disturbed McKinley and Alger, who feared that Toral was

---

61 Blanco to Correa y García, 9 July 1898, cited in John L. Offner, *An Unwanted War: The Diplomacy of the United States and Spain over Cuba, 1895–1898* (Chapel Hill, NC, 1992), p. 205.

62 Linares to Correa y García, 12 July 1898, cited in Alger, *Spanish-American War*, p. 202.

63 Blanco's instructions authorizing Toral to negotiate with Shafter were approved by Sagasta on 15 July.

64 See Alger, *Spanish-American War*, p. 216.

65 Miles to Alger, 14 July 1898, cited in Alger, *Spanish-American War*, p. 211.

employing delaying tactics to gain a military advantage. But Shafter's patience was rewarded. Late on 15 July Toral received the necessary authority from his government. Next day the commissioners duly signed the articles of capitulation. Despite the adoption of the term 'capitulation', the Spaniards were essentially accepting unconditional surrender.

The first article stated that 'all hostilities between American and Spanish forces in this district absolutely and unequivocally cease'. The Spaniards were to give up all weapons, although officers could retain their side arms, a reference to their ceremonial swords and pistols. In return, Spanish troops were to be repatriated to Spain at American expense and 'with as little delay as possible'. In what had been a totally unexpected bonus for the Americans, Toral had included in the capitulation not just the city's garrison but all the men in his command throughout the military division of Santiago de Cuba.[66] The total of Spanish troops surrendered eventually came to 22,700, of whom 13,558 came from the city of Santiago de Cuba and the rest from the other garrisons.

The actual capitulation was formally enacted on Sunday, 17 July. Shafter and Toral, each with an escort of 100 men, met between the lines at 9.30 a.m. and confirmed the settlement. The mood was anything but sombre. 'One might have thought it was a meeting of old friends and not the acknowledgement of defeat,' reported one American journalist.[67] Once the official ceremony was completed, both official parties proceeded together into Santiago de Cuba. At noon the American flag was symbolically raised over the governor's palace. Throughout the day the Spanish garrison systematically turned over its weapons, including 16,000 rifles and 3 million rounds of ammunition, and marched out of the city to a temporary detention camp located in the San Juan Heights. The honour of the Spanish army was maintained because it technically remained 'undefeated' in the battle for the city.

The euphoria of victory muted the criticism of General Shafter that he had been too cautious and indecisive. He was now praised for his astuteness in correctly judging that the city could be captured by a combination of siege and negotiation. Shafter was personally relieved that it had not been necessary to repeat the frontal assault of 1 July. Even so, American combat casualties had been high, and

66 For the 'Articles of Capitulation' see Alger, *Spanish-American War*, pp. 217–18.
67 James F.J. Archibald, 'The Day of the Surrender of Santiago', *Scribner's* 24 (1898), p. 413.

amounted to 243 killed and 1,445 wounded. Nevertheless, the President's orders had been successfully carried out. Within less than a month the Fifth Corps had landed on enemy territory, defeated a brave and resolute Spanish army, and taken more than 20,000 prisoners. The American army could also boast the capture of Cuba's second largest city and the possession of the eastern section of the island. In the process, the Spanish cause had suffered yet another devastating setback. Despite its inauspicious beginning, Alger concluded that 'the expedition was successful beyond the most sanguine expectation'.[68]

68 Alger, *Spanish-American War*, p. 296.

7 WINDING DOWN THE WAR

EVACUATION FROM SANTIAGO DE CUBA

The Spanish capitulation meant that Shafter could finally feel militarily secure. The outlying garrisons offered no resistance and accepted the terms agreed at Santiago de Cuba. Arrangements were made to assemble the prisoners in camps outside Santiago de Cuba and at Guantánamo. Although they were unarmed, Shafter was concerned about the presence of such a substantial number of Spanish soldiers and sought to repatriate them as soon as possible. The unavailability of American shipping meant that the War Department asked foreign steamship companies to bid for the contract to transport the troops. By bidding $800,000 less than its British and German competitors, the Spanish Transatlantic Company won the contract. Ironically, this meant that the troops would return to Spain in Spanish-owned ships sailing under the Spanish flag! Between 9 August and 17 September 22,864 soldiers were repatriated at a cost to the United States of $513,860.[1] Although Alger was clearly delighted at gaining a very good financial deal for his government, he did not seek to reduce costs at the expense of the well-being of the Spanish soldiers. The contract stipulated that the ships should not be overcrowded and that adequate rations must be supplied. The repatriation proposal was judged an unqualified success because it had constructively assisted both the negotiation and the implementation of the capitulation of Santiago de Cuba. 'To no other cause can be ascribed the alacrity with which 12,000 Spanish regulars, in the province of Santiago, outside of the city, surrendered without having fired a shot,' Alger proudly claimed.[2]

Personal relations between the victors and vanquished were remarkably cordial. Shafter commented that the Spanish prisoners

---

1 Spanish sailors who had been taken prisoner were held in Portsmouth, New Hampshire. Similar arrangements were made for their repatriation to Spain.

2 Russell A. Alger, *The Spanish-American War* (New York, 1901), p. 277.

were 'the most orderly, tractable, and generally best-behaved men that I have known'.[3] The respect and sympathy shown by the Americans towards the Spaniards contrasted very visibly with the unfriendly attitude which was increasingly apparent in dealings between Americans and insurgents. More than 1,000 insurgents had fought side by side with American soldiers at El Caney and the San Juan Heights, but this was apparently forgotten by Americans in their anger over the alleged failure of García's men to prevent the arrival of Escario's relief column from Manzanillo.[4] A typical American view of the insurgents was expressed by Roosevelt: 'They turned out to be nearly useless ... so far as the Santiago campaign was concerned.'[5] The low esteem accorded the insurgents was underlined by Shafter's pointed exclusion of García from both the peace negotiations and the formal ceremonies marking the capitulation of Santiago de Cuba. By contrast, Shafter treated the Spanish commander with the utmost respect and praised his men for their valiant defence of the city. Cubans might be forgiven for believing that they, not the Spaniards, were being treated as the enemy.

In fact, worse humiliation was to follow. The insurgents had expected to assume administrative control of Santiago de Cuba. They had been fighting for this objective for three years, and believed that it had been promised to them by Shafter in his meeting with García at Aserradero on 20 June. Instead García was informed by Shafter that the insurgents would not be allowed to enter the city under arms. The order was ostensibly justified as a measure to prevent possible public disorder and reprisals against the defeated Spanish troops. What most disturbed García, however, was the implication that Santiago de Cuba was under American military control. On the day of the capitulation he protested to Shafter over the humiliating restrictions unilaterally placed on the movements of his men:

A rumour, too absurd to be believed, General, describes the reason of your measures and of the orders forbidding my army

3 Ibid., p. 279.
4 Calixto García argued that Shafter's instructions to move the main insurgent army from Aserradero to Siboney prevented the deployment of a force strong enough to block Escario. Even so, the relief column was harried by insurgents throughout its march.
5 Theodore Roosevelt, *The Rough Riders* (New York, 1902), p. 75.

to enter Santiago for fear of massacres and revenge against the Spaniards. Permit me, sir, to protest against even the shadow of such an idea. We are not savages ignoring the rules of civilized warfare. We are a poor, ragged army as ragged and poor as was the army of your forefathers in their noble war for independence, but like the heroes of Saratoga and Yorktown, we respect our cause too deeply to disgrace it with barbarism and cowardice.[6]

García also announced that he was withdrawing himself and his forces from joint military operations with the Americans. His dignified protest, however, had no influence upon Shafter, who maintained the prohibition upon armed Cubans entering the city. García retaliated by ordering his forces north in the direction of Holguín. Americans regarded this as simply further proof of Cuban unreliability and ingratitude.

The removal of García's insurgent army partly eased Shafter's other major administrative burden of providing adequate supplies of food, shelter, clothing and medical supplies. Shafter's responsibilities initially included not only 20,000 American soldiers and an equivalent number of insurgents and prisoners of war but also humanitarian assistance for the masses of starving civilians who returned to the city after the signing of the capitulation. Little advantage was gained from the capture of the city because the spoils of war were minimal. Indeed, the defeated Spanish garrison left more ammunition than food. The opening of the harbour on 19 July facilitated the transport of supplies,[7] but most goods and equipment still had to be brought from the cargoes already landed at Siboney and Daiquirí. Consequently, the vast majority of American soldiers experienced only a marginal improvement in their living conditions. The most visible change for the better occurred in Santiago de Cuba. An efficient system of distribution was imposed by Leonard Wood,

6 García to Shafter, 17 July 1898, cited in Aníbal Escalante Beatón, *Calixto García: Su campaña en el 95* (Havana, 1978), p. 623. For an English translation of García's letter, see Philip S. Foner, *The Spanish-Cuban-American War and the Birth of American Imperialism, 1895–1902* (2 vols; New York, 1972), vol. ii pp. 369–70.

7 The first vessel to enter the harbour was the *City of Texas*, a steamer owned and operated by the American Red Cross. Clara Barton, the Director of the American Red Cross, went ashore to assist the hungry and sick people of Santiago de Cuba. The Red Cross was estimated to be providing food for 10,000 civilians every day. See George Kennan, *Campaigning in Cuba* (Port Washington, NY, 1971), p. 191.

whom Shafter had appointed Military Governor of Santiago de Cuba on 20 July. Wood employed autocratic methods to ensure a fair provision of food rations for civilians and to embark upon a major programme to improve sanitation. According to George Kennan, Santiago de Cuba 'always had the reputation of being the dirtiest city in Cuba'.[8] Within a few weeks of assuming office, Governor Wood felt able to claim that, except for the existence of tropical fever, conditions in Santiago de Cuba were as healthy as those in any major city in the United States.

The incidence of fever was not confined to civilians. Its seemingly inexorable spread within the American army became Shafter's major concern during the weeks following the capitulation of Santiago de Cuba. By authorizing American soldiers to fight in Cuba during the disease-ridden rainy season, President McKinley had, in effect, taken a calculated risk with the army's health. It was hoped that the campaign would be concluded quickly before disease could set in. Unaware of the dangers of mosquitoes in transmitting disease, expert American medical opinion of the day linked tropical fevers with poor sanitation, downpours of rain and vapours arising from so-called 'infected' soil. To avoid the latter it was recommended that campsites for troops be established on virgin land, preferably at higher elevations. The reasoning for this was that fever was relatively rare in mountainous regions. The risk of contracting disease would be further reduced by moving troops to new campsites every two to three days. Where cases of fever were reported, the individuals should be isolated and quarantined in army hospitals.

The most feared tropical disease was yellow fever. Popularly referred to as 'Yellow Jack', there was no known cure for this scourge which annually claimed hundreds, if not thousands, of lives in the tropical regions of the Caribbean and Brazil. American surgeons knew very little about the disease. In fact, a combination of anxiety and medical inexperience initially resulted in their failing to distinguish between yellow fever and the much more common and less deadly malarial fever. The first suspected cases of yellow fever among American troops were identified at Siboney on 6 July. Fearful of the outbreak of an epidemic and, in accordance with the best medical advice available, Alger instructed Shafter to move his troops from the lowland 'fever belt' to high ground as soon as the fighting

8 Ibid., p. 174.

was over.[9] Alger stated that cases of yellow fever were to be isolated, but he also added that they should not be put on transports for return to the United States. The prohibition was extended to include not only individuals but the rest of their regiment. Clearly, Alger was determined not to risk the spread of yellow fever to the United States. The men would be brought home when it was judged safe to do so. Meanwhile, they must stay in Cuba 'until the fever has had its run'.[10]

Shafter did not attempt to move the army to higher ground. One reason was the need to retain a sufficient number of troops to guard the Spanish prisoners awaiting repatriation. Another factor was the poor physical condition of the American soldiers and the sheer impracticability of marching them and their equipment along virtually impassable trails into the mountains. Roosevelt remarked that, whenever his regiment moved camp even a short distance, this resulted in a doubling of the sick-roll on the next morning. 'To have gone up the mountains', he believed, 'would have meant early starvation.'[11] The satisfaction of having defeated the Spaniards had diverted attention in Washington from the fact that thousands of American soldiers continued to suffer from the oppressive climate, lack of medical care and poor food. 'With a few exceptions', reported Kennan, 'the soldiers had nothing but hard bread and bacon after they left the transports at Siboney, and short rations at that.'[12] During the days following the capitulation there was a steady spread of disease, mainly malaria, typhoid and dysentery. On 22 July Kennan estimated that no more than half of the American troops were fit for active duty. He placed the blame not on the Cuban climate but 'bad management, lack of foresight, and the almost complete breakdown of the army's commissary and medical departments'. Kennan's views were published in the American press on 30 July, and formed part of a growing chorus of concern and anger emerging in the United States that official neglect and incompetence were causing the unnecessary suffering of brave American soldiers in Cuba.[13]

In his official communications with the War Department, Shafter acknowledged the increase in cases of malarial fever, but he

---

9 Alger to Shafter, 13 July 1898, cited in Alger, *Spanish-American War*, p. 256.

10 Cited in Graham A. Cosmas, *An Army for Empire: The United States Army and the Spanish-American War* (Columbia, MO., 1971), p. 255.

11 Roosevelt, *Rough Riders*, p. 206.

12 Kennan, *Campaigning in Cuba*, p. 217.

13 Ibid., pp. 215–6.

did not appear to be unduly alarmed. There was, therefore, no real warning of the crisis which was to strike Washington during the first week of August. On 2 August Alger was surprised to receive a telegram from Shafter stating: 'I am told that at any time an epidemic of yellow fever is liable to occur. I advise that the troops be moved as rapidly as possible whilst the sickness is of a mild type.'[14] After consulting the Surgeon-General, George M. Sternburg, Alger repeated his advice that the army be moved to high ground. Shafter wrote back on 3 August saying that this was 'practically impossible' given the weakened state of his men, of whom 75 per cent had been or were currently suffering from malaria. 'In my opinion', he stated, 'there is but one course to take, and that is to immediately transport the 5th Corps and the detached regiments that came with it to the United States. If that is not done, I believe the death-rate will be appalling.'[15] Within an hour Alger replied that Shafter should 'move to the United States such of the troops under your command as are not required for duty at Santiago'.[16] The resulting shortfall of active troops at Santiago de Cuba would be met by despatching regiments of 'immunes' and volunteers from the United States.

Prior to this exchange of telegrams Shafter had held a meeting of his generals and senior surgeons on 3 August. The atmosphere was just as gloomy as that of a similar meeting held a month earlier to consider withdrawal from the San Juan Heights. Indeed, the threat of disease was more serious than that of a Spanish counter-attack. All those present concurred that the only way to escape a major epidemic of yellow fever was for the army to return to the United States as quickly as possible. Concern was expressed, however, that the War Department would continue to insist that the troops remain in Cuba. To assist Shafter in his dealings with Washington, it was decided to prepare a separate statement of support. The resulting document was signed in turn by each general and Colonel Roosevelt, and became known as the 'Round Robin'. Its main recommendation was bluntly worded: 'This army must be moved at once or it will perish. As an army it can be safely moved now. Persons responsible for preventing such a move will be responsible for the unnecessary loss of many thousands of lives.'[17]

14 Shafter to Alger, 2 August 1898, cited in Alger, *Spanish-American War*, p. 262.
15 Shafter to Alger, 3 August 1898, cited in ibid., p. 263.
16 Alger to Shafter, 3 August 1898, cited in ibid., p. 265.
17 The text of the 'Round Robin' is printed in ibid., p. 266.

Shafter sent the 'Round Robin' to Washington on 3 August and it was received the next day by Alger at the War Department. However, the text of the document had been secretly leaked to a correspondent of the Associated Press at the general's headquarters on 3 August. The result was the publication of the 'Round Robin' in the American press on the morning of 4 August before Alger had officially received the note. The leak not only severely embarrassed the War Department but also threatened to disrupt diplomatic negotiations which were taking place in Washington to end the war. Alger described the 'Round Robin' as 'one of the most unfortunate and regrettable incidents of the war'.[18]

President McKinley was indignant. Without success, he sought to discover the source of the leak. The view at the time placed the blame on Roosevelt. Indeed, appearing as the champion of the ordinary American soldier against a heartless government did not hurt Roosevelt's personal political ambitions. However, he later claimed that Shafter was the true culprit. Whoever was responsible, the fact was that the 'Round Robin' successfully achieved its objective. The press was duly informed by the War Department on 4 August that instructions were on their way to Shafter to prepare the evacuation of his troops 'as fast as transportation can be provided'.[19] Even though Alger had actually sent similar instructions to Shafter the previous day, the controversy over the 'Round Robin' made it appear that an insensitive administration was being forced to act belatedly and out of shame. The evacuation of the Fifth Corps proceeded rapidly. It began on 7 August and was completed in less than three weeks. Among the last to leave was General Shafter, on 25 August. The destination for the evacuees was Montauk Point, New York.

War Department officials had given little thought to preparing a camp in the United States to receive troops returning from Cuba. The matter was not considered to be particularly urgent. Following the capitulation of Santiago de Cuba, the Fifth Corps would be moved to higher ground and was expected to remain in Cuba for some weeks until all signs of yellow fever had been eradicated. Meanwhile, on 28 July Alger approved Montauk Point in the state of New York as the site of the proposed reception camp. Situated at the east of Long Island and 125 miles from New York City, it comprised 5,000 acres of virtually uninhabited land owned by the

18 See ibid., p. 269.
19 Corbin to Shafter, 4 August 1898, cited in ibid., pp. 271–2.

Long Island Railroad Company. The principal advantage of Montauk was its geographical remoteness. Troops could be landed and quarantined there until they were judged to be free from yellow fever. The War Department leased the land, and on 2 August signed contracts with local private companies to construct housing and provide a supply of water. It was envisaged that a camp and medical facilities would be established for about 5,000 men.

Hardly had these arrangements been made when it was announced that the evacuation of the whole Fifth Corps was to begin at once. Quite simply, Montauk was not ready. The drilling of wells and laying down of wooden floorboards only started on 6 August. The disorder and confusion reminiscent of Tampa was once again repeated, as large quantities of equipment and supplies were frantically despatched to Long Island. Ironically, Montauk's very remoteness became a disadvantage because it meant a lack of roads and available local supplies. The single-track railway linking Montauk with New York City was soon congested. Nevertheless, a 'camp' consisting mainly of thousands of tents speedily came into existence. It was named Camp Wikoff, in honour of the colonel who had been killed in the battle for the San Juan Heights.

The first troops from Santiago de Cuba reached Camp Wikoff on 14 August. Every day new units arrived, consisting of weak, emaciated men many of whom were suffering from malarial fever or its after-effects. Theodore Roosevelt remarked on the 'great confusion' and 'lack of almost everything' during this period.[20] Visiting relatives, the public and press witnessed the inadequate provision of housing, food and medical facilities and castigated the War Department and especially Secretary Alger. But conditions steadily improved in September as shortages were remedied and the camp's affairs came under the energetic administration of General Wheeler, who had assumed command on 15 August. Once the first chaotic days were over, Roosevelt stated that 'we were very well cared for and had abundance of all we needed'. He made a special note of the ample supply of tobacco, 'the lack of which during portions of the Cuban campaign had been felt as seriously as any lack of food'.[21]

As men recovered their health, they were allowed to leave for their homes. Serious cases of illness were transferred to hospitals in New York and other cities. The last batch of soldiers left Camp

20 Roosevelt, *Rough Riders*, p. 220.
21 Ibid.

Wikoff on 28 October. In a period of almost eleven weeks the camp received more than 20,000 evacuees. Of these 257 died while at the camp. Cases of yellow fever were minimal and no epidemic occurred. Alger claimed that the camp's record of achievement was 'creditable', and cited the comment of Shafter that 'it was the best camp I ever saw'.[22] The seal of official approval was also given by President McKinley's visit to the camp on 3 September. None the less, the controversy surrounding the 'Round Robin' and the attested reports of emaciated men returning from Cuba only to endure further suffering at Camp Wikoff undermined the best efforts of McKinley and Alger. Public criticism was directed specifically at Alger, whose reputation was further damaged by revelations of similar deplorable conditions in the volunteer camps at Chickamauga Park and Camp Alger. Alger and his officials at the War Department, however, had worked hard to ensure that the evacuation of the Fifth Corps was a success. At least for the men of the Fifth Corps, the alarm over yellow fever meant that they had been allowed to return to the United States instead of being sent to fight in Puerto Rico and the Philippines.

THE CONQUEST OF PUERTO RICO

In addition to Cuba, Spain's other colonial possession in the Caribbean was the island of Puerto Rico. Situated to the east of the Dominican Republic, Puerto Rico was essentially a garrison fortress which lay astride the main shipping route from Europe to Cuba. In terms of strategic significance, Mahan likened the island to Malta.[23] But Puerto Rico had long been overshadowed by Cuba. It was less than one-tenth the size of Cuba and had never been accorded a historical importance or status similar to that of the 'ever-faithful isle'. In 1898 Puerto Rico possessed a population of just under 1 million whose main economic activity revolved around the sugar industry. Despite the existence of a local movement for constitutional reform, political affairs were more peaceful in Puerto Rico than in Cuba. The Spanish authorities did not have to contend with internal armed rebellion. Consequently, the presence of the Spanish military was much less visible, and consisted of about 8,000

---

22 Alger, *Spanish-American War*, pp. 438, 448.
23 Alfred T. Mahan, *Lessons of the War with Spain, and Other Articles* (Boston, 1899), p. 29.

regular soldiers who were stationed in garrisons spread over the island. These numbers were considered adequate because Spanish governments did not regard the external defence of Puerto Rico as a major priority. In cases of emergency local volunteer militia forces were expected to assist the regulars. Naval defences were limited to a small number of light cruisers and gunboats with support from light artillery located in the principal ports.

Although Puerto Rico was known to be less well-defended than Cuba, it attracted relatively little attention from American political and military leaders. In marked contrast to Cuba, Puerto Rico was considered to be geographically remote from the United States. The journey from Key West to San Juan was more than 1,000 miles. Moreover, there was no brutal civil war taking place to arouse American public consciousness. The prevailing attitude of American indifference was not shared by General Miles, who advocated that the Expeditionary Force should attack Puerto Rico as an alternative to campaigning in Cuba during the rainy season. He also emphasized the strategic importance of the island and argued that its capture would deprive Spain of a valuable naval base in the Caribbean from which it could supply Cuba and launch raids against American ships and territory. Miles's ideas did not go entirely unheeded. In May 1898 the War Department sent Lieutenant Henry F. Whitney on a secret mission. Whitney entered the island on a British merchant ship and spent ten days at the southern city of Ponce gathering information about local defences.

At the beginning of the war, however, American military effort was firmly concentrated on Cuba and the Philippines. The marginal importance attached to Puerto Rico was demonstrated on 12 May when, in search of Cervera's squadron, Admiral Sampson approached San Juan, briefly shelled the city and then departed. However, the discovery a few weeks later that Cervera was at Santiago de Cuba suddenly shifted the geographical focus of American attention from northern to eastern Cuba and from the Atlantic to the Caribbean. Eager to exercise command of an overseas expedition, Miles seized the opportunity to urge the immediate conquest of Puerto Rico. 'The possession of Puerto Rico', he stressed, 'would be of very great advantage to the military, as it would cripple the forces of Spain.'[24] McKinley was not averse to an attack on Puerto Rico, but he gave priority to the expedition against Santiago de Cuba. Only when the latter objective had been

24 Miles to Alger, 27 May, 1898, cited in Alger, *Spanish-American War*, p. 51.

successfully achieved would Miles be allowed to proceed with an operation against Puerto Rico.

Without a great deal of personal enthusiasm, Alger worked with Miles in late June to mobilize an expeditionary force to campaign in Puerto Rico. In contrast to Cuba, the absence of a guerrilla movement in Puerto Rico meant that American troops would have to land and fight without local assistance. According to Miles, an army of 30,000 was required. Major-General John R. Brooke was instructed to organize three divisions drawn from the First, Third and Fourth Army Corps. Transports would be assembled at Tampa, Newport News, Virginia, and Charleston, South Carolina.[25] Activities at the latter port were significantly speeded up in early July when the McKinley administration became greatly disturbed by rumours of Shafter's ill-health and the fragility of the American defensive line at Santiago de Cuba. Miles was instructed to take whatever regiments were available and leave for Cuba. He was expected, first, to assist Shafter to bring about the surrender of Santiago de Cuba, and then to proceed to Puerto Rico. On 8 July Miles left Charleston. The forces under his command numbered almost 3,500 and consisted mainly of two volunteer regiments.

Miles arrived at Siboney on 11 July and became actively involved in the negotiations between Shafter and Toral which resulted in the capitulation of Santiago de Cuba. From 15 July onwards Miles was able to concentrate on preparing for the campaign in Puerto Rico. The first task was to choose which regiments would make up the expeditionary force. Miles's longstanding concern over the dangers of tropical fever had been heightened by the growing number of cases he witnessed among American soldiers in Cuba. As a result he decided against taking units from the Fifth Corps to Puerto Rico. He also kept his own troops on board their transports at Siboney as a precautionary measure and eventually moved them to Guantánamo Bay. A combination of Miles's preventive health-care, the provision of more ample supplies than had been available to Shafter's forces, and the fact that the climate was healthier in Puerto Rico than in Oriente, resulted in few cases of tropical disease among the soldiers of the Puerto Rican expedition.

American victory in Puerto Rico was to be achieved by

25 To avoid a repetition of the confusion surrounding the embarkation of the American Expeditionary Force at Tampa, the War Department had sensibly decided to make use of other American ports in despatching troops overseas.

attacking and capturing San Juan, the major stronghold and centre of Spanish power. Miles favoured landing 30 miles east of the capital at Cape Fajardo, a remote headland in the northeastern corner of the island. Once a beachhead had been established and reinforced with troops from the United States, he would move against San Juan by land while the navy would bombard the city from the sea. Miles personally discussed these plans with Sampson on 16 July and, at the same time, requested a naval escort including armoured warships to protect the transports on their journey from Cuba to Puerto Rico. The American general acted quickly and positively, because he recognized that the strategic significance of Puerto Rico had been considerably diminished by the capture of Santiago de Cuba and the destruction of Cervera's squadron. Miles's anxiety, however, was unnecessary because McKinley saw the operation as a useful means of exerting additional military pressure on Spain to sue for peace. The President also believed that the victory at Santiago de Cuba should be exploited as rapidly as possible. On 18 July Miles was authorized to proceed immediately to Puerto Rico. He was expected to establish a beachhead with the troops whom he had brought from Charleston. Substantial reinforcements would arrive from the United States within a week of his landing.

The sailing of the expedition received an unanticipated delay when Miles complained to the War Department that Sampson would not release any armoured ships for convoy duty. Sampson argued that light cruisers were adequate for the purpose. Perhaps, as Alger later suggested, the admiral was still brooding over his absence from the naval battle on 3 July. Sampson may also have been retaliating against the army on account of Shafter's exclusion of naval officers from the negotiations leading to the capitulation of Santiago de Cuba. Whatever the admiral's rationale, McKinley was annoyed to learn of another case of inter-service squabbling, which, in this instance, threatened to endanger the safety of American troops. On 20 July the President ordered an armoured ship to be made available. Accordingly, Sampson released the battleship *Massachusetts* for convoy duty. Miles and the army had, therefore, triumphed over Sampson and the navy. The fact that the dispute had become personal was not so much the fault of the individuals concerned as the lack of institutional machinery in Washington to coordinate the actions of separate government departments. On a number of occasions throughout the war inter-service disputes were only resolved by the intervention of the President.

On 21 July, Miles's expeditionary force of almost 3,500 men left Guantánamo Bay. The convoy intended to cover 700 miles in three days by steaming north through the Windward Passage and then eastwards to Puerto Rico. Reinforcements from the United States would have to travel double the distance. In fact, Major-General James H. Wilson with 3,600 troops had already departed the previous day from Charleston. On 24 July an additional 2,900 men under the command of Brigadier-General Theodore Schwan left Tampa. An additional detachment amounting to 5,000 soldiers commanded by General Brooke departed on 28 July from Newport News. The combined total of these forces numbered about 15,000. Although this was less than Miles' initial target of 30,000, the forces were equivalent to the estimated combined strength of the Spanish army and militia in Puerto Rico.

On his second day at sea the mercurial Miles confounded everyone by switching the expedition's destination from Fajardo to Guánica, a small town at the opposite end of the island. Miles later explained that the Spaniards were expecting a landing at Fajardo and he chose to maintain the element of surprise by going elsewhere. He had also studied the report made by Lieutenant Whitney[26] in which Guánica was judged preferable to Fajardo because it possessed a deep-water harbour and good docking facilities. The choice of Guánica meant that the city and port of Ponce, which was 15 miles to the east, would become the first American military target. According to Whitney, Ponce was weakly defended and its inhabitants were sympathetic to the United States. On 24 July, to the confusion of the Spaniards, the American expedition steamed past Fajardo and set its course for Guánica. When news of the change was reported next day in the New York press, Alger was similarly baffled. 'Why did you change?' he cabled Miles on 26 July.[27] Instructions were quickly sent to redirect the transports carrying reinforcements from the United States.

The decision to land at Guánica certainly surprised the Spaniards, but it also delayed land operations against San Juan, the centre of Spanish power and authority. Not only were Guánica and San Juan at opposite ends of the island but they were also divided by an extensive mountain range. Alger, however, approved Miles's

---

26 Whitney had been promoted to captain and was assigned to Miles's staff for the expedition to Puerto Rico.

27 Alger to Miles, 26 July, 1898, cited in Alger, *Spanish-American War*, p. 305.

action and reckoned later that 'it probably saved a battle'.[28] Indeed, Miles correctly judged that Spanish resistance at Guánica would be minimal. On the morning of 25 July a small force of American marines drove away the Spanish defenders and raised the American flag. No casualties were incurred on the American side. Shortly afterwards, the transports docked at the harbour to disembark troops and unload supplies. The beachhead had been successfully established without a single American casualty.

Miles's first aim was to capture Ponce. The same tactics designed originally for use against San Juan were put into effect. On 26 July troops advanced along the road from Guánica to Ponce. The march was conducted at deliberate rather than rapid speed in order to coordinate operations with the navy. On 27 July General Wilson arrived with reinforcements of 3,600 men. Miles ordered Wilson's transports not to dock at Guánica but to proceed to Ponce. The ships would be accompanied by the *Massachusetts*, which had instructions to bombard Ponce ahead of an American landing. As Miles's troops approached the city on 28 July, Wilson's convoy entered the harbour. After a brief engagement in which four Americans were wounded, the Spanish garrison retreated to the north. Miles entered the city and in proconsular fashion issued a proclamation declaring that Americans came to liberate the people of Puerto Rico and to give them 'the advantages and blessings of enlightened civilization'.[29] Whether it was a result of Miles's show of personal consideration for local sensitivities, a straightfoward bowing to superior American military force or the realization that Spanish power was in terminal decline, the inhabitants of Ponce confirmed Whitney's prediction and openly welcomed the invaders. 'At least four-fifths of the people hail with great joy the arrival of United States troops,' Miles proudly reported.[30] This was corroborated a short time later by a visiting British journalist, who reported that 'the sentiment of dislike towards Spain was unmistakably genuine'.[31]

The American military position was considerably strengthened by the possession of Ponce and the addition of Wilson's reinforcements. Within a week the total strength of the expedition

28 Ibid., p. 307.

29 28 July 1898, cited in Nelson A. Miles, *Serving the Republic: Memoirs of the Civil and Military Life of Nelson A. Miles* (New York, 1911), p. 302.

30 Miles to Alger, 30 July 1898, cited in Alger, *Spanish-American War*, p. 307.

31 John Black Atkins, *The War in Cuba: The Experiences of an Englishman with the United States Army* (London, 1899), p. 234.

was further increased by the arrival of Schwan on 31 July with 2,900 men and Brooke on 3 August with an even bigger detachment of 5,000. Most of these troops were drawn from volunteer regiments representing most of the states of the United States. The fact that such disparate units could be assembled, transported and disembarked overseas in less than four weeks contrasted with the disorganization which had plagued Shafter's preparations and testified to the improved skill of War Department officials and army staff officers. Nor did Miles encounter the supply difficulties faced by Shafter. Guánica and Ponce provided sheltered harbours and docking facilities. Goods could also be moved inland more easily because the local roads were in much better condition than those in Cuba.

Whereas Shafter's military strategy had basically evolved according to events, Miles developed a complicated tactical plan. The ultimate goal was the capture of San Juan. No doubt, influenced by the example of Spanish resistance at El Caney and the San Juan Heights, Miles wished to avoid a pitched infantry battle. Instead of a frontal assault, Miles sought to isolate and surround the enemy by advancing in four separate columns. General Schwan and Brigadier-General Guy Henry would operate in the west and eventually link up at Arecibo on the northern coast. General Wilson would advance and attack Aibonito, an important garrison that was strategically located at a pass in the mountains which intersected with the main road from Ponce to San Juan. In the meantime, General Brooke would be a few miles to the east at Cayey, a position from which he would be able to outflank the Spanish defenders at Aibonito and, if necessary, cut off their retreat. Miles's strategy envisaged the Spaniards falling back in disorder to San Juan, where they would be effectively trapped and compelled to surrender.

The offensive began on 6 August and proceeded according to plan. The most rapid advance was made in the west by General Schwan, who won two skirmishes and captured the city of Mayagüez on 11 August. Enemy resistance was weak, largely because the Spanish forces were already demoralized by the loss of Santiago de Cuba and reports that the government at Madrid was seeking an early end to the war. Captain General Manuel Macías y Casado had also followed the usual Spanish tactics of spreading troops too thinly so that the individual garrisons were outnumbered by American units consisting of more than 1,000 soldiers. Contrary to the hopes of Spanish commanders, the local militia failed to make up the numerical deficiencies. Most units chose to desert rather than confront the Americans. Although the Spanish cause appeared doomed, Macías was known to have concentrated at least 1,300 regulars at Aibonito, the gateway to San Juan. If the Americans stormed the garrison, they might well run into the same resolute resistance that Spanish troops had displayed at El Caney and the San Juan Heights.

The battle of Aibonito, however, did not materialize. On 12 August the War Department sent a telegram to Miles informing him that the governments of the United States and Spain had signed a peace protocol in Washington. All military operations were to be halted immediately. In Puerto Rico Spanish forces surrendered to the Americans. Reviewing the campaign, Miles believed that his offensive needed four more days to have achieved total victory. His assumption was based on the relatively easy success enjoyed up to 12 August by the American invading force. Whereas American casualties were only seven killed and thirty-six wounded, Spanish losses were estimated at ten times the American number. Furthermore, Ponce and Mayagüez, two of the three principal cities on the island, had fallen. Miles could justly take considerable satisfaction in his military achievement. Almost alone among American leaders, he had persistently urged the sending of an expeditionary force to Puerto Rico. While he had not faced the difficulties encountered by Shafter at Santiago de Cuba, Miles had conquered the island at relatively little cost in American blood and treasure. Even Alger, who was hardly sympathetic to Miles, was complimentary. 'The campaign in Puerto Rico had been well conceived and skilfully executed,' summed up the Secretary for War.[32]

THE CAPTURE OF MANILA

While stirring military events took place in Cuba and the Caribbean, Admiral Dewey waited patiently in Manila Bay for supplies and reinforcements from home. By destroying the entire Spanish fleet, Dewey enjoyed complete naval supremacy in local waters. Although the Spaniards retained control of the city of Manila, they were blockaded by sea and dared not launch a counter-attack or fire on the American squadron for fear of provoking a naval bombardment

---

32 Alger, *Spanish-American War*, p. 317.

in retaliation. A similar constraint, however, applied to Dewey. He had landed marines to seize the Cavite arsenal, but any further advance onshore was ruled out by the fact that the forces under his command amounted to little more than 1,700 men while the Spanish garrison in Manila comprised over 10,000 regulars and an equivalent number of local militia. The total would be doubled if additional Spanish units in the rest of Luzon and the other islands of the archipelago were included. But Dewey remained as optimistic as the day he had left Mirs Bay. When asked by Long how many soldiers would be required to capture Manila, the admiral replied on 13 May that 5,000 would be sufficient.

The Philippines were 7,000 miles in distance from the west coast of the United States. An expeditionary force had to be assembled at the Presidio, San Francisco, organized and then sent on an ocean voyage that would take from seven to eight weeks. One pressing concern of American officials was that Spain would similarly despatch its own reinforcements to relieve Manila. This eventually materialized on 16 June, when a powerful squadron, including the armoured warships *Pelayo* and *Carlos V*, left Cádiz *en route* to Manila via the Suez Canal. It would be some weeks, however, before the squadron arrived in the Philippines. In the meantime Dewey was distracted by a naval problem arising from an unexpected source. The fighting in Manila Bay had aroused the attention of foreign powers who sent warships to the scene of the conflict. Such action was standard practice in the trouble spots of the world and was designed not to intervene in the conflict but to report on events and, if necessary, provide naval protection for foreign citizens and their property. Consequently, within a few days of Dewey's victory, ships from the navies of Britain, France, Germany and Japan had entered the bay.

What was unusual and puzzling was the size of the German naval contingent. During May and June six German vessels arrived, including the battleship *Kaiser* and the cruiser *Kaiserin Augusta*, the flagship of the German Asiatic Squadron with Vice-Admiral Otto von Diederichs on board. The appearance of such large warships and the presence of von Diederichs aroused American suspicions of German ulterior motives. Moreover, the habit adopted by the German ships of going in and out of the bay without signalling their intentions greatly annoyed Dewey, who regarded such action as a deliberate flouting of the American blockade. On one occasion the admiral was so irate that he threatened to fire on vessels which did not properly identify themselves. Von Diederichs was conciliatory, and appears to have acted as a neutral observer rather than an advance agent of German imperialism. Nevertheless, Dewey's reports of German awkward behaviour contrasted with the friendly attitude shown by British naval officers, and aroused suspicions among officials in Washington that Germany had selfish territorial designs on the Philippines.

Eager to grasp any glimmer of hope, Captain General Basilio Augustín regarded the presence of the German fleet as a sign of sympathy for the Spanish cause. An even greater boost to morale was the news that Admiral de la Cámara's squadron had left Spain in mid-June. In the meantime, however, the Spanish garrison in Manila remained in an extremely precarious position. The problem was that they were involved not only in defending the city against the Americans but also in fighting the resurgence of local nationalist rebellion. Political developments in the Philippines were similar to Cuba in that the overthrow of the Spanish monarchy in 1868 and the influence of European liberalism had stimulated demands for constitutional change. The leading reformers were native-born mestizos of mixed Spanish, Filipino and sometimes Chinese parentage. They were known as '*ilustrados*', a reference to the fact that they were educated and wealthy. A separate and more radical organization appealing to the masses emerged during the early 1890s. This was the *Katipunan*, a secret society which attracted support especially among the Tagalog-speaking people of Luzon. On 22 August 1896, the leader of the *Katipunan*, Andrés Bonifacio, proclaimed the *grito* of Balintawak and initiated a guerrilla uprising demanding independence from Spain. During the ensuing rebellion Emilio Aguinaldo, a mestizo of Tagalog and Chinese descent, replaced Bonifacio as the military commander of the *Katipunan*. Despite some early success for the *Katipuneros*, the Spanish army was successful in driving the guerrillas into the mountains of central Luzon and persuaded them to accept the Pact of Biyak-na-Bató in December 1897. In return for a financial payment and vague promises of political reform, Aguinaldo and other *Katipunero* leaders agreed to surrender their weapons and go into voluntary exile. Soon after Aguinaldo's departure to Hong Kong, however, the renewal of Spanish repression sparked off a resumption of the insurgency in March 1898. It was significant that the new uprisings spread beyond Luzon to the islands in the south. They also coincided with the outbreak of war between Spain and the United States.

Aguinaldo was at Singapore *en route* from Hong Kong to

Europe when he learned that the United States was officially at war with Spain. Conversations took place between Aguinaldo and the American consul at Singapore, E. Spencer Pratt, after which Pratt telegraphed Dewey on 24 April to inform him that the Filipino leader wished to offer his assistance. Dewey replied: 'Tell Aguinaldo come soon as possible.'[33] The fact that Dewey left for Manila the next day indicated that he did not consider Aguinaldo's personal participation to be vitally important. Aguinaldo proceeded to Hong Kong, took passage on the *McCulloch* and eventually arrived in Manila Bay on 19 May. After meeting with Dewey on board the *Olympia*, Aguinaldo established his headquarters at Cavite, assumed dictatorial powers and began conducting military operations against the Spaniards. American assistance included the exchange of information, the gift of captured Spanish weapons and ammunition and permission for insurgent vessels to use the bay. This aid formed the basis of Aguinaldo's later claim that Pratt and Dewey had approved and promised to support the struggle for Filipino independence and self-government. Military cooperation with the insurgents, whether in Cuba or the Philippines, was an integral element of American strategy, especially at the beginning of the war. It is very likely, therefore, that Aguinaldo was given verbal statements of support by Pratt and Dewey, although this has not been substantiated by documentary evidence.[34]

The potential for political entanglements was appreciated by President McKinley and his closest advisers in Washington. They viewed the capture of Manila principally as an opportunity to exert additional military pressure upon Spain to force it to sue for peace. The actual political future of the Philippine Islands was a question which had not yet been addressed. To retain flexibility in making policy, it was essential that American officials on the spot should not give any guarantees or commitments to local leaders. On 26 May, Secretary of the Navy Long informed Dewey: 'It is desirable, as far as possible, and consistent with your success and safety, not to have political alliances with the insurgents or any faction in the islands that would incur liability to maintain their cause in the

33 Dewey to Pratt, 24 April 1898, cited in Ronald Spector, *Admiral of the New Empire: The Life and Career of George Dewey* (Baton Rouge, LA, 1974), p. 88.

34 See Henry F. Graff, ed., *American Imperialism and the Philippine Insurrection: Testimony Taken from Hearings on Affairs in the Philippine Islands before the Senate Committee on the Philippines – 1902* (Boston, 1969). Aguinaldo's views are expressed in Emilio Aguinaldo and Vincente Pacis, *A Second Look at America* (New York, 1957).

future.' Dewey replied a week later that he had carefully avoided making entangling alliances 'from the beginning'.[35] Nevertheless, he acknowledged shortly afterwards that his personal relations with Aguinaldo were 'cordial' and that he respected the character and abilities of the Filipinos. 'In my opinion', Dewey noted, 'these people are far superior in their intelligence and more capable of self-government than the natives of Cuba.'[36]

The destruction of the Spanish fleet and the return of Aguinaldo had given a significant impetus to the rebellion against Spain. Local Filipino militia on Luzon who had originally been recruited to suppress the *Katipunan* switched their allegiance in droves and boosted the size of Aguinaldo's army to more than 10,000. Like most Spanish commanders, Augustín had followed the practice of locating his forces in numerous small garrisons. In the context of the Philippines, this meant that they were scattered over a large geographical area comprising a large number of islands. Cut off from Manila, many of the garrisons were quickly surrounded and overwhelmed by larger insurgent forces. During June the rebels took control of central Luzon. Aguinaldo remained in Cavite where he consolidated his personal authority and prepared to lay siege to Manila. On 12 June Aguinaldo declared the independence of the Republic of the Philippines and on 23 June decreed the establishment of a provisional government with himself as President. The fact that Dewey made no objection was interpreted by the insurgents to signify tacit American recognition of their political authority. In reality, Dewey was indifferent to these developments. He was much more concerned by naval matters such as dealing with the antics of the German warships in the bay and monitoring the progress of the squadron sent out from Spain to relieve Manila.

Dewey would have liked the presence of an American battleship in Manila Bay. Despite the significant diversion of military resources to prepare an expeditionary force for service in the Philippines, the strategic priority of the McKinley administration remained fixed on Cuba. This was demonstrated by the refusal to detach any armoured warships from blockading duty off Cuba. The only ships that could be spared for Dewey were those vessels currently based in the Pacific – namely, the protected cruiser *Charleston* and the slow-moving but

---

35 Long to Dewey, 26 May 1898 and Dewey to Long 3 June 1898, cited in French E. Chadwick, *The Relations of the United States and Spain: The Spanish American War* (3 vols; London, 1911), vol. iii pp. 366–7.
36 Dewey to Long, 27 June 1898, cited in ibid., vol. iii p. 368.

powerfully armed monitors *Monterey* and *Monadnock*. The *Charleston* left San Francisco on 21 May, the *Monterey* on 11 June and the *Monadnock* on 25 June. The monitors would not arrive in the Philippines until August. It was learned in mid-June, however, that Admiral de la Cámara's squadron was definitely headed for the Philippines and would reach its destination towards the end of July. Dewey found himself therefore in a similar position to that experienced some months earlier by Montojo. Unlike Montojo, however, Dewey was determined not to be a sitting target for the more powerful Spanish warships. His intention was to leave Manila Bay and either link up with the ships of the Expeditionary Force *en route* from San Francisco or sail to the south and attempt to outmanoeuvre the Spanish commander. The contingency planning proved unnecessary because Spain, in the aftermath of Cervera's disastrous defeat at Santiago de Cuba, recalled de la Cámara on 7 July.

In contrast to the limits placed on naval reinforcements for the Philippines, McKinley allowed the army contingent to be considerably expanded in size. The number of men ultimately assigned to what would become the Eighth Army Corps was increased from Dewey's original request for 5,000 to 20,000. About one-quarter were regulars and the rest volunteers drawn from the western states. In command of the expedition was Major-General Wesley Merritt, a Civil War veteran, who, after General Miles, was the next senior ranking general in the army. Merritt understood that his specific task was to join forces with Dewey and capture the city of Manila. Beyond this objective, however, the expedition's aims were never precisely defined. On 19 May McKinley sent written orders to Merritt outlining the mission's 'two-fold purpose of completing the reduction of Spanish power in that quarter and giving order and security to the island while in the possession of the United States'. 'Order and security' would be enforced by the establishment of an American military government whose powers would be 'absolute and supreme'.[37] American military occupation was therefore clearly envisaged, though it was not certain how long this would last or whether it would be extended beyond Manila and Luzon. Evidently, the direction of American policy towards the Philippines would be shaped pragmatically according to the unfolding of events.

---

37 McKinley to Merritt, 19 May 1898, cited in ibid., vol. iii pp. 396–7.

Compared to Tampa, the well-established port of San Francisco was much better suited and equipped for the organization and despatch of a large overseas military expedition. However, like Tampa, there was the same difficulty in procuring steamers to be used as transports. The lack of available shipping resulted in the expedition being sent in three separate convoys spread out over more than four weeks. An advance party of three transports left San Francisco on 25 May and consisted of almost 2,500 men under the command of Brigadier-General Thomas M. Anderson. A second contingent of 3,500 under Brigadier-General Francis V. Greene departed on 15 June. The third and largest detachment of almost 5,000 troops, commanded by Brigadier-General Arthur MacArthur and including General Merritt, embarked on 25–29 June. In total the three convoys carried 407 officers and 10,437 men. The expedition was well stocked with supplies including light artillery, tropical uniforms, medical stores and six months' supply of food. It was also the first American expeditionary force to go beyond the Western Hemisphere.

On 1 June the first group of transports reached Honolulu and linked up with the *Charleston*, which had departed from San Francisco on 21 May. The next stop more than 3,000 miles to the west was Guam, the principal island of the Spanish Ladrones (present-day Marianas Islands). Captain Henry Glass of the *Charleston* was under instructions from the Navy Department to take possession of Guam. This was carried out on 21 May, and marked the first American territorial conquest of the war. No resistance was forthcoming from the tiny Spanish garrison. In fact, the Governor interpreted the three warning shots fired by the *Charleston* on her approach to port as a naval salute and apologized for lacking a cannon to return the courtesy. He was quite unaware that Spain was officially at war with the United States. The conquest of Guam contained a strong element of comedy, but it gave the United States the possession of an island which afterwards became a vital link of communication across the Pacific Ocean.

Another consequence of the decision to despatch an expeditionary force to the Philippines was the annexation of the Hawaiian Islands. Throughout the nineteenth century the United States had developed close political, economic and cultural links with the islands. Their strategic importance also grew as the United States became a nation of continental extent. 'The safety and welfare of the Hawaiian group is obviously more interesting and important to the United States than to any other nation,' declared Secretary of

State Thomas F. Bayard in 1887.[38] In contrast to Cuba, however, the 'laws of gravitation' did not apply to the Hawaiian Islands, which were more than 2,000 miles from California. Efforts were made in 1854 and 1893 to annex the Islands to the United States, but these failed largely on account of traditional American opposition to acquiring overseas colonies. In 1897 a new treaty of annexation was approved by McKinley and the government of the Hawaiian Republic. The treaty encountered stiff opposition in the United States Senate.

The outbreak of war with Spain, and especially Dewey's attack upon the Philippines, dramatically raised the strategic and military significance of Hawaii. Despite the fact that the Hawaiian Republic voluntarily opened its ports to American warships, advocates of annexation argued that the United States must control the islands in order to ensure the flow of reinforcements to Dewey in the Philippines. They also feared that, if the United States did not act, another power would take over the islands. 'We need Hawaii just as much and a good deal more than we did California,' President McKinley told an aide.[39] In an attempt to circumvent the opposition of the Senate, McKinley and Republican Party leaders astutely decided to implement annexation by means of a joint resolution rather than a formal treaty which required a two-thirds majority vote. In 1845, Texas had been admitted to the Union in this way. The joint resolution was introduced on 4 May 1898, and passed the House of Representatives on 15 June by 209 to 91 votes. The Senate voted in favour on 6 July by 46 to 21 votes. McKinley signed the joint resolution on 7 July. The Hawaiian Islands were officially annexed to the United States on 12 August. The political manoeuvres to achieve annexation had little material impact on the conduct of the American military campaign at Manila. On the other hand, the extension of the war to the Philippines had been instrumental in highlighting the strategic importance and desirability of establishing a chain of American naval bases across the Pacific Ocean.

Meanwhile, in the Philippines the advance contingent of the Expeditionary Force reached Manila Bay on 30 June. General Anderson's initial task was to establish a base onshore where he could land his men and make preparations for the forthcoming

---

38 8 January 1887, cited in Charles C. Tansill, *The Foreign Policy of Thomas F. Bayard, 1885–1897* (New York, 1940), pp. 382–3.

39 Cited in Margaret Leech, *In the Days of McKinley* (New York, 1959), p. 213.

assault on the city. In contrast to Shafter at Santiago de Cuba, Anderson was under instructions to avoid formal cooperation with the Filipino insurgents. But contact could not be avoided. The American general met personally with Aguinaldo on only one occasion, and carefully avoided doing anything which might imply recognition of the latter's political authority. According to Anderson, Aguinaldo was disconcerted by the arrival of American troops because this upset his plan to capture Manila with his own men. The Filipino leader 'seemed very suspicious and not at all friendly', reported Anderson.[40] The signs of future American–Filipino conflict were clearly apparent. Significantly, Aguinaldo made no offer to place himself under American orders as Calixto García had done in Cuba. Nevertheless, he did not oppose an American landing. Anderson selected a site on the beach 3 miles south of the city and directly behind the insurgent lines. The base became known as Camp Dewey.

In Manila, the Spanish garrison numbered 13,000 regulars most of whom were located within 'Old' Manila. This part of the city was a virtual fortress protected to the north by the River Pasig and to the east and south by ancient stone walls. Just over a mile away in the suburbs of Paco, Singalong and Malate was an outer defensive line consisting of trenches interspersed with blockhouses and ending at Fort San Antonio Abad on the coast. Although the defences had not yet been seriously tested, the morale of the Spaniards had substantially declined throughout June and July. Not only was there a chronic shortage of food and water, but also hopes of external aid were severely dashed in July by reports of Cervera's defeat and the subsequent turning back of Admiral de la Cámara's squadron. In the midst of this depressing news, American troops began to arrive in large numbers, and an insurgent army estimated to be in excess of 10,000 gradually surrounded the outskirts of the city.

The second detachment of the American Expeditionary Force, under General Greene, reached Manila on 17 July. Just over a week later General Merritt arrived and assumed command. Unknown to the Spaniards, who dreaded a combined attack on the city by the American and insurgent forces, Merritt was determined to mount a purely American military operation. Like Anderson, however, he had to deal directly with the insurgents because they occupied the land

---

40 Anderson to Corbin, 9 July 1898, cited in John Morgan Gates, *Schoolbooks and Krags: The United States Army in the Philippines, 1898–1902* (Westport, CT, 1973), p. 18.

directly in front of the Spanish defensive line. Mindful of his instructions to avoid entangling alliances, Merritt deliberately avoided personal contact with Aguinaldo. Fortunately for Merritt, Aguinaldo had moved his headquarters 12 miles east of Cavite to Bacoor. This enabled General Greene fortuitously to bypass Aguinaldo and make a private arrangement with the local Filipino commander, General Mariano Noriel, in which the insurgents under Noriel's command agreed to evacuate their trenches to the north of Camp Dewey. On 29 July, American troops advanced to these positions and pushed forward a further 100 yards so that they were less than 400 yards from the outer Spanish defensive line. The operation was conducted in torrential rain and men soon found themselves in trenches full of water. 'The service in the trenches', reported Greene, 'was of the most arduous character, the rain being almost incessant and the men having no protection against it.'[41] A more deadly hazard emerged during the night of 31 July and subsequent nights, when the Spaniards fired on these forward positions. This resulted in the first American infantry casualties of the campaign in the Philippines. Losses numbered twenty-five dead and fifty wounded.

The monsoon rains also seriously hindered the disembarkation of the third contingent of American troops, commanded by General MacArthur. When the landing was eventually completed on 7 August, an army of 10,000 American soldiers had been assembled for the assault on Manila. The delay actually suited Dewey because the *Monterey* arrived in the meantime thereby adding the monitor's 10-inch and 12-inch guns to the firepower of the American squadron. Dewey was also keen to pursue secret negotiations with Captain General Augustín in the belief that they might lead to the surrender of the city without an assault having to be made. The Belgian consul, Edouard André, acted as the confidential go-between in these talks. To increase pressure on the Spaniards, Dewey and Merritt issued an ultimatum on 7 August stating that, if surrender was not forthcoming, military operations against the city would commence at any time after 9 August. The new Captain General, Fermín Jáudenes y Alvarez, who had replaced Augustín on 5 August, replied that he had no authority to surrender.

Like Toral at Santiago de Cuba, Jáudenes could see little point in fighting on against overwhelming enemy forces. What he and his fellow Spaniards feared most was not so much an American military

---

41 Cited in Chadwick, *United States and Spain*, vol. iii p. 401.

victory but the retribution that the Filipino insurgents would exact on their former rulers. This resulted in a complicated subterfuge by which the Spaniards hoped to retain both their *pundonor* and their lives. André informed Dewey that Jáudenes would capitulate on condition that the Americans prevented the insurgents from entering the city. The Spanish Captain General also required that a token battle be fought on the outskirts of Manila to preserve Spanish military honour and appease the government in Madrid. After a suitable passage of time Jáudenes would raise a white flag to signal surrender and allow American troops to occupy the walled city. Although no details were ever written down and no formal undertakings were made on either side, the pattern of subsequent events demonstrated that a definite arrangement had been agreed upon.

The American attack was scheduled for 13 August. Merritt was not entirely confident that Jáudenes would keep his word, so he did not divulge details of the secret arrangement to his generals. At 9.35 a.m. Dewey's flagship, the *Olympia*, supported by three of the squadron's smaller ships, opened fire on Fort San Antonio Abad. The desultory bombardment lasted for almost an hour. The Spanish guns did not return fire. As the shelling came to an end, half of the American infantry forces under General Greene advanced along the beach on the left, while the other half commanded by General MacArthur led the attack from the right. Greene's troops, consisting mainly of the First Colorado Volunteers, entered the fort and found it unoccupied. However, their advance beyond the fort into Malate encountered Spanish resistance in which one American was killed and fifty-four wounded. After a brief engagement Greene's troops proceeded quickly to the walled city. About half a mile away on the right flank, MacArthur was halted by heavy fire from blockhouses and trenches. The ensuing skirmish lasted for two hours and claimed five American dead and thirty-eight wounded before the Spaniards retreated.

Meanwhile, at 11 a.m., Dewey's flagship had hoisted the letters 'DWHB', the international naval signal for 'Do you surrender?' The white flag was observed in the walled city some 20 minutes later. Lieutenant-Colonel Charles A. Whittier and Lieutenant Thomas M. Brumby, representing the army and navy respectively, went ashore to arrange the terms of capitulation. Shortly after they arrived, advance units of Greene's troops began entering the walled city. At 2.30 p.m. Brumby reported the official capitulation of the city. Troops of the Second Oregon Volunteers were landed to disarm the

Spanish garrison and establish a guard around the walled city. The American flag was raised at 5.43 p.m., marking an end to the 'Battle of Manila'. Although the victory had been won with relatively light American casualties, Dewey regarded the losses as unnecessary. He considered that the Spaniards and the American navy had kept to their part of the bargain, but the 'army was too brash and rushed in too soon'.[42]

The events of 13 August confirmed Aguinaldo's worst fears. From his headquarters at Bacoor, he had received reports of the steady American military build-up. It was evident that Merritt regarded the insurgents as redundant to his military plans and intended to exclude them from participation in the assault on Manila. Aguinaldo might have launched his own assault on the city, but he chose to bide his time and adopt a policy of non-cooperation with the American forces. Consequently, relations grew even colder and more distant than ever. According to Dewey, his former protégé had become 'aggressive and even threatening towards our army'.[43] On 12 August, Aguinaldo received a message from General Merritt requesting that the insurgent forces not join in the attack which was about to be made on the city. It is not known what precise instructions Aguinaldo gave his men, but they could not resist the temptation to follow MacArthur's advance and join in the fighting against the Spaniards. Merritt had hoped that Greene and MacArthur would be able to link up and form a cordon which would block the insurgents from entering the city. But MacArthur was not able to advance quickly enough to achieve the junction with Greene. As a result, several thousand insurgents swarmed into the suburbs adjoining the walled city. Merritt assigned American troops to isolate and segregate the insurgents.

On 14 August a commission of American and Spanish officers drew up the terms for the capitulation of Manila. As at Santiago de Cuba, the defeated enemy were treated sympathetically. Spanish troops were required to hand over their weapons, though officers were allowed to retain their side arms. Like Calixto García at Santiago de Cuba, Aguinaldo was not invited to participate either in the negotiation of the peace terms or the official ceremony marking the capitulation. Merritt and Dewey requested instructions from Washington on how they should treat the insurgents. A telegram was sent from Washington on 17 August stating:

42 20 September 1898, cited in Spector, *Admiral of the New Empire*, p. 97.
43 Cited in Alger, *Spanish-American War*, p. 349.

The President directs that there must be no joint occupation with the insurgents. ... The insurgents and all others must recognize the military occupation and authority of the United States and the cessation of hostilities proclaimed by the president. Use whatever means in your judgment are necessary to this end. All law-abiding people must be treated alike.[44]

In fact, Merritt had already rejected Aguinaldo's request for a joint occupation of the city. By granting this he would have conferred American recognition of the government of the Republic of the Philippines. Instead, Merritt asserted his own authority and ordered the insurgents to withdraw from Manila in the interests of order and security. The action was commended by Alger, who noted later that 'the horrors of a Filipino horde let loose in the town to indulge in the expected carnival of loot, arson, and rapine, had been avoided'.[45] Aguinaldo accepted that he had been out-manoeuvred, and withdrew his forces to the outskirts of the capital. An uneasy truce came into being between the insurgents and the American occupation forces. Meanwhile, the government and people of the United States rejoiced in the news that Manila had been captured. Ironically, the Battle of Manila had marked the last fighting between American and Spanish troops in the Spanish-American War and had taken place after peace had been signed in Washington on the previous day. The lack of telegraphic communications with the rest of the world meant that this news did not actually reach Manila until 16 August.

---

44 Corbin to Merritt, 17 August 1898, cited in Chadwick, *United States and Spain*, vol. iii p. 423.
45 Alger, *Spanish-American War*, p. 340.

8 PEACE

THE PEACE PROTOCOL

The outbreak of war between the United States and Spain on 21 April signified the collapse of American and Spanish diplomatic efforts to bring peace to Cuba. Diplomacy was temporarily put aside as both powers formally broke off relations with each other and sought to resolve their disagreement by force of arms. At some point, however, diplomacy would be revived to facilitate an end to the fighting and, ultimately, to negotiate and confirm a peace settlement. Whenever the opportunity presented itself, the great powers of Europe were ready to offer their good offices to bring the belligerents together. The rapidity and completeness of Dewey's victory at Manila Bay on 1 May suggested that these services might be utilized sooner rather than later. On 8 May, the American ambassador in London, John Hay, reported a private conversation with the British colonial minister, Joseph Chamberlain, during which the latter stated that Britain was willing to act as a diplomatic go-between. This was followed up two days later by the British prime minister, Lord Salisbury, telegraphing Julian Pauncefote, the British ambassador in Washington: 'If you should think now or at any future stage in this unhappy war that offers from European powers would be welcomed or received favourably by the United States, please inform me.' After sounding out his diplomatic contacts, Pauncefote replied that such an approach was premature. According to the ambassador, McKinley was 'anxious for the termination of the war' but believed that Spain would have to suffer 'a further naval disaster' to persuade it to seek peace.[1]

McKinley's judgement was proved correct. Despite the humiliating setback at Manila Bay, the Spanish government was

---

1 Salisbury to Pauncefote, no. 100, 10 May 1898, London, Public Record Office, Foreign Office Records [hereafter cited as FO], 5/2364. Pauncefote to Foreign Office, no. 68, 16 May 1893, FO 5/2365.

evidently not deterred from continuing the war. As Cervera's squadron sailed westwards to the Caribbean, the United States prepared to send expeditionary forces to Cuba and the Philippines. Nevertheless, the flurry of diplomatic activity and the victory in the Philippines prompted the McKinley administration to review its terms for a peace settlement. These were expressed in a note sent on 3 June to Hay by Secretary of State William Day.[2] The basic priority was unchanged: Spain must withdraw its military forces from Cuba and hand over control of the island to the United States. The achievement of this objective would have satisfied McKinley and Congress prior to 21 April. Since that date, however, the United States had suffered the pain and expense of war. Spain was held responsible for this and must pay compensation. But Spain was known to be virtually bankrupt. Consequently, instead of demanding a financial indemnity, the United States asked for the cession of Puerto Rico. The acquisition of this island served not only an economic purpose but would also eliminate the Spanish colonial presence in the Caribbean. In addition, the United States would gain possession of a valuable naval base. The extension of the war to the Pacific Ocean had also underlined the importance of overseas bases and resulted in a similar American request for Spain to cede a port in both the Ladrones and the Philippines. Ominously for the Spaniards, Day's note revealed that American terms for peace were much stiffer than they had been at the start of the conflict in April.

The information relayed to Hay was highly confidential and was not to be made public. Disclosure would imply that the United States was seeking peace and would be interpreted as a sign of weakness. Hay's task was to communicate his government's views to the British Foreign Office so that the latter could act as an unofficial go-between. In accordance with the arcane procedures of peacemaking diplomacy the next stage was a meeting in Vienna between the British envoy at that capital and the Austrian foreign minister. The British diplomat learned that Spain was unwilling to enter into peace talks. In fact, the Spanish government simultaneously launched a diplomatic counter-offensive by proposing that the European powers send troops to the Philippines as a temporary measure designed to protect lives and property from attack by the insurgents. Lord Salisbury rejected what was obviously an attempt to assist Spain by entangling neutral countries in the war.

2 William R. Day had replaced John Sherman as secretary of state on 26 April 1898.

Although the State Department remained wary of diplomatic developments in Europe, the great powers studiously refrained from becoming directly involved in the hostilities. The powers were generally displeased to see an 'Old World' monarchy militarily humiliated by the upstart republic from the 'New World'. They were also concerned that American commercial and military influence was being extended not only in the Caribbean but also in the Pacific. On the other hand, there was no desire for conflict of any kind with the United States. Consequently, the European powers exerted a negligible influence on the course of the war and the peacemaking process. In mid-July Salisbury remarked that negotiations for peace would only be held when Spain and the United States both agreed. 'It is obvious', he noted, 'that the other powers will not take any active part in a quarrel in which they are not concerned.'[3]

The destruction of Cervera's squadron on 3 July and the capitulation of Santiago de Cuba on 17 July enabled Prime Minister Sagasta to take the decisive step and formally open negotiations for peace. Only a few months earlier the Spanish government had resolutely opposed granting an armistice to the Cuban insurgents. Now that the Americans were clearly in the military ascendancy, Sagasta wished to arrange a cessation of hostilities as soon as possible before Spain lost further territory. To ask publicly for an armistice would be interpreted, however, as an admission of Spanish military defeat. This would not only be humiliating but would also seriously weaken Spain's bargaining position in any forthcoming negotiations to end the war. Consequently, Sagasta resorted to communicating indirectly with the American government via a third party. On 18 July the Spanish foreign minister, the Duke of Almodóvar del Río, asked the the French government to authorize its ambassador in Washington, Jules Cambon, to act as an official intermediary between Spain and the United States. The selection of Cambon was logical because the French government had already agreed to look after Spanish diplomatic and consular interests in Washington for the duration of the war.[4]

Sagasta and Almodóvar hoped for a speedy response, but an unexpected delay was experienced when the French foreign minister stated that the Spanish request required the specific approval of the

---

3 Salisbury to Wolff, no. 89, 16 July 1898, FO 72/2067.
4 Cambon's role became more than simply an intermediary. The Spanish government gave him full powers to negotiate on their behalf in his meetings with McKinley.

French President and cabinet. Almodóvar's inner concerns were revealed in a telegram which he immediately sent to the Spanish ambassador at Paris, informing him that the Americans were about to attack Manila and Puerto Rico so that 'the loss of hours, not to speak of days, might be of grave consequence' and 'might result in greater claims'.[5] The necessary permission of the French government was promptly given, but Cambon was unable to meet formally with President McKinley until 26 July.[6] On the previous day American troops had invaded Puerto Rico and General Merritt had assumed command of the projected attack on Manila. The time-consuming nature of diplomatic communications had often served Spain's diplomatic interests well in the past. Ironically, on this occasion it thwarted Spanish hopes of swiftly bringing about a cease-fire and preventing a significant extension of the war beyond Cuba.

On 26 July McKinley and Day received Cambon in the library of the White House. The French ambassador delivered a letter nominally from the Queen Regent which requested the President to state his government's terms to end the war and establish 'a political status in Cuba'.[7] The undisguised attempt to limit discussions to Cuba was rejected by Day, who told Cambon that other Spanish territories must be included. The French ambassador made no objection. It was evident to him that the Americans were intent on adopting a firm and resolute stance. After Cambon left, the waiting press corps were informed that peace negotiations had officially commenced, though this did not mean that the actual fighting had ended. During the next four days, amid the oppressive heat and humidity of summer in Washington, McKinley prepared his formal reply to the Spanish government. The document handed to Cambon on 30 July was very similar to the terms outlined by Day on 3 June. To the principal demand that Spain relinquish its sovereignty over Cuba was added the stipulation that Spanish military forces must evacuate the island immediately. But there was no desire to impose harsh or humiliating conditions. In what he described as an offer of 'signal generosity', McKinley reaffirmed that Spain cede Puerto Rico

---

5 Almodóvar to León y Castillo, 20 July 1898, cited in French E. Chadwick, *The Relations of the United States and Spain: The Spanish American War* (3 vols; London, 1911), vol. iii p.428.

6 A further delay was caused by the fact that the despatch from Madrid was written in code. The key to the code was held by the Austrian minister, who was temporarily absent from Washington.

7 María Cristina to McKinley, 22 July 1898, cited in Chadwick, *United States and Spain*, vol. iii p. 430.

and an island in the Ladrones, most likely Guam, in exchange for a financial indemnity. The question of the Philippines was more controversial and reflected a division within the American cabinet. A majority favoured American annexation, but were uncertain whether this should be restricted to the city of Manila, the island of Luzon or the whole archipelago. A form of words was eventually agreed upon in which the United States would insist on occupying Manila 'pending the conclusion of a treaty of peace which shall determine the control, disposition and government of the Philippines'.[8] This essentially meant that the issue was deferred until the forthcoming peace conference, which McKinley proposed be held in Washington.

The forthright statement of American terms reflected the strong bargaining position earned by military success. By contrast, the Spanish cause appeared hopeless. Faced by the threat of enemy naval raids on its coastline, a hostile army advancing in Puerto Rico, and an assault about to take place against Manila, it seemed that Spain had no option but to submit. On the question of the future of Cuba, Almodóvar accordingly told Cambon that 'Spain is disposed to accept the solution which may please the United States'.[9] But 'victories' can be won at the diplomatic table as well as on the battlefield. The task of Spanish diplomacy was to try and limit Spain's losses solely to the island of Cuba. Almodóvar instructed Cambon to suggest to McKinley that the cession of Cuba was 'the richest of indemnification' and that American demands for additional territory were unjustified and excessive.[10] The foreign minister also claimed that American occupation of Manila could only be temporary because Spain held sovereignty over the Philippines.

Cambon duly raised these points in a meeting with McKinley at the White House on 4 August. But the President 'showed himself inflexible'.[11] He insisted on the cession of Puerto Rico, and stated that the question of the Philippines would be decided by negotiation. On the peace conference itself, McKinley raised no objection to a Spanish proposal that the meeting be convened in Paris rather than Washington. After leaving the White House Cambon was later

8 Day to Almodóvar, 30 July 1898, cited in US Department of State, *Papers Relating to the Foreign Relations of the United States, 1898* [hereafter cited as *FRUS* with year number], (Washington DC, 1862–), pp. 820–1.

9 Almodóvar to Cambon, 28 July 1898, cited in Chadwick, *United States and Spain*, vol. iii p. 431.

10 Almodóvar to Cambon, 31 July 1898, cited in ibid., vol. iii p. 433.

11 Cambon to Almodóvar, 4 August 1898, cited in ibid., vol. iii p. 435.

visited by Day, who reaffirmed that the United States demanded the 'immediate' evacuation of Cuba and Puerto Rico 'without awaiting the treaty of peace'. The French ambassador was not surprised by American firmness. He wrote privately to the French foreign minister that Day was seeking Spanish 'scalps': 'One cannot imagine what it is to treat with the Americans when one is defeated; they have the blood of Indians in their veins.'[12] In Cambon's opinion, Spanish diplomatic manoeuvring no longer served much purpose. 'I cannot but persist in the idea', he cabled Almodóvar on 4 August, 'that all vacillation will further aggravate the severity of the conditions.'[13]

The Spanish government appreciated Cambon's timely advice, but was concerned by the implications of Day's insistence on immediate military withdrawal. If this was carried out, it would mean the army having to act dishonourably and abandon Havana and San Juan to the enemy without a fight. An attempt was therefore made to try and modify the American terms. On 7 August Almodóvar instructed Cambon to inform McKinley that Spain's acquiescence to any agreement was conditional upon securing prior approval from the Cortes. This effectively ruled out the immediate evacuation of Spanish forces. Cambon faithfully communicated Almodóvar's views to McKinley on 9 August. The result was predictable. McKinley was clearly annoyed at what he regarded as Spanish duplicity. Cambon sensed that the President was on the point of calling the meeting to an end. In effect, McKinley was calling the Spanish bluff. Cambon gave way. To save the peace negotiations, he asked the President how Spain could prove its good faith. In that moment it was evident that McKinley's astute combination of firmness mixed with generosity and brinkmanship had won the decisive diplomatic victory. The President proposed that the American terms be drawn up in the form of a protocol which would be signed by both governments. The issue of constitutional approval would not be relevant because the protocol was an executive agreement and, unlike a peace treaty, did not require ratification by either the American Congress or the Spanish Cortes. The protocol would allow hostilities to be formally suspended while both sides made arrangements for the forthcoming peace conference to be held in Paris.

12 Cambon to Delcassé, 4 August 1898, cited in John Offner, 'The United States and France: Ending the Spanish-American War', *Diplomatic History* 7 (1983), p. 15.
13 Cambon to Almodóvar, 4 August 1898, cited in Chadwick, *United States and Spain*, vol. iii p. 436.

Cambon duly received the protocol on 10 August. The terms were identical to those stated by McKinley on 30 July, except for the inclusion of a provision to extend the time allowed for Spanish military evacuation from Cuba and Puerto Rico. If the document was not accepted, Cambon warned that 'Spain will have nothing more to expect from a conqueror resolved to procure all the profit possible from the advantages it has obtained'.[14] On 11 August the Spanish government telegraphed its consent. In the White House on Friday, 12 August, at 4.30 p.m., President McKinley and Ambassador Cambon signed the protocol and officially brought hostilities in the Spanish-American War to an end. Spain was definitely to give up Cuba and Puerto Rico, but the question of the territorial disposition of the Philippines was still unresolved. This particular issue was made even more complicated by the fact that the Americans had shown no desire to involve any Filipinos in the discussions leading to the protocol. Indeed, the deliberate exclusion of not only Filipinos but also Cubans and Puerto Ricans from both the negotiations and the signing of the protocol signified the determination of the McKinley administration to dominate the peace process and unilaterally impose what it considered to be the best and most appropriate terms.

THE PARIS PEACE CONFERENCE

A few days after the signing of the protocol, senior army and naval officers were appointed by both the United States and Spain to supervise Spanish military withdrawal from Cuba and Puerto Rico. The evacuation was successfully completed in the latter island by 24 October. The task proved more time-consuming in Cuba, and a deadline of 1 December was set. This was later extended to 1 January 1899. No such arrangements had been provided for in the Philippines, where General Merritt had established a military government to rule Manila. In fact, the Spanish government challenged the legal basis of Merritt's authority on the grounds that the capitulation of Manila on 13 August had taken place after the signature of the peace protocol in Washington. Although the Spanish claim was well supported by historical precedents, it was rejected outright by McKinley. First, he stated that the suspension of hostilities at Manila came into effect not on 12 August but four days

---

14 Cambon to Almodóvar, 10 August 1898, cited in ibid., vol. iii p. 440.

later, on 16 August, when Merritt and Dewey first received official notification of the protocol. Secondly, the President bluntly asserted that the American military government at Manila derived its authority to rule by right of conquest.

Prior to Dewey's victory at Manila Bay, American political and military leaders had given scant attention to the Philippines. An apocryphal story mischievously stated that McKinley was initially uncertain of the geographical location of the islands and believed they were somewhere in the centre of the Pacific Ocean. However, the decisions to send reinforcements to Dewey and annex the Hawaiian Islands and Guam demonstrated the President's apparent endorsement of what was called an 'expansionist' or 'large' foreign policy. The logical next step was to acquire possession of the Philippines. The peace protocol, however, stipulated that the United States would only initially occupy Manila and that the future political status of the Philippines would be decided by the peace conference scheduled to begin in Paris on 1 October.

The likelihood of an outcome in favour of expansionism was indicated by the composition of the American Peace Commission. Of the five members appointed by McKinley, three were well-known expansionists from the Republican Party – Whitelaw Reid, publisher of the *New York Tribune* and former ambassador to France, Senator Cushman K. Davis of Minnesota and Senator William P. Frye of Maine. On the other hand, the commission included Senator George Gray of Delaware, who was a notable critic of acquiring overseas territories. Gray was also a Democrat and thereby contributed to the bipartisan image of the commission. William Day resigned as secretary of state to act as chairman. In effect, Day would represent McKinley who remained in Washington and kept in contact by telegraph. Until Woodrow Wilson made the break with tradition in 1918, it was regarded as unthinkable for a serving President to leave the United States for any length of time. Consequently, the question of McKinley's personal presence at the conference was not raised. Nor was any concern expressed over the absence of representatives from the Cuban or Filipino insurgents. They were reckoned to have played no part in winning the war and were therefore not invited to participate in the conference.

McKinley's paramount influence was evident at all stages of the conference. Prior to the commission's departure for France, he arranged a final meeting with the commissioners at the White House on 16 September. His parting instructions stressed that the articles of the peace protocol were to be strictly enforced. He reminded the commissioners that American intervention in Cuba had been prompted by humanitarian motives and a desire to end Spanish colonialism in the Western Hemisphere. The Philippines, however, were considered to 'stand on a different basis'. The President remarked:

> ... we cannot be unmindful that, without any desire or design on our part, the war has brought us new duties and responsibilities which we must meet and discharge as becomes a great nation on whose growth and career from the beginning the Ruler of Nations has plainly written the high command and pledge of civilization.[15]

To fulfil this sense of 'duty and responsibility', McKinley believed that the United States should retain control of Manila and extend its jurisdiction to the whole of Luzon. Nothing specific was said about the rest of the archipelago. This omission would form the basis of considerable discussion at the peace conference.

While McKinley had not yet completed half of his elected term of office, Práxedes Mateo Sagasta wondered how long he would remain as Spanish prime minister. The Liberal government was deeply unpopular. Both Sagasta and Foreign Minister Almodóvar were personally blamed for the humiliation inflicted upon the Spanish people by the protocol. A prominent critic was Francisco Silvela, the leader of the Conservative Party, who confirmed the collapse of *caciquismo* by ensuring that no Conservative offered to join the Spanish Peace Commission. Consequently, the five Spanish members consisted of three leading Liberal politicians, Eugenio Montero Ríos, Buenaventura de Abarzuza y Ferrer and José de Garnica y Díaz, plus a diplomat, Wenceslao Ramírez de Villaurrutia y Villaurrutia and an army representative, General Rafael Cerero y Sáenz. Montero Ríos would act as president of the commission.

The first meeting of the Paris Peace Conference took place on Saturday 1 October in the Quai d'Orsay. The business-like American commissioners wished to concentrate first on Cuba and Puerto Rico before dealing with the more controversial question of the Philippines. But the Spaniards adopted a different strategy. They realized that the disposition of the Philippines was the one major issue which remained open to discussion and negotiation. In an

---

15 'Instructions to the Peace Commissioners', 16 September 1898, *FRUS* (1898), p. 907.

attempt to restore Spanish control over the islands they reaffirmed the argument that the capitulation of Manila on 13 August was nullified on the grounds that the peace protocol had been already signed in Washington the day before. By challenging the legality of American actions, the Spanish commissioners sought to please public opinion in Spain. 'Since they have to consent to the dismemberment of their country', Whitelaw Reid noted in his diary, 'they wish ... to show to their countrymen that they protested and struggled at every turn, using every resource to avert their unhappy fate.'[16] None the less, the Americans were unyielding. At the second meeting on 3 October, Day bluntly stated that his government had already made its opinion categorically clear on this particular matter. Any further discussion must be conducted at government level and not by the peace commissioners. The Spaniards had little option but to acquiesce.

The following sessions of the conference focused on Cuba. Although the Spanish commission was resigned to losing the island, they sought to proceed slowly on this issue in order not to appear too submissive. There was also the pragmatic consideration that skilfull diplomacy might moderate American terms. An opportunity to prolong and complicate discussions arose over the question of the so-called 'Cuban debt'. This was estimated at more than $400 million, and consisted mainly of financial charges and obligations owed to Spanish citizens by the colonial administration in Cuba. In what seemed like a mere legal quibble, Montero Ríos proposed that the wording in the protocol be changed so that Spain would 'transfer' rather than 'relinquish' sovereignty over Cuba to the United States. The change was highly significant, because the 'transfer' of sovereignty to the United States meant that the latter should automatically assume liability for the payment of the Cuban debt. A similar arrangement would also apply to Puerto Rico.

Two weeks of debate ensued in which the American commissioners totally rejected what Reid described as 'an insidious scheme' which effectively required the United States to pay the costs of decades of Spanish tyranny in Cuba.[17] The resulting impasse threatened to bring the conference to a close. This was evidently not desired by either side. A face-saving compromise emerged on 26 October after a private conversation between Montero Ríos and the

---

16 3 October 1898, cited in H. Wayne Morgan, ed., *Making Peace with Spain: The Diary of Whitelaw Reid, September–December 1898* (Austin, TX, 1965), p. 53.

17 7 October 1898, cited in ibid., p. 63.

American ambassador in Paris, Horace Porter. The ambassador suggested that his government might make concessions on the Philippines if an understanding was reached on the Cuban debt. In effect, the American commissioners wished to move on to a discussion of the future of the Philippines. Montero Ríos agreed. Though no specific undertaking had been given by the Americans, he accepted the original wording in the protocol pertaining to Cuba, Puerto Rico and Guam. However, Spanish approval was provisional and subject to confirmation in the final peace treaty.

As discussion switched to the Philippines, the longstanding divisions among the American commissioners became clearly apparent. Davis, Frye and Reid advocated annexation of the whole archipelago, but this was opposed by Day and Gray. They looked to McKinley for guidance. In fact, the President's views had undergone a significant change since the opening of the conference. From 11 to 21 October he had toured the Midwest ostensibly to explain his administration's policies though, in reality, he was seeking to influence the forthcoming mid-term Congressional elections. Large crowds turned out to greet and applaud the man who had led the country to victory over Spain. In speech after speech McKinley stressed that America had entered the war for humanitarian reasons and must do its 'duty' to help those people who had been liberated from Spanish tyranny. The response was invariably enthusiastic. McKinley returned to the White House convinced that the American people wanted an expansionist foreign policy which included the acquisition of all the Philippines. But this created a moral dilemma for a President who regarded the seizure of territory by conquest as repugnant. He recalled later that his doubts were finally resolved by prayer and divine inspiration: 'There was nothing left for us to do but to take them all, and to educate the Filipinos, and uplift and civilize and Christianize them, and by God's grace do the very best we could by them, as our fellow-men for whom Christ also died.'[18]

18 Account of an interview given by McKinley to a group of Methodist clergymen at the White House, 21 November 1899, cited in Charles S. Olcott, *The Life of William McKinley* (3 vols; Boston, 1916), vol. ii pp. 110–11. For a discussion of the authenticity and significance of the statement, see Lewis L. Gould, *The Presidency of William McKinley* (Lawrence, KS, 1980), pp. 140–2; and Ephraim K. Smith, ' "A Question from which We could not Escape", William McKinley and the Decision to Acquire the Philippine Islands', *Diplomatic History* 9 (1985), pp. 363–75. One eminent American historian has argued that McKinley's stress on 'duty' exemplified a wider 'psychic crisis' from which American society was suffering. See Richard Hofstadter, 'Manifest Destiny and the Philippines', in Daniel Aaron, ed., *America in Crisis* (New York, 1952), pp. 173–200.

The stress on religious duty was genuine, but McKinley's decision was also motivated by the desire to increase America's international prestige and overseas trade. John Hay, who had replaced Day as secretary of state, informed the commissioners by telegram on 26 October:

> The information which has come to the President since your departure convinces him that the acceptance of the cession of Luzon alone, leaving the rest of the islands subject to Spanish rule, or to be the subject of future contention, cannot be justified on political, commercial, or humanitarian grounds. The cession must be of the whole archipelago or none. The latter is wholly inadmissible, and the former must therefore be required.[19]

On 31 October Day announced his government's desire to annex all of the Philippines. Montero Ríos expressed 'amazement'.[20] Anticipating American concessions, the Spanish commissioners found themselves presented instead with an imperious demand which went far beyond the terms outlined in the peace protocol. Spain was being asked to accept the burden of the Cuban debt and to give up not only Cuba, Puerto Rico and Guam but also all the Philippines, even though American troops only currently controlled Manila. In effect, the Americans were demanding the dissolution of Spain's overseas empire. When news reached Madrid, Almodóvar condemned what he described as 'the greatest extreme imaginable in the claims of the United States'.[21] Some weeks of tense diplomatic manoeuvring followed. It seemed that a breakdown in negotiations was averted only because it would technically lead to a resumption of the war. Reid believed, however, that the Spaniards were 'sparring for time' in what he correctly predicted was the forlorn hope that Democratic victories in the Congressional elections on 8 November might be to their advantage. The American commissioner was also fairly confident that Spain wished 'to get rid of the Philippines'.[22] In fact, the likelihood of an agreement was greatly assisted by a proposal emanating from Senator Frye that the United

19 Hay to Day, 26 October 1898, *FRUS* (1898), p. 935.
20 Montero Ríos to Almodóvar, 1 November 1898, cited in Chadwick, *United States and Spain*, vol. iii p. 456.
21 See Morgan, *Reid Diary*, p. 130, n. 5.
22 4 November 1898, cited in ibid., p. 134.

States should offer financial compensation in exchange for the Philippines. Some protracted haggling resulted in which Spain expressed a willingness to sell all its island possessions in the Pacific Ocean, including the Ladrones and the Carolines. Eventually, on 21 November, the American commissioners made their 'final offer' of $20 million for the Philippines.[23] Day warned that Spanish rejection would mean an end to the negotiations.

On 25 November, Almodóvar instructed the Spanish commissioners to agree to a peace treaty incorporating the American terms. He considered that further resistance was pointless, and that, 'in order to avoid greater evils, the painful necessity of submitting to the will of the conqueror becomes imperative'.[24] Montero Ríos announced Almodóvar's decision to the conference on 28 November. Reid observed that the Spaniards 'sat in their places with a certain air of mournful dignity'. In his opinion, they were simply submitting 'to the inevitable'.[25] After additional meetings to clarify various technical points, the peace treaty was finally ready for signature on 10 December. Spain 'relinquished' its sovereignty over Cuba, and thereby remained liable for debts contracted before and during the war. It ceded Puerto Rico, Guam and the Philippines to the United States. In return for the Philippines, the United States agreed to pay Spain $20 million.[26] The American peace commissioners had worked long and hard to fulfil the President's instructions. But the peace process was not yet over. A period of six months was allowed for each government to secure formal ratification of the treaty. According to American law, this meant that the Treaty of Paris had to come before the United States Senate.

RATIFICATION OF THE TREATY OF PARIS

Foreshadowing the role of 'War President' that would be assumed by several of his presidential successors in the twentieth century, McKinley used his authority as Commander-in-Chief to direct the prosecution of a foreign war and the negotiation of the peace settlement. The significant expansion of presidential power was

23 Day to Adee, 22 November 1898, *FRUS* (1898), p. 958.

24 Almodóvar to Montero Ríos, 25 November 1898, cited in Chadwick, *United States and Spain*, vol. iii p. 469.

25 28 November 1898, cited in Morgan, *Reid Diary*, p. 168.

26 For the text of the treaty, see Moore to Hay, 10 December 1898, *FRUS* (1898), p. 965.

summed up by the establishment of a 'War Room' in the White House from which radiated numerous telephone and telegraph wires connecting the President with senior government and military personnel. The influence of Congress was consequently diminished, as it assumed a supportive and largely invisible function while the war was in progress. But this was dramatically changed by the conclusion of the peace treaty. The American Constitution states that the President has the power to make treaties, but they only become law upon securing ratification by the United States Senate. This requires a vote of concurrence by two-thirds of the Senators present. In order to facilitate the process of ratification, McKinley astutely appointed three Senators to the American Peace Commission, thereby ensuring that the Senate participated directly and actively in the negotiation of the peace treaty. Moreover, the potential for political conflict was diminished by choosing a Republican and a Democrat from the Senate Foreign Relations Committee. Senator Davis was the Republican chairman of that committee, while Senator Gray served as the leading Democrat.

The adoption of a bipartisan political approach was sensible because the Republican majority in the Senate was not large enough to secure automatic ratification. With all ninety senators present, the treaty would require 60 votes for approval. Currently there were fifty Republicans, thirty-five Democrats and five Populists. It was essential, therefore, for McKinley and Republican Party bosses to persuade a number of Democrats and Populists to vote for the treaty. The preferred method of achieving this was to present the Treaty of Paris as a national rather than a party political issue. Indeed, the large majority of articles in the treaty received senatorial approval precisely because they were regarded as the just rewards for a glorious American military triumph. There was also an awareness that to disturb the arrangements made in Paris would not only embarrass the President and the peace commissioners but would also technically mean a return to a state of war between the United States and Spain. Nevertheless, a controversy could not be avoided. The single issue which most upset McKinley's political arithmetic and provoked a 'great debate' over the future direction of the United States was the provision to annex the Philippines. Two prominent Republican Senators, George Frisbie Hoar of Massachusetts and Eugene Hale of Maine, openly declared their total opposition to annexation and thereby dashed McKinley's hopes of achieving Republican unity. The likelihood of cooperation from the Democrats was similarly undermined on 12 December, when a

Democratic Senator, George Vest of Missouri, introduced a resolution stating that 'under the Constitution of the United States no power is given to the federal Government to acquire territory to be held and governed permanently as colonies'.[27] Despite the treaty being reported favourably from the Senate Foreign Relations Committee on 4 January 1899, it was evident that a very close contest was under way and that a handful of votes would determine the outcome.

The criticism of the treaty within the Senate was echoed outside Congress. Under the leadership of the businessman Edward Atkinson, the Anti-Imperialist League had been formed in Boston on 19 November 1898 'to oppose, by every legitimate means, the acquisition of the Philippine Islands, or of any colonies away from our shores, by the United States'.[28] Similar 'Leagues' were soon formed throughout the nation. By activities such as holding rallies, circulating literature and organizing petitions, the Anti-Imperialist League led the public campaign against annexation of the Philippines. Several cogent arguments were employed to persuade the Senate not to ratify the peace treaty. The League stressed that America had gone to war to free the Cuban people from political oppression and was morally bound to extend the same purpose to the Philippines. The idea of Americans ruling an overseas people without their consent was condemned as unconstitutional and undemocratic. There were also practical problems to consider in that the Filipinos were quite different from Americans in their race, religion and history and could not be easily incorporated into the political system of the United States. Moreover, it was argued that the creation of an overseas 'empire' would inevitably lead to foreign entanglements, economic ruin and the creation of large standing military forces. 'When Rome began her career of conquest, the Roman Republic began to decay,' noted the anti-imperialist leader, Moorfield Storey. He warned that the acquisition of overseas colonies must consign America to an identical fate.[29]

The Anti-Imperialist League attracted wide and varied endorsement. Its views were approved by prominent Republicans such as ex-President Benjamin Harrison, the self-made millionaire, Andrew Carnegie, and the German-American political leader, Carl Schurz. Leading Democratic supporters included ex-President Grover

27 *Congressional Record*, 55th Congress 3rd Session, p. 93.
28 'Draft Constitution of the Anti-Imperialist League', cited in Maria C. Lanzar, 'The Anti-Imperialist League', *Philippine Social Science Review* 3 (1930), p. 16.
29 Cited in ibid., p. 9.

Cleveland, and William Jennings Bryan, the presidential candidate defeated by McKinley in 1896 and the favourite for the Democratic nomination in 1900. In addition, the campaign against imperialism was joined by non-political figures including the author Mark Twain, the newspaper editor E. L. Godkin, the philosopher William James, the social worker Jane Addams, and the trade-union leader Samuel Gompers.

Despite its impressive list of adherents, the Anti-Imperialist League failed to arouse mass support. As McKinley had discerned in October, the mood of public opinion was running strongly in favour of territorial expansion and the adoption of the 'large policy'. Indeed, Congress had already demonstrated this by voting in favour of acquiring the Hawaiian Islands. The annexation of the Philippines was an obvious next step. Expansionists pointed out that the constitutionality of such a measure was upheld by the Louisiana Purchase of 1803 which had not involved seeking the consent of the governed. In fact, by following Rudyard Kipling's advice to 'take up the white man's burden', Americans would be fulfilling a duty to bestow the blessings of civilization upon the less fortunate Filipinos. There were also influential economic arguments which saw the Philippines as a 'stepping-stone' to the potentially vast and lucrative 'China market'. Nor was there an acceptable alternative to American annexation. Even anti-imperialists acknowledged that the Philippines could not be returned to Spanish misrule. If the United States did not annex the archipelago, some other nation would certainly do so. Most likely this would be either Germany or Japan, powers generally perceived by Americans as hostile to democratic government.

While McKinley carefully stood above the political fray, the administration's case was skilfully presented in the Senate by Henry Cabot Lodge of Massachusetts, Nelson Aldrich of Rhode Island and Mark Hanna of Ohio. With the notable exceptions of Hoar and Hale, Republican Senators remained loyal to McKinley. By contrast, the opposition to the treaty lacked effective leadership. Arthur Pue Gorman of Maryland attempted to lead the Democratic Senators, but his authority was challenged by William Jennings Bryan who, though not a Senator, was recognized as the nominal head of the Party. Bryan was an avowed anti-imperialist, but he worried over the fact that failure to ratify the peace treaty would lead to the resumption of war. He reluctantly concluded that the Democratic Party should support ratification. The exact extent of Bryan's influence upon the votes of Democratic Senators is uncertain.

Nevertheless, it did sow dissension among the opponents of the treaty and thereby aided the expansionist cause.[30]

In the meantime, relations between the McKinley administration and the Filipino insurgents had steadily deteriorated. Hostilities were avoided because neither side wished open military conflict with the other. Ever since his return to Manila in May, Aguinaldo had stressed the need for American aid to defeat the Spaniards and establish an independent Filipino republic. But he was dismayed when, after the capitulation of Manila, McKinley ruled against joint occupation of the city. Local tensions were increased by the frequently insensitive attitude of Major-General Elwell S. Otis, who replaced Merritt as Military Governor in late August. In October, Otis secured the withdrawal of the insurgent forces from the outskirts of Manila by threatening military action. At the same time McKinley delivered a series of diplomatic rebuffs to the Filipino nationalists. Although the President received Aguinaldo's representative, Felipe Agoncillo, at the White House in October, he simply listened to the emissary and pointedly refused to grant the meeting official status. Moreover, the Filipinos were given no part in the Paris peace conference. They were further alarmed by developments at Paris which suggested that the United States intended to annex the archipelago. Any lingering hopes that McKinley favoured Filipino independence and self-government were finally dashed by the conclusion of the peace treaty in December 1898.

In September 1898 Aguinaldo had summoned a constitutional convention to meet at Malolos, a city 30 miles to the north of Manila which served as the temporary capital of the Philippine Republic. The stated purpose was to counter American claims to sovereignty over the archipelago. Responding to the news of the conclusion of the Treaty of Paris, the convention defiantly proclaimed the constitution of the Republic of the Philippines on 27 January 1899. If American diplomatic recognition was not forthcoming, then hostilities could not be long delayed. The first serious fighting occurred on Saturday 4 February after Private William Grayson of the First Nebraska Volunteers fired on a patrol of Filipino insurgents that had ignored his order to halt at a sentry post in 'disputed territory' just outside Manila. The news signalling the beginning of what would become known in the United States as

---

30 See Paolo E. Coletta, 'Bryan, McKinley, and the Treaty of Paris', *Pacific Historical Review* 27 (1957), pp. 131–46.

the 'Philippine Insurrection' was speedily cabled to Washington. Critics of expansionism were dismayed by the turn of events. The Filipinos 'have undoubtedly injured their cause', lamented *The Nation*.[31] McKinley described the report of fighting as 'unexpected', and concluded: 'This means the ratification of the treaty; the people will insist on its ratification.'[32]

The gloom of the anti-imperialists was justified because the startling news that American soldiers were under attack in the Philippines arrived just as the Senate prepared to vote on the treaty on Monday, 6 February. Of the 84 Senators present, 57 voted in favour and 27 against. This gave the treaty the necessary two-thirds concurrence plus one. The crucial margin of victory had come from 11 Democrats who had joined the Republican majority. 'It was the closest, hardest fight I have ever known,' Lodge informed Roosevelt.[33] Indeed, the delicate balance of votes was underlined a few days later, on 14 February, when an amendment introduced by Augustus O. Bacon of Georgia came to a vote. Copying the language of the Teller Amendment, the Bacon Amendment sought to give a specific promise of future independence for the Philippines. The resulting tied vote of 29 to 29 was broken by Vice-President Hobart's use of his casting vote against the amendment. However, despite the strength of feeling against acquiring overseas colonies, the anti-imperialists had failed in their efforts to defeat or amend the peace treaty. Their defeat provided a signal political and personal triumph for McKinley who had never wavered from insisting throughout the ratification process that the United States annex the Philippines.

The treaty, however, still required formal ratification by Spain. A period of six months had been allowed for this purpose. The Spanish government sensibly decided to defer reassembling the Cortes until the United States Senate had voted on the peace treaty. Prime Minister Sagasta did not expect that Spanish ratification would be a contentious issue. It was evident that Spain accepted the loss of its colonies and had no desire to renew the fighting or re-open the negotiations concluded at Paris. Defeat had been a painful experience, but Spaniards generally showed no hatred or bitterness towards their American victors. Moreover, Cuba was no longer a divisive issue between Spain and the United States. That

---

31 *The Nation* (New York), 9 February 1899.
32 Cited in Margaret Leech, *In the Days of McKinley* (New York, 1958), p. 358.
33 See ibid.

island's political future would now be the responsibility of other powers and races. 'Soldiers and civilians alike', noted *The Times*, 'have settled down, with a dreary and fatalistic calm, into the acceptance of their disaster and its consequences.'[34] If anything, the mass of the Spanish people were greatly relieved by the end of hostilities and the lifting of what had become an intolerable financial and military burden.

In the search for reasons to explain their country's humiliating defeat, most Spaniards freely acknowledged the superiority of the American people not only in economic and military power but also in political organization and racial attributes. While some writers and politicians pessimistically concluded that the Iberian race was intrinsically inferior to the Anglo-Saxons, others favoured a political analysis which identified *caciquismo* as the principal cause of the nation's relative backwardness. According to this view, *caciquismo* had imposed upon the Spanish people an inordinately expensive and inefficient administrative establishment whose priority lay in responding to the machinations of selfish and corrupt cliques rather than promoting the national interest. Indeed, the reactionary nature of the system had stifled political development not only in Spain but also in Cuba, where the obstinate denial of local autonomy had ultimately provoked the outbreak of the 1895 revolt. Critics argued that the ensuing sequence of military disasters had merely underlined the deficiencies of *caciquismo*. The initial demands for its overthrow arose not from politicians but primarily from members of the middle class who had long felt exploited both politically and economically by an elitist and unrepresentative political system. A national pressure group was formed by various chambers of commerce meeting at Zaragoza in November 1898. While pressing for practical measures such as a retrenchment in government spending and a substantial reduction in the number of civil servants, the emerging reform movement also stressed broader demands for major improvements in public services such as education, transportation and irrigation. The stated aim was to modernize and 'regenerate' Spain so that it might reverse generations of national decline. As Admiral Cervera remarked, the disastrous war with the United States had actually produced a positive aspect in that Spain could now 'concentrate her efforts on an inner regeneration'.[35]

34 *The Times* (London), 20 September 1898.
35 28 November 1898, cited in José Varela Ortega, 'Aftermath of Splendid Disaster: Spanish Politics before and after the Spanish American War of 1898', *Journal of Contemporary History* 15 (1980), p. 329.

Radical reform, however, was not easily implemented. Indeed, the inherent difficulty of enacting legislation in what had become an increasingly fragmented political system was exemplified by the government's attempts to ratify the Treaty of Paris. Just before the Cortes assembled on 20 February 1899, Prime Minister Sagasta appeared outwardly confident of securing a smooth passage for the treaty. He told the press that the recent American ratification had 'simplified the situation'.[36] But Sagasta's show of political bravado was misplaced. Although the particular articles of the treaty aroused little controversy in the Cortes, opposition members seized upon the ratification process as a means not only of berating the government for its conduct of the war but also to voice the urgent need for 'regeneration'. The predictable result was legislative stalemate accompanied by rumours of ministerial crisis. During the first week in March Sagasta resigned and was replaced as prime minister by his political arch-foe, Silvela. The new government promised to 'regenerate' the nation, but was soon immersed in political intrigues and manoeuvring. In the process, ratification was withheld from the Treaty of Paris. 'The first object of every Spanish politician at the present time', cynically observed *The Times*, 'is to avoid formal responsibility for the ratification of a treaty which all know to have been necessary and unavoidable.'[37]

The failure of Spain to ratify the treaty within the allotted period of six months would inevitably lead to embarrassing diplomatic complications with the United States. This prompted the constitutional intervention of the Queen Regent, María Cristina, who closed the Cortes on 6 March. Only a year earlier it had been feared that the loss of Cuba would mean the overthrow of the Spanish monarchy. Despite the subsequent military disasters, the monarchy still remained as the symbol of national unity and political stability amid the general mood of postwar malaise. Indeed, María Cristina would continue as Queen Regent until May 1902, when her son came of age and was crowned as King Alfonso XIII. In accordance with the political settlement which had prevailed in Spain since December 1874, it was fitting in 1899 that she should fulfil the crown's constitutional obligations and serve the national interest by defusing political tensions over the peace treaty. Having closed the Cortes, María Cristina simply made use of the royal prerogative and signed the treaty in her own name on 19 March

---

36 *The Times* (London), 8 February 1899.
37 Ibid., 18 March 1899.

1899. Shortly afterwards, on 11 April, the Spanish-American War was officially brought to an end when the governments of Spain and the United States formally exchanged their ratifications of the Treaty of Paris.

9 THE AFTERMATH

MILITARY POST-MORTEMS

With the exception of the resolute defence of El Caney and the San Juan Heights and the brave attempt of Cervera's squadron to out-run the powerful fleet of American battleships, Spain derived precious little military glory from three years of warfare. In retrospect it seemed the height of folly to have gone to war against the United States. Indeed, Spaniards would forever remember 1898 as the year of '*el desastre*' (the disaster). However, the scale of national humiliation was such that it was not enough to attribute defeat simply to the greater size and overwhelming power of the United States. A search for scapegoats ensued which was primarily directed at the country's political leaders and eventually secured the resignation of Prime Minister Sagasta. However, senior military officers did not escape public censure. 'Why have these incompetent generals not been shot?' provocatively asked one critic in the Cortes.[1] Despite being given vast national resources, the Spanish army and navy had suffered a succession of crippling reverses. More than 200,000 troops had failed to force the Cuban insurgents to sue for peace. In the process, what had begun as a colonial rebellion was transformed into a war with the United States in which Spain suffered military defeats not only confined to Cuba but also involving the Philippines and Puerto Rico. The cost was truly disastrous in terms of Spanish life, treasure and national spirit. Three years of stubbornly fighting 'to the last peseta and last drop of blood' claimed the lives of more than 50,000 soldiers and sailors, bankrupted the country and brought about the effective dissolution of the empire.

In the opinion of a leading British newspaper, Spain's 'prestige

---

1 Speech of the Count de Almenas, cited in Melchor Fernández Almagro, *Historia política de la España contemporánea* (3 vols., Madrid, 1968), vol. iii p. 211.

as a fighting-power, by land or sea, has disappeared'.[2] The war exposed glaring shortcomings in Spanish military organization, ranging from the shortage of rations for the infantrymen at the front line to the inability to equip warships with their proper complement of weapons. It was also evident that the high military command had failed to provide competent leadership. From the beginning of the rebellion in 1895 Spanish army commanders were held to have pursued a misguided defensive strategy which had resulted in what was essentially the transfer of one half of the army from the peninsula to Cuba. The *trocha* was the most visible product of a siege mentality which concentrated large numbers of troops in defensive positions where they waited for the enemy to appear. Such tactics failed to defeat the insurgents and had little chance of succeeding against the superior resources of the Americans. Indeed, the sheer size of Spanish forces in Cuba proved to be a distinct liability, especially when they were denied supplies from outside by the imposition of the American naval blockade. Despite his aggressive public statements, Captain General Blanco remained on the defensive and did not attempt to break the blockade. A similar defensive mentality was displayed by other Spanish commanders. For example, Linares allowed Shafter to land unimpeded at Daiquirí and deployed only a small fraction of his available forces to halt the American advance on Santiago de Cuba. In the opinion of *The Times*, Spanish generals had shown 'incredible ineptitude' throughout the war.[3]

On the other hand, the Spanish army in Cuba could not logistically mount a land invasion of the United States, and had therefore little option but to dig in and await the arrival of the enemy. Consequently, the role of the navy assumed crucial importance. Both Captain General Blanco and Prime Minister Sagasta wanted the Spanish navy to adopt a positive strategy of directly confronting the enemy and, where possible, launch raids against the American mainland. However, as Cervera repeatedly pointed out, the difficulty with this policy was that the Spanish navy was not only substantially inferior in strength to the American fleet but would be operating too far away from its principal sources of supplies and repairs. He advocated, therefore, a defensive naval strategy in which the priority of the Spanish navy would be to defend the peninsula. But this was countered by Blanco who insisted

2 *The Times* (London), 12 December 1898.
3 Ibid., 17 August 1898.

that the presence of the squadron was absolutely necessary to boost local morale. In order to please Blanco and the loyalists, the Spanish government rejected Cervera's views and ordered him to proceed to the Caribbean.

The Spanish naval tactics were sound in theory. Indeed, Americans were greatly alarmed by the threat of attack from the reputedly swift Spanish warships roaming the Atlantic and the Caribbean. However, the danger never materialized because Cervera chose to locate his ships in Santiago de Cuba. Moreover, the Spanish admiral remained in port and thereby gave the Americans time to mount a naval blockade and to despatch a large expeditionary force. Cervera's lethargy was greatly to the advantage of the Americans in that the major battle of the war did not take place, as was generally expected, in the centre of Spanish power around Havana but in the much less well-fortified and relatively isolated city of Santiago de Cuba. Athough the resulting capitulation of the city was a severe military blow for Spain, the destruction of Cervera's squadron had more immediate ramifications. The establishment of American naval supremacy meant that Spain was unable either to relieve or supply its colonial armies. The surrender of Cuba, Puerto Rico and Manila became purely a matter of time.

In late July 1898 the Spanish government accepted the inevitable and sued for peace, even though the large majority of Spanish troops in Cuba had not entered into combat against the Americans. Ironically, by claiming not to have been actually defeated in battle, the Spanish army technically retained its *pundonor* so that the opprobrium of defeat was thrown on the politicians. Moreover, the demands for the 'regeneration' of Spanish political life were not extended to the military, whose institutional power was sufficient to resist public pressure for a full-scale investigation into its conduct of the war. Nevertheless, the military high command did not attempt to portray the war as anything other than a disaster. The honour of the armed services required that those who had acted dishonourably must be punished. Accordingly, the senior officers who had capitulated to the Americans were taken into custody and subjected to lengthy and humiliating internal inquiries. While Cervera and Toral were eventually acquitted, Montojo and Jáudenes were compelled to take early retirement. The only prominent military figure who gained advancement after the war was General Weyler. His recall to Spain in 1897 meant that he had not taken an active role in the conflict with the Americans. Ironically, the man who had once so disturbed relations between civilians and the military was appointed Minister of War in 1902.

Whereas Spaniards brooded on the reasons for their defeat, the relative brevity of the war and its lack of hard fighting was a cause for much joy and congratulation in the United States. On learning that Spain was seeking peace, John Hay wrote to Theodore Roosevelt: 'It has been a splendid little war; begun with the highest motives, carried on with magnificent intelligence and spirit favored by that fortune which loves the brave.'[4] Hay's celebrated phrase, 'splendid little war', summed up the conflict for many Americans. They basked in the glory of the naval victories of Manila Bay and Santiago de Cuba, the charge up the San Juan Heights, the capitulation of Santiago de Cuba, and the capture of Puerto Rico and Manila. Success was attributed to superior American skill and character exemplified on the battlefield by the likes of Commodore Dewey and Colonel Roosevelt, both of whom would be spoken of as future American presidential material.[5] More prosaically, Mahan concluded: 'The short brilliant moments of triumph in war are the sign and the seal of the long hours of obscure preparations, of which target practice is but one item.'[6]

Prewar planning and training certainly contributed to the remarkable success achieved by the American navy in 1898. However, just like the Spaniards, the implementation of American policy did not always proceed smoothly. The public perception that the coastline was inadequately defended created political pressures which resulted in splitting the armoured fleet into two main squadrons. Mahan condemned the decision as 'contrary to sound practice'.[7] Naval operations were also hampered by personality conflicts among senior officers, especially between Sampson and Schley. Even more directly damaging to the successful prosecution of the war effort was Sampson's awkward working relationship with General Shafter. Sampson believed that the Expeditionary Force had been sent to Santiago de Cuba to assist the navy to destroy the Spanish fleet. But Shafter ignored Sampson's advice and unilaterally embarked on a land campaign in which the navy was assigned only

4 Hay to Roosevelt, 27 July 1898, cited in Walter Millis, *The Martial Spirit* (Boston, 1931), p. 340.

5 Theodore Roosevelt was elected Vice-President in 1900. He became President on 14 September 1901 after the death of William McKinley from a gunshot wound suffered in an attempt to assassinate him on 6 September.

6 Alfred T. Mahan, *Lessons of the War with Spain, and Other Articles* (Boston, 1899), p. 88.

7 Ibid., p. 56.

a peripheral role. The tension between the two commanders was illustrated by the absence of a navy representative at the ceremony marking the capitulation of Santiago de Cuba. The inter-service conflict was continued between Sampson and Miles over the provision of protective cover for the expedition to Puerto Rico. The dispute was only resolved by the direct intervention of President McKinley.

The inter-service rivalries at the front line were replicated in Washington, where no administrative machinery existed for combining land and sea forces in joint operations overseas. Secretary of the Navy Long and Secretary of War Alger displayed little understanding of or sympathy for each other's particular difficulties. Long saw the army as subordinate to the navy, but Alger stressed that only a land invasion of Cuba by the army would secure the final victory. Whereas a powerful American navy already existed in 1898, Alger and his officials at the War Department faced the enormous task of creating an army virtually from scratch. Within three months they had mobilized more than 200,000 men and despatched expeditionary forces to Cuba, Puerto Rico and the Philippines. However, there was dissatisfaction over the length of time taken to organize the expeditionary force for Cuba and the great confusion marking its embarkation from Tampa. Jubilation over the army's capture of Santiago de Cuba was soon swamped by growing public discontent aroused over the publication of the 'Round Robin' and the subsequent return of thousands of emaciated soldiers to Montauk Point during August 1898.

Blame for the appalling state of affairs was increasingly personalized and fastened, not upon President McKinley or senior military officers, but upon Secretary of War Alger. In popular speech the word 'Algerism' was used as a term of abuse to denote maladministration and callous insensitivity. To relieve public anxieties McKinley appointed a special presidential commission to investigate the War Department's conduct of the war. Under the chairmanship of General Grenville M. Dodge, the 'Dodge Commission' commenced its proceedings on 26 September 1898 and continued until 9 February 1899. No sensational revelations were forthcoming until General Miles appeared before the Commission on 21 December 1898 and revived his longstanding feud with Alger by accusing the War Department of including in the army's rations large stocks of canned roast beef treated with chemicals. Miles declared that soldiers in Cuba had suffered considerable sickness after eating what he described as 'embalmed beef'. The final report of the Commission dismissed Miles's allegations and found no incriminating evidence of corruption or maladministration by the War Department. However, the commissioners adopted an ambivalent attitude towards Secretary of War Alger, and ended their report with the concluding statement that 'there was lacking in the general administration of the War Department during the continuance of the war with Spain that complete grasp of the situation which was essential to the highest efficiency and discipline of the Army'.[8]

Alger let it be known privately that he felt personally maligned by the report's conclusion. After a short interval he resigned his office in August 1899. The Dodge Commission was successful not only in alleviating public anxieties over alleged administrative scandals but also provided a thorough report extending to eight volumes which proved invaluable to the new Secretary of War, Elihu Root. The work of the Commission greatly facilitated Root's implementation of an extensive programme of reform and reorganization of the War Department, including the establishment in 1903 of an Army General Staff and a Joint Army and Navy Board on National Defense. The number of regular soldiers in the federal army was also considerably increased and training procedures were improved in the state militias. Similar reforms were also introduced in the navy. In 1900, the Navy Department created a General Board of the Navy to plan and advise on the execution of naval policy. The Office of the Chief of Naval Operations was later established in 1913.

The Spanish-American War was so short and lacking in great battles that it attracted little attention from contemporary military experts. Consequently, the conflict is generally accorded scanty mention in the annals of the history of war. 'There are few, if any, lessons for the British Army to learn from the conduct of this campaign,' concluded a British military attaché who had accompanied the American Expeditionary Force to Santiago de Cuba.[9] With the benefit of hindsight, however, the Spanish-American War provided a foretaste of the terrible slaughter which would strike Europe in 1914. The advantages of troops being

8 Report of the Commission Appointed by the President to Investigate the Conduct of the War Department in the War With Spain, 56th Congress 1st Session, Senate Document No. 221 (8 vols; Washington DC, 1900), vol. i pp. 115–61.

9 The comments of Captain Arthur H. Lee, cited in Edward Ranson, 'British Military and Naval Observers in the Spanish-American War', *Journal of American Studies* 3 (1969), p. 51.

positioned in well-fortified trenches and equipped with magazine rifles firing high-velocity, smokeless bullets at long range were demonstrated at El Caney and the San Juan Heights, where a relatively small number of Spanish defenders provided stiff resistance to the advancing American forces. Like the generals of the First World War, Shafter chose to overwhelm the enemy with thousands of men. It was an unimaginative policy which resulted in gaining the desired territory but at the cost of heavy casualties. Shafter emerged from the war with the reputation of a blunderer rather than a hero.

The importance of possessing a powerful navy, especially one which included modern armoured warships, was underlined by the Spanish-American War. The destruction of Cervera's squadron at Santiago de Cuba was attributed to the greater tonnage and firepower of the American battleships. American success was also explained by the adoption of an offensive naval strategy which sought to gain the command of the seas even if this necessitated a major battle of the fleets. The views of strategists such as Mahan appeared to be vindicated when American naval supremacy compelled the Spanish government to seek peace. 'Sea power has again triumphantly asserted its dominant influence,' noted *The Times*.[10] The practical lesson deduced in the United States was that the American navy should acquire more and bigger battleships and also the overseas facilities and bases requisite for a large battle fleet. The Spanish-American War therefore contributed to the international arms race in capital warships and the 'scramble for empire' among the great powers, including the United States.

Finally, the guerrilla warfare between the Spaniards and the insurgents, which predated the American military intervention in 1898, provided an example of the so-called 'dirty war' which would become a frequent feature of the twentieth-century world. Within only a few months of the end of fighting in Cuba, the British were embroiled in suppressing colonial rebellion in South Africa. Similar missions were soon undertaken by the American army in the Philippines and the Spanish army in North Africa. The strategy and tactics employed showed that, if the colonial powers had learned any lesson from Spain's disastrous experience in Cuba, it was to prosecute their own war just as ruthlessly and, if anything, to aim to be more efficient in the application of force. When confronted by movements for national liberation, they invariably adopted the same military strategy of despatching ever-increasing numbers of soldiers

10 *The Times* (London), 15 August 1898.

to crush the guerrillas and, where this proved ineffective, introduced policies of 'pacifying' or 'reconcentrating' the local civilian population. Like the example of Spain in Cuba, the cost of colonial war would often become not so much militarily but politically insupportable and would compel face-saving concessions in favour of local self-government or independence. In the particular case of the Spanish-Cuban War in 1898, this sequence of events was interrupted by the intervention of the United States.

THE NEW AMERICAN 'EMPIRE'

Military victory in 1898 presented the United States with the perplexing problem of deciding the political organization of Spain's former colonies in the Caribbean and the Pacific. 'We are facing administrative difficulties in our island possessions with which nothing in our experience fits us to cope,' summed up *The Nation*.[11] Despite the underlying assumption that self-government would shortly be granted, the strains of adjusting from war to peace and the perceived inability of the local peoples to rule themselves resulted in the establishment of government by the American military authorities. This temporary arrangement gradually assumed a more permanent form. As the debate over the ratification of the Treaty of Paris demonstrated, the elation of victory over Spain combined with the perceived dictates of 'duty and responsibility' to break down the traditional aversion of Americans to foreign entanglements and the acquisition of colonies. The Spanish-American War was therefore directly instrumental in bringing about the emergence of an American overseas 'empire' at the beginning of the twentieth century.

According to the Joint Resolution and the Teller Amendment of April 1898, the United States had entered into war with Spain to bring peace and freedom to the Cuban people. Having achieved victory over Spain, it was expected that President McKinley would proclaim the formation of an independent Cuban republic and withdraw American troops from the island. However, the McKinley administration had paid minimal attention to postwar planning. 'It is doubtful whether many Americans have endeavoured to think out the problems of Cuba,' remarked a British newspaper at the outset of the war.[12] Nevertheless, there were clear indications as to the

11 *The Nation* (New York), 1 September 1898.
12 *The Times* (London), 15 April 1898.

likely direction of American policy. For example, McKinley never openly espoused the cause of Cuban independence or *Cuba libre*. Moreover, he steadfastly pursued a unilateral policy which was characterized by the refusal to give official recognition to the Cuban Provisional Government and to the Cuban Army of Liberation. As Martí had feared, the 'Spanish-Cuban War' became the 'Spanish-American War' in which a struggle for national liberation was transformed into a war of American military conquest. Americans used their superior power to dictate military strategy and the peace settlement. General Shafter treated the Cuban insurgents as expendable. Their representatives were excluded from the negotiations leading to the capitulation of Santiago de Cuba, the Peace Protocol and the Treaty of Paris. The pre-eminence of the United States in Cuba was symbolically demonstrated on 1 January 1899 when the American military authorities refused to allow armed insurgents to participate in the ceremonies marking the evacuation of Spanish troops from Havana. Máximo Gómez deliberately stayed away from the capital, and lamented that the Americans 'have soured the joy of the victorious Cubans'.[13]

On 1 January 1899, the United States formally replaced Spanish rule in Cuba with a military government headed by General John R. Brooke. According to the Teller Amendment, such an arrangement would be temporary. The duration of the occupation, however, was not specified. Consequently, the future political status of Cuba remained uncertain. The question was complicated by the low opinion which Americans possessed concerning the capacity of the Cubans to exercise self-government. American soldiers and journalists had already conveyed highly unfavourable accounts of their personal encounters with Cubans. They presented an image of Cubans as thieves and scroungers who were more likely to run away than fight or work. American contempt was also fuelled by the perception that the majority of Cubans were illiterate and apparently black or of mixed race. Conditioned by Anglo-Saxon racist prejudice towards blacks and also influenced by the fashionable Social Darwinist theories of the time which stressed the 'survival of the fittest', Americans readily believed that Home Rule for Cuba was premature and, if granted, would result in the island becoming poor and unstable like the notorious black republic of Haiti. One particularly disparaging comment made by General Shafter in December 1898 was widely reported in the American press:

13 Máximo Gómez, *Diario de campaña, 1868–1899* (Havana, 1968), pp. 371–2.

'Self-government! Why, these people are no more fit for self-government than gun-powder is for hell.'[14] The answer was to establish American civil and military administration while providing Cubans with instruction in the art of government until such time as they were deemed ready for independence. Reports from American officials in Cuba reassuringly suggested that there would be local acceptance of a period of tutelage. Indeed, leading Cuban politicians and businessmen were known to favour the continuation of an American governmental role and military presence as a safeguard against economic and social disorder. In effect, they wanted the United States to replace Spain as the guarantor of order and stability on the island.

The new role envisaged for the United States was even supported by Senator Teller. On 8 September 1898, in a speech at Colorado Springs, Teller declared that the Cubans were not yet ready for self-government. In the meantime, the United States must 'put a strong hand on them and give them a good government.'[15] Citing 'the laws of gravitation', other American political leaders such as Senator Henry Cabot Lodge went further, and advocated the annexation of Cuba to the United States. Although McKinley endorsed the acquisition of the Philippines, he remained ambivalent over the question of Cuba. In his Annual Message to Congress of December 1898, he stated that the United States was obligated to help the Cubans set up 'a government which shall be free and independent', but he warned that the American military occupation would continue 'until there is complete tranquillity in the island and a stable government inaugurated'.[16]

For more than three years, from 1 January 1899 to 20 May 1902, the people of Cuba were ruled by the United States army. A military governor was appointed by the President of the United States and was directly accountable to the Secretary of War. As soon as the rainy season ended in October 1898 several American regiments were transferred from the United States. By March 1899 American forces in Cuba numbered 50,000, a figure almost three times the size of the American Expeditionary Force sent to Santiago

14 *New York Tribune*, 19 December 1898.

15 Cited in David F. Healy, *The United States in Cuba, 1898–1902: Generals, Politicians, and the Search for Policy* (Madison, WI, 1963), p. 85.

16 'Annual Presidential Message for 1898', cited in *FRUS* (1898), p. xvii. Ironically, the Teller Amendment actually justified the continuation of military government in Cuba. The amendment disclaimed American control over Cuba 'except for the pacification thereof'.

de Cuba. There was virtually no organized Cuban resistance to the imposition of American military control. No longer able to forage and live off the land, the insurgents had become increasingly destitute. Demoralized and fragmented, they were vulnerable to American economic pressure which offered rations and jobs in exchange for giving up their weapons. By the spring of 1899 the Cuban Liberation Army was effectively disbanded. In June, Máximo Gómez took his leave of his soldiers and returned to Santo Domingo.

The American military government, first under Brooke and later under Leonard Wood, who became Military Governor in December 1899, embarked upon a major programme of emergency relief, administrative reform and public works. Wood was particularly interested in improving education and public health, especially the eradication of yellow fever. Nevertheless, despite the economic benefits of military rule, Cubans began to chafe under Wood's evident desire to turn the island into a mirror-image of the United States. In particular, they showed increasing impatience over American reluctance to state when the pledge given in the Teller Amendment would be fulfilled and the occupation ended. Secretary of War Elihu Root was concerned that disaffected Cubans might imitate the example of the Filipino nationalists and launch a revolt against American rule. In a statement made public in December 1899, Root referred to 'our temporary occupation' and affirmed that it would not 'continue any longer than is necessary'.[17]

In order to demonstrate American good intentions, elections were organized in September 1900 for a convention to undertake the task of drafting a constitution for an independent Cuba. But the old American suspicions soon surfaced that life and property were in danger. Wood alarmingly described some of the delegates who had been elected as 'the worst agitators and political rascals in Cuba'.[18] Secretary of War Root concurred. Pre-empting the work of the convention, he sought to ensure future stability in Cuba by devising a scheme in which the current military government would be replaced by an American protectorate. The idea was based upon British policy towards Egypt, which, according to Root, allowed Britain 'to retire and still maintain her moral control'.[19] The United States would exercise a similar influence over Cuba by securing a

---

17 2 December 1899, cited in Healy, *United States in Cuba*, p. 121.

18 Wood to Root, 26 September 1900, cited in Louis A. Pérez, Jr, *Cuba Between Empires, 1878–1902* (Pittsburgh, 1983), p. 316.

19 Root to Hay, 11 January 1901, cited in Healy, *United States in Cuba*, p. 154.

constitutional right to intervene by armed force. The matter was not to be resolved by discussion or concession. If the Cubans did not consent, it was to be made clear that the American military occupation would continue. The scheme was endorsed by Senator Orville H. Platt of Connecticut, the chairman of the Senate Committee on Relations with Cuba. Platt included Root's proposals in the form of an amendment to the annual Army Appropriations Bill. The 'Platt Amendment' was duly approved by Congress in March 1901.

The Platt Amendment consisted of eight articles designed 'to define the future relations of the United States with Cuba'. The most famous and controversial was the third article, which stated that 'the United States may exercise the right to intervene for the preservation of Cuban independence, the maintenance of a government adequate for the protection of life, property, and individual liberty'. Other notable clauses restricted Cuba's powers to contract financial debts and to enter into treaties with foreign nations. The United States was also allowed to purchase what would become a major American naval base at Guantánamo Bay.[20] The Cuban delegates at the constitutional convention in Havana argued that the amendment was a serious curtailment of Cuba's sovereign rights. But all counter-proposals were firmly rejected by McKinley and Root. After considerable debate, the convention eventually accepted the Platt Amendment on 12 June 1901 by a vote of 16 to 11 with 4 abstentions.[21] Almost one year later, at a ceremony in Havana on 20 May 1902, Wood declared an end to the occupation and formally transferred the powers of government to Tomás Estrada Palma, the elected President of the new Republic of Cuba. Estrada Palma had lived in New York for a number of years and had succeeded Martí as the leader of the Cuban Revolutionary Party. The new President, however, held strong pro-American sympathies and represented the 'better class' of Cuban much preferred by Wood and the American military authorities.[22]

The Platt Amendment was essentially a substitute for annexation, and provided the means by which the United States granted independence to Cuba but withheld sovereignty from the

---

20 The text of the Platt Amendment is printed in *Congressional Record*, 56th Congress 2nd Session, p. 2954.

21 The convention had approved a modified version of the Platt Amendment on 28 May 1901. The modifications were unacceptable to the United States government.

22 Cited in Louis A. Pérez, Jr, *Cuba Under the Platt Amendment, 1902–1934* (Pittsburgh, 1986), p. 39.

new republic. In reality, Cuba became an American protectorate. Root's insistence that the amendment be incorporated into the Cuban constitution reflected not only his legalistic mind-set but also the stereotyped view held by many American political and military leaders that Cubans were unfit for self-government. 'In many respects they are like children,' noted Platt.[23] The constitutional right to intervene provided the ultimate safeguard should the island collapse into disorder. The United States would therefore be able to protect life and property on the island and obviate any need for intervention from any foreign power. Despite criticism that it betrayed the Teller Amendment, the Platt Amendment was attractive to Americans because it promised future stability and brought an end to the lengthy and increasingly expensive military occupation. Cubans had virtually no alternative but to accept the amendment. If they refused, the American military occupation would be maintained. Cubans generally felt humiliated by the imposition of the Platt Amendment and came to regard it as a symbol of American oppression. Nevertheless, in 1902 it gave them a measure of self-government and an opportunity to affirm their national identity.

American policy towards Cuba from 1898 to 1902 was not systematic. It basically evolved according to circumstances. After more than three years of savage warfare, Cuba was in ruins in 1898. The existing political vacuum was filled by the American army. Military government did not lead to political annexation, primarily because American political leaders felt constrained by the Teller Amendment. Curiously, American business interests were initially hesitant to enter into close economic links with Cuba. One main reason for this was the fear of Cuban competition expressed by sugar growers in the United States. In fact, economic relations flourished after the creation of the republic when Cuban sugar was given preferential access to the American market. Though nominally an independent nation, Cuba was effectively an American 'colony'. The one-sided nature of the relationship would provoke Cuban resentment and ultimate retaliation, but Americans in 1902 believed that the question of Cuba's political status had been satisfactorily resolved, and wished that a similarly successful outcome would materialize in the Philippines.

In contrast to Cuba, American policy towards the Philippines was not bound by the provisions of the Teller Amendment. Using

23 Cited in Philip S. Foner, *The Spanish-Cuban-American War and the Birth of American Imperialism* (2 vols; New York, 1972), vol. ii p. 584.

his powers as Commander-in-Chief, McKinley decided that the United States should replace Spain as the sovereign ruler of the islands. In the same way as he dealt with the question of postwar Cuba, the American President refused to recognize the existence of a Filipino government and showed no disposition to consult the people of the Philippines regarding their future political status. The Filipinos were essentially regarded as a backward race who should be treated as if they were children. Their individual rights were to be protected, but independence would not be granted until a time in the future when the United States judged them capable of exercising self-government. In practice, however, Americans serving in the Philippines treated the local people as racial inferiors. While American soldiers were openly contemptuous of the Filipinos and generally referred to them as 'niggers', official American policy vigorously denied that the United States had any intention of acting as a colonial oppressor. Indeed, the mood of taking up 'the white man's burden' was very much in evidence. In instructions sent to Major-General Elwell S. Otis on 21 December 1898, McKinley stressed 'that the mission of the United States is one of benevolent assimilation, substituting the mild sway of justice and right for arbitrary rule'.[24]

Imbued with the sense of 'benevolent' mission and elated by the rapid military victory over the Spaniards, officials in Washington did not anticipate armed Filipino resistance to American rule. The insurgents led by Aguinaldo were regarded as an unrepresentative minority. In Alger's opinion, they were merely 'armed natives'.[25] This proved to be a grievous miscalculation. The fighting which broke out on 4 February 1899 marked the beginning not of a brief skirmish but the 'Philippine Insurrection' or 'Filipino-American War' which lasted for more than three years. After the fall of Manila, masses of Filipinos had flocked to join the insurgent army. With around 50,000 men under his command, Aguinaldo initially sought to engage the Americans in full-scale infantry battles. Although American troops were outnumbered, their superior weaponry and discipline enabled them to drive the insurgent army from the outskirts of Manila. By the end of March 1899 the insurgent capital at Malolos had fallen and Aguinaldo was forced to seek refuge in the mountains of northeastern Luzon. The American advance,

---

24 21 December 1898, cited in John M. Gates, *Schoolbooks and Krags: The United States Army in the Philippines, 1898–1902* (Westport, CT, 1973), p. 36.
25 Russell A. Alger, *The Spanish-American War* (New York, 1901), p. 356.

however, was halted by the onset of the rainy season. Like the Spanish army in Cuba, American soldiers found themselves at war thousands of miles from home in a tropical country where the heat was intense, the rain torrential and disease a constant danger.

Realizing that pitched battles must be avoided, Aguinaldo switched to guerrilla tactics with the deliberate aim of prolonging the war until the American army succumbed to fatigue and the ravages of the climate, or domestic political pressures in the United States compelled a reversal of McKinley's policies. Although the strategy proved ultimately unsuccessful, the resort to guerrilla warfare was effective in dispelling American expectations of a quick military victory. American commanders found it a frustrating task to track down an elusive enemy who was often indistinguishable from the civilian population. General Otis summed up:

> Little difficulty attends the act of taking possession of and temporarily holding any section of the country. A column of 3,000 men could march through and successfully contend with any force which the insurgents could place in its route, but they would close in behind it and again prey upon the inhabitants, persecuting without mercy those who had manifested any friendly feeling toward the American troops.[26]

To defeat the insurgents it became necessary to pacify the civilian population especially in the countryside. Like the Spaniards in Cuba, this resulted in American generals requesting substantial reinforcements so that total American forces in the Philippines rose to 70,000 during 1900. The appointment in May 1900 of Major-General Arthur MacArthur as Military Governor inaugurated a period of aggressive counter-insurgency measures. Though on a smaller scale than that practised by Weyler in Cuba, a policy of reconcentration was pursued which relocated civilians in towns and villages garrisoned and protected by American troops.

Despite heavily censored press communications, allegations began to emerge of atrocities committed by American forces against Filipino civilians. The most shocking related to Brigadier-General Jacob Smith, who was later court-martialled for his orders to his men to turn the island of Samar into a 'howling wilderness' by shooting every Filipino male above the age of 10.[27] In their own

26 31 August 1899, cited in Gates, *Schoolbooks and Krags*, p. 102.
27 See Brian M. Linn, *The US Army and Counterinsurgency in the Philippine War, 1899–1902* (Chapel Hill, NC, 1989), p. 27.

defence, American officers pointed out that the insurgents were treacherous and ruthless enemies who were guilty of terrorizing civilians and massacring American soldiers. However, instead of boosting patriotic sentiment, such statements only served to diminish public support in the United States for a war which was certainly not 'splendid' and threatened to drag on indefinitely. *The Nation* critically observed that 'the war of 1898 "for the cause of humanity" has degenerated ... into a war of conquest, characterized by rapine and cruelty worthy of savages'.[28]

McKinley's declared aim of 'benevolent assimilation' in which the Filipino people would be 'uplifted' and 'civilized' was undermined by reports of the American army ruthlessly crushing the insurgents. In an effort to find a viable political solution, McKinley sent a commission headed by Jacob Gould Schurman, president of Cornell University, to visit the Philippines in March 1900. The Schurman Commission reassured American consciences by reporting that the insurgents were in a minority and that the majority of Filipinos favoured American rule. It confirmed that the Filipinos were not yet capable of self-government, but recommended that they be granted a measure of limited local government and also representation in the government advisory council which served under the American governor.

The main recommendations of the Schurman Commission were put into effect by William H. Taft, who became the first civilian governor of the Philippines in July 1901. Legal affirmation was forthcoming in July 1902, when the United States Congress passed the Philippine Organic Act which gave the Philippines the status of an 'unincorporated territory' under the sovereign control of the United States. The use of the word 'unincorporated' was significant because it meant that the Philippines were regarded as an American possession and did not have a right of eventual admission to statehood.[29] The passage of the Organic Act came at a time when the war had come to an end. Taft's appointment had coincided with a period of American military successes against the insurgents, including the capture of Aguinaldo in March 1901. In fact, the nationalist movement had already become demoralized by military

28 *The Nation* (New York), 20 April 1899.
29 The term 'unincorporated territory' was used by the United States Supreme Court in a series of rulings made between 1901 and 1904 and known as the 'Insular Cases'. The key ruling was Downes *v.* Bidwell in 1901. The United States eventually granted full independence to the Philippines in 1946.

defeat. It was also divided by regional and ethnic rivalries. The prominent leadership role assumed by Tagalogs had long aroused suspicion, especially among the peoples of the islands south of Luzon. Moreover, the policy of terrorizing the peasantry increasingly alienated rural support and became counter-productive. By contrast, Taft stressed American goodwill and benevolent purpose. Despite its racist overtones, Taft's public references to 'our little brown brothers' reflected a genuinely sympathetic approach towards the Filipino people which had been lacking during the previous military administration.[30] While submission to American rule signified the suppression of nationalist aspirations, it also offered Filipinos the appealing prospect of political stability and economic prosperity.

Although sporadic guerrilla resistance would continue in remote areas for at least another five years, American military ascendancy had become so evident that on 4 July 1902 President Theodore Roosevelt formally declared an end to the fighting in the archipelago. The American army had successfully achieved its objective of defeating the insurgents. But the costs were high. The Filipino-American War had lasted more than three years, from February 1899 to July 1902. The total number of American troops sent to the Philippines was 126,468, of whom 4,234 were killed and 2,818 wounded. The insurgents were estimated to have suffered from 16,000 to 20,000 fatalities. Even more destructive was the impact of the war on the countryside, which resulted in as many as 200,000 civilian deaths. American officials calculated that fighting the war cost the United States $400 million or twenty times the amount paid to Spain for the archipelago.[31] In addition to the human and financial losses, the Filipino-American War delivered an unquantifiable but no less damaging blow to America's image as a nation dedicated to the promotion of freedom and democracy.

The extension of American sovereign control over Puerto Rico, Hawaii and Guam was less complicated and was achieved much more peacefully than in Cuba and the Philippines. These islands were considerably smaller in size and offered minimal political and military resistance. In the case of Puerto Rico, Congress passed an Organic Act in April 1900 which established a political system headed by an American governor. The Congressional Joint

30 Morrell Heald and Lawrence S. Kaplan, *Culture and Diplomacy: The American Experience* (Westport, CT, 1977), p. 148.
31 See Richard E. Welch, Jr., *Response to Imperialism: The United States and the Philippine-American War, 1899–1902* (Chapel Hill, NC, 1979), p. 42.

Resolution of July 1898 had already made a similar constitutional provision for the Hawaiian Islands, though closer historical and cultural ties with the United States resulted in Hawaii being given 'incorporated' territorial status. Like the Philippines, however, Puerto Rico was regarded as 'unincorporated'. The McKinley administration also acquired the Pacific islands of Guam, Wake Island and Tutuila (American Samoa), so that by 1899 the United States possessed a chain of naval bases extending across the Pacific Ocean. These remote and sparsely populated islands were placed under the administration of American naval officers accountable to the Department of the Navy.

WORLD POLITICS

Throughout the nineteenth century the United States was an anomaly in world politics. Except during the American Civil War (1861–65), the American republic deliberately chose not to translate its abundant geopolitical resources into the large diplomatic and military establishment which the European nations equated with world power and prestige. By contrast, Spain grimly held on to the trappings of great power status. At the onset of war in April 1898 it even seemed that the two countries were equally matched in military terms. The ensuing events confirmed, however, the end of Spanish pretensions to be an imperial power and the emergence of the United States as an active force in world affairs. Not only did the United States achieve impressive military victories, but it acted like a world power in aggressively seizing territory in the Caribbean and Pacific. 'The American people', declared Henry Cabot Lodge in 1900, 'have decided that the United States should play its great part among the nations of the earth.'[32]

The diplomats of the Old World felt threatened. With the exception of Britain, the sympathies of the European foreign offices

---

32 Speech dated 23 November 1900, cited in William C. Widenor, *Henry Cabot Lodge and the Search for an American Foreign Policy* (Berkeley, CA, 1980), p. 120. The exact timing of the rise of the United States to the status of a world power has attracted considerable discussion among American historians. Though it questions the significance of 1898 as a watershed date, a useful introduction to this debate is Thomas A. Bailey, 'America's Emergence as a World Power: The Myth and the Verity', *Pacific Historical Review* 30 (1961), pp. 1–16. See also James A. Field, Jr, 'American Imperialism: The Worst Chapter in Almost Any Book', *American Historical Review* 83 (1978), pp. 644–83.

both before and during the war had rested with monarchical Spain rather than the republican United States. Typical of this attitude was the description of Kaiser Wilhelm II of Germany of American designs upon Cuba as 'the insolence of the Yankee'.[33] The great powers, however, were taken aback by the speed and completeness of the American victory and the uncompromising manner in which Spain was dispossessed of its empire during the negotiations for the Treaty of Paris. A concern was expressed that the United States would seek further territorial gains at the expense of existing colonial powers. The awareness that America's military potential was underpinned by a rapidly growing economy contributed an additional cause of alarm in Europe, and prompted some writers, especially in France, to warn of the dangers of the 'American peril' or the 'American menace'.

The power of the United States was illustrated most clearly in the Western Hemisphere. This was hardly a new development. America's special hemispheric role had been asserted in the Monroe Doctrine of 1823 and more recently had been proclaimed by Secretary of State Richard Olney in 1895: 'To-day the United States is practically sovereign on this continent, and its fiat is law upon the subjects to which it confines its interposition.'[34] Indeed, America's vital interests in this region were highlighted by its close interest in Cuban affairs and the decision to go to war with Spain in 1898. Moreover, the non-interventionist policy pursued by the great powers of Europe reflected their recognition of American political and military pre-eminence in questions relating to the Caribbean. This pre-eminence was further underlined by victory over Spain and the extension of protectorates over Cuba and Puerto Rico. In addition, the McKinley administration proceeded to seek naval bases and announced its determination to control any future trans-isthmian canal which might be constructed between the Atlantic and Pacific. American trade and investment also benefited significantly from this active policy which would soon be popularly referred to as 'dollar diplomacy'. The Spanish-American War facilitated, therefore the development of the Caribbean as an 'American lake', a region which the United States sought to dominate politically, militarily and economically.

---

33 Cited in Ernest R. May, *Imperial Democracy: The Emergence of America as a Great Power* (New York, 1961), p. 196.
34 Olney to Bayard, no. 804, 20 July, 1895, *FRUS* (1895), p. 558.

The war in Cuba also affected the neighbouring countries of Central and South America. Fully aware of the geopolitical might of the United States, these governments were wary of annoying the 'colossus of the north' and adopted policies of neutrality towards the conflict. The short duration of the war effectively prevented the emergence of disputes over maritime rights or the need for any offer of diplomatic mediation. Nevertheless, the outward show of official neutrality concealed strong undertones of anti-American sentiment among the educated creoles who made up the ruling class in Latin America. Although the Latin American creoles were generally critical of Spanish political repression in Cuba, once American intervention occurred they privately sympathized with Spain rather than the United States. Part of the reason for this was a century of regarding the United States as an alien and aggressive power. Latin Americans instinctively distrusted, therefore, the idealistic motives proclaimed by President McKinley in justifying war in April 1898. There was also the suspicion that the 'Yankees' were deliberately bent on humiliating the Spanish race. Consequently, expressions of Latin American public opinion during the war frequently adopted an anti-American tone. For example, money was openly raised in Mexico to assist Spain, while public demonstrations were held in Buenos Aires to affirm Argentine support for the Spanish cause. The notable exception was Brazil, whose Portuguese background and diplomatic ambitions to become a greater hemispheric power than its arch-rival Argentina resulted in the adoption of a conspicuously friendly and helpful Brazilian attitude towards the United States. The American navy purchased two Brazilian warships, which were renamed the *New Orleans* and *Albany*, and was able to make use of Brazilian ports for the purpose of taking on fuel and carrying out repairs.

The stunning military defeat of Spain followed by the denial of home rule to Cuba and Puerto Rico, and the establishment instead of American military governments in those islands, served to confirm and harden anti-American sentiment in Latin America. Nevertheless, the removal of Spanish imperial power from the New World was a reality and only made the Latin American nations even more vulnerable to the political, economic and military influence of the United States. The Latin American predicament was eloquently expressed by the Uruguayan writer José Enrique Rodó, whose celebrated work *Ariel* was published in 1900. Echoing the warnings made by José Martí, Rodó implicitly likened the United States to 'Caliban', a monster respected for its great energy and strength but feared for its insensitivity and apparently unquenchable appetite for material expansion.

The Spanish-American War coincided with a period of increasing international rivalry in the Far East, where the great powers were absorbed in extending their respective 'spheres of influence' in China. The European powers and Japan were concerned by the strategic implications of America's territorial acquisitions in the Pacific. 'The Philippine Islands, rich, coal-bearing, and with fine harbors', noted the American writer Brooks Adams, 'seem a predestined base for the United States in a conflict which probably is as inevitable as that with Spain.'[35] However, American diplomacy was already active in China, so that the statement of national policy expressed by the 'Open Door Notes' in 1899 and 1900 was not dependent upon the new American military presence in the Philippines.

A more direct consequence of American involvement in the Philippines was a worsening of diplomatic relations between the United States and Germany. Admiral Dewey had interpreted Admiral von Diederichs's manoeuvres in Manila Bay as unfriendly, and privately regretted that he had not sunk the German squadron. In 1898 the American public perceived Germany as an intriguing and hostile rival. This negative image persisted into the twentieth century.

By contrast, Britain emerged from the Spanish-American War as the principal foreign friend of the United States. Americans generally regarded the British as sympathetic and supportive in 1898. For example, it was widely believed that the British warships in Manila Bay had saved Dewey's fleet from German skulduggery.[36] Relations were so amicable that European diplomats suspected the existence of a secret Anglo-American alliance. The bonds of history, shared ideals, racial affinities and common national interests were eloquently argued by leading British politicians such as Joseph Chamberlain and influential Americans such as Admiral Mahan. The British press generally approved of the Americans taking up 'the white man's burden' in Cuba and the Philippines. 'She will govern

---

35 Brooks Adams, 'The Spanish War and the Equilibrium of the World', *The Forum*, 25 (1898), p. 650.

36 This refers to the fact that two British warships had placed themselves between the American and German squadrons when Dewey bombarded Manila on 13 August. The intention of the British captain was not to protect Dewey but to gain a clearer picture of the naval proceedings. See Thomas A. Bailey, 'Dewey and the Germans at Manila Bay', *American Historical Review* 45 (1939), pp. 74–8.

them [The Philippines] well enough, much better than any Power except ourselves,' condescendingly remarked the *Spectator*.[37] Moreover, the United States was welcomed by British diplomats as a potential ally against Germany. Consequently, the Spanish-American War was significant in strengthening Anglo-American relations and contributed to the diplomatic *rapprochement* that was taking place between the two nations.

Contrary to the expectations of some European statesmen, the United States did not play a leading role in world politics during the first decade of the twentieth century. In fact, this had already been foreshadowed in American diplomacy towards the crisis in Cuba and the ensuing war with Spain. Both the Cleveland and McKinley administrations stressed American freedom of action and remained suspicious of the intentions of the European powers. Although McKinley later appeared to be joining the great powers in taking up 'the white man's burden', he carefully refrained from entering into formal alliances or cooperative arrangements with other governments. Indeed, American rule over subject peoples was described as being very different in kind and intent from that practised by the European imperial powers. In 1900 McKinley explained how the United States was helping the Filipinos: 'Every effort has been directed to their peace and prosperity, their advancement and well-being, not for our aggrandizement, not for pride and might, not for trade or commerce, not exploitation, but for humanity and civilization.'[38]

Despite the bold acquisition of an overseas empire, American diplomacy was essentially cautious and pragmatic during the period from 1895 to 1903. The hesitation to go to war with Spain, the inclusion of the Teller Amendment and the 'great debate' over the ratification of the Treaty of Paris underlined the ambivalence of Americans towards their country's assuming an active role in world politics. Moreover, public uncertainty was heightened by the subsequent difficulties encountered in administering distant peoples with quite different historical backgrounds and cultures. Americans were also unwilling to assume the financial and military burdens of great power status. There was no disposition to fight in the

---

37 *Spectator* (London), 21 May 1898, cited in A.E. Campbell, *Great Britain and the United States, 1895–1903* (London, 1960), p. 152.

38 8 September 1900, cited in Göran Rystad, *Ambiguous Imperialism: American Foreign Policy and Domestic Politics at the Turn of the Century* (Stockholm, 1975), p. 222.

Philippines 'to the last man or the last dollar'. Just as 'the disaster' of 1898 prompted Spaniards to forsake imperial ambitions in favour of concentrating on internal regeneration, Americans quickly lost interest in overseas empire and directed their energies to domestic affairs and what would become known as the 'progressive movement'. The suppression of nationalist movements in Cuba, Puerto Rico and the Philippines would later arouse criticism and controversy both within and outside the United States, but, in the immediate aftermath of the Spanish-American War, Americans were jubilant over winning what they fondly depicted as the 'splendid little war'.

CHRONOLOGY OF MAIN EVENTS

1895

24 February	*Grito* of Baire marks start of the Spanish-Cuban War
19 May	Martí killed in ambush
30 November	Insurgents under Gómez and Maceo begin 'Invasion of the West'

1896

10 February	Weyler replaces Martínez Campos as Captain General
7 April	Secretary of State Olney offers US good offices to end fighting in Cuba
6 December	Maceo killed in ambush
7 December	President Cleveland renews offer of US good offices and warns that American patience is not unlimited

1897

4 March	McKinley inaugurated as US President
8 August	Spanish Prime Minister Cánovas assassinated
August	Outbreak of rebellion against Spanish rule in the Philippines
October	Sagasta becomes Spanish Prime Minister and replaces Weyler with Blanco
6 December	McKinley condemns policy of reconcentration and hints at likelihood of US military intervention
14 December	Pact of Biyak-na-Bató brings temporary end to rebellion in the Philippines

1898

12 January	Riots by loyalists in Havana
9 February	Publication of De Lôme letter in New York press

15 February	USS *Maine* blown up in Havana harbour
11 April	McKinley sends 'War Message' to Congress
19 April	Congress passes Joint Resolution approving US military intervention
22 April	US North Atlantic Squadron under Sampson institutes blockade of Cuba
23 April	Spain recognizes state of war with United States McKinley issues call for 125,000 volunteers
25 April	US Congress declares retrospectively that state of war with Spain had begun on 21 April
27 April	US Atlantic Squadron under Dewey leaves Mirs Bay
29 April	Spanish naval squadron under Cervera leaves Cape Verdes for Caribbean
1 May	Dewey wins Battle of Manila Bay
19 May	Cervera's squadron arrives at Santiago de Cuba Aguinaldo returns to Manila
21 May	US navy takes possession of Guam
29 May	Schley confirms sighting of Cervera and institutes American blockade of Santiago de Cuba
1 June	Sampson assumes command of blockade of Santiago de Cuba
12 June	Aguinaldo declares independent Republic of the Philippines
14 June	American Expeditionary force under Shafter embarks from Tampa
16 June	Spanish naval squadron under de la Cámara leaves Cádiz for Philippines via Suez Canal
20 June	American Expeditionary Force arrives off Santiago de Cuba
22 June	American troops begin landing at Daiquirí and Siboney
24 June	American victory in skirmish at Las Guásimas
1 July	Battles of El Caney and San Juan Hill
3 July	Cervera's squadron is destroyed at the Naval Battle of Santiago de Cuba
7 July	Spanish government recalls de la Cámara's squadron McKinley signs Congressional Joint Resolution annexing Hawaiian Islands to the United States
17 July	Spanish 'capitulation' of Santiago de Cuba

25 July	Expeditionary force under Miles lands at Guanica and begins invasion of Puerto Rico
26 July	McKinley and Cambon start peace talks in Washington
4 August	Publication in American press of 'Round Robin'
6 August	Miles launches major offensive in Puerto Rico
7 August	Evacuation begins of American army from Santiago de Cuba to Montauk Point, NY
12 August	Governments of the United States and Spain sign the Peace Protocol and institute cease-fire
13 August	Dewey and Merritt launch attack on Manila. Spaniards surrender the city
1 October	Paris peace conference begins
10 December	Treaty of Paris formally concluded

1899

1 January	Spanish army officially withdraws from Cuba. US military occupation of Cuba formally begins
4 February	Fighting erupts at Manila between American troops and Filipino insurgents and marks beginning of the Philippine-American War
6 February	US Senate ratifies Treaty of Paris
19 March	Queen Regent of Spain ratifies Treaty of Paris
11 April	United States and Spain exchange ratifications and formally end Spanish-American War

1900

6 November	McKinley elected President and Theodore Roosevelt elected Vice-President

1901

23 March	Capture of Aguinaldo by US army
12 June	Cuban Constitutional Assembly approves Platt Amendment
14 September	Theodore Roosevelt becomes President on death of McKinley

1902

20 May	US Military Occupation ends and Cuba becomes an independent republic
4 July	Roosevelt declares the end of the Philippine-American War

GLOSSARY

caciquismo Spanish political system operated by political bosses.

capitulation An act of surrender containing conditions negotiated by both sides

cortes Spanish parliament.

Cuba española Idea that Cuba should remain an integral part of the mother country.

Cuba libre Idea that Cuba should separate itself politically from Spain.

expeditionary force Units of American army deployed in overseas military campaign.

grito Public proclamation of revolt against oppressive rule.

katipunan Filipino secret society which sought national liberation from Spanish rule.

manigua Literally means 'the jungle'. To the Cuban insurgents it represented the front line in the struggle for national liberation from Spain.

pundonor Point of honour.

reconcentration The policy of relocating the civilian population in fortified towns protected by the Spanish army.

rough riders The most famous unit of American volunteer cavalry, which included Theodore Roosevelt among its commanding officers.

trocha A massive ditch which formed a defensive barrier against the insurgents in Cuba.

SELECTIVE GUIDE TO FURTHER READING

BIBLIOGRAPHY AND SOURCES

A most useful guide to the historical literature in English is Anne Cipriano Venzon, *The Spanish-American War: An Annotated Bibliography* (New York, 1990) which lists more than 1,000 books and articles and includes brief comments on their contents. Araceli García Carranza, *Bibliografía de la guerra de independencia (1895–1898)* (Havana, 1976) concentrates on Spanish materials. A forthcoming major work of reference, which consists of articles by leading scholars, is Benjamin R. Beede, ed., *Garland Encyclopedia of American Wars: The Spanish-Cuban/American War, the Philippine War, and the Small Wars* (New York, in press).

For readers unable to consult the diplomatic archives at the National Archives, Washington DC, and the Ministry of Foreign Affairs, Madrid, the study of the Spanish-American War has been greatly assisted by the publication in the United States of a substantial amount of official documentary material. Much of this was published shortly after the close of the war. For example, many of the most important American diplomatic despatches appear in the annual volume for 1898 of United States Department of State, *Papers Relating to the Foreign Relations of the Untied States* (Washington DC, 1901). Similarly, there is considerable information concerning, military matters in United States Department of War, *Correspondence Relating to the War with Spain and Conditions Growing out of the Same, Including the Insurrection in the Philippine Islands and the China Relief Expedition* (2 vols; Washington DC, 1902). Of the many Congressional publications especially valuable is the multi-volume *Report of the Commission Appointed by the President to Investigate the Conduct of the War Department in the War with Spain*, 56th Congress 1st Session, Senate Document No. 221 (8 vols., Washington DC, 1900). Extracts from Congressional Hearings on American policy towards the

Philippines are contained in Henry F. Graff, ed., *American Imperialism and the Philippine Insurrection: Testimony Taken from Hearings on Affairs in the Philippine Islands before the Senate Committee on the Philippines – 1902* (Boston, 1969).

Contemporary American political and public interest in the war also resulted in the translation into English and publication of official Spanish diplomatic correspondence. In 1898–99 the Spanish government issued three volumes of diplomatic correspondence known as the 'Red Books'. These appeared in English translation as *Spanish Diplomatic Correspondence and Documents, 1896–1900, Presented to the Cortes by the Minister of State* (Washington DC, 1905). Accounts of the war by senior Spanish military figures were also translated and published in the United States. They included: Pascual Cervera y Topete, *The Spanish-American War: A Collection of Documents Relative to the Squadron Operations in the West Indies* (Washington, DC, 1899); Victor M. Concas y Palau, *The Squadron of Admiral Cervera* (Washington DC, 1900); and José Müller y Tejeiro, *Battles and Capitulation of Santiago de Cuba* (Washington DC, 1899).

The above material was extensively used in French Ensor Chadwick, *The Relations of the United States and Spain: The Spanish-American War* (3 vols; London, 1911); Russell A. Alger, *The Spanish-American War* (New York, 1901); and Herbert H. Sargent, *The Campaign of Santiago de Cuba* (3 vols; Chicago, 1907). In fact, the substantial studies by Chadwick, Alger and Sargent contain so many extracts from government documents that I have often preferred to cite these authors as the source of the official quotations used in my own work rather than refer to the original publication which is likely to be much less accessible to readers.

SECONDARY WORKS

General overviews

The best one-volume study is David F. Trask, *The War with Spain in 1898* (New York, 1981), which gives a comprehensive and masterly overview of all aspects of the subject from the *grito* of Baire in 1895 to the ratification of the Treaty of Paris. H. Wayne Morgan, *America's Road to Empire: The War with Spain and Overseas Expansion* (New York, 1965) is an excellent and concise text. Readers seeking a detailed and virtually blow-by-blow account of diplomatic and military events should consult French Ensor Chadwick, *The Relations of the United States and Spain: The Spanish-American War* (3 vols; London, 1911). Chadwick's volumes are valuable in presenting not only the considered views of a participant in the naval war but also a large number of official documents relating to the military campaigns.

The Spanish-Cuban war

Raymond Carr, *Modern Spain, 1808–1975* (Oxford, 1982), and Stanley G. Payne, *Politics and the Military in Modern Spain* (Stanford, CA, 1967) provide a useful introduction to the political history of late-nineteenth-century Spain. More detailed studies are Melchor Fernández Almagro, *Historia política de la España contemporánea* (3 vols; Madrid, 1968), and José Varela Ortega, *Los amigos políticos: partidos, elecciones y caciquismo en la Restauración (1875–1900)* (Madrid, 1977).

The link between politics and diplomacy is discussed in José Varela Ortega, 'Aftermath of Splendid Disaster: Spanish Politics before and after the Spanish American War of 1898', *Journal of Contemporary History* 15 (1980), pp. 317–44.

The general history of Cuba is surveyed in the massive tome by Hugh Thomas, *Cuba: The Pursuit of Freedom* (London, 1971), and Louis A. Pérez, Jr, *Cuba: Between Reform and Revolution* (Oxford, 1988).

The late-nineteenth-century background is expertly analyzed in Louis A. Pérez, Jr, *Cuba between Empires, 1878–1902* (Pittsburgh, 1983). The first volume of Philip S. Foner, *The Spanish-Cuban-American War and the Birth of American Imperialism, 1895–1902* (2 vols; New York, 1972) is extremely informative on events in Cuba. Among studies by Cuban historians, José Miro y Argenter, *Cuba: Crónicas de la guerra* (3 vols; Havana, 1909), and Miguel Angel Varona Guerrero, *La guerra de independencia de Cuba, 1895–1893* (3 vols; Havana, 1946) are sound factual accounts.

Martí has attracted considerable attention. Jorge Manach, *Martí, Apostle of Freedom* (New York, 1950) is uncritical and old-fashioned and should be compared with the more modern approach of John M. Kirk, *José Martí: Mentor of the Cuban Nation* (Gainesville, FL, 1983), and Peter Turton, *José Martí: Architect of Cuba's Freedom* (London, 1986).

Philip S. Foner, *Antonio Maceo: The 'Bronze Titan' of Cuba's*

Struggle for Independence (New York, 1977) does not disguise his admiration for Maceo.

There is no satisfactory biography of Gómez in English, but insights into his life and times are contained in Máximo Gómez, *Diario de campaña, 1868–1899* (Havana, 1968), and Grover Flint, *Marching with Gómez* (Boston, 1898), which tells the story of an American journalist's brief travels with the insurgents in 1896.

Aníbal Escalante Beatón, *Calixto García: Su campaña en el 95* (Havana, 1978) is a thorough account of the fighting in Oriente.

An invaluable source of information on the Spanish campaign against the insurgents is Valeriano Weyler, *Mi mando en Cuba* (5 vols; Madrid, 1910–11).

For an example of a personal memoir see Manuel Corral, *¡El desastre! Memorias de un voluntario en la campaña de Cuba* (Barcelona, 1899).

American intervention

On late-nineteenth-century American diplomacy in general, good introductions are Charles S. Campbell, *The Transformation of American Foreign Relations, 1865–1900* (New York, 1976), and Robert L. Beisner, *From the Old Diplomacy to the New, 1865–1900* (Arlington Heights, IL, 2nd edition, 1986). Walter LaFeber, *The New Empire: An Interpretation of American Expansion, 1860–1898* (Ithaca, NY, 1963) is an influential and often cited work which stresses the significance of economic factors. The same approach has been applied to a number of studies of American relations with Cuba. The most recent is Jules R. Benjamin, *The United States and the Origins of the Cuban Revolution: An Empire of Liberty in an Age of National Liberation* (Princeton, NJ, 1990). James W. Cortada, *Two Nations Over Time: Spain and the United States, 1776–1977* (Westport, CT, 1978) is a guide to the main themes in diplomatic relations between Spain and the United States. Ernest R. May, *Imperial Democracy: The Emergence of America as a Great Power* (New York, 1961) is based upon American and European archival sources and provides a balanced analysis of the diplomatic efforts to avert war in 1898. Orestes Ferrara, *The Last Spanish War: Revelations in 'Diplomacy'* (New York, 1937), and Julian Companys Monclus, *España en 1898: entre la diplomacia y la guerra* (Madrid, 1991), stress European aspects. The British diplomatic role is competently described by Robert G. Neale, *Britain and American Imperialism, 1898–1900* (Brisbane, Queensland,

1965). The outstanding work on American diplomacy has long been John L. Offner, 'President McKinley and the Origins of the Spanish American War', (PhD dissertation, Pennsylvania State University, 1957). After decades of further impressive research in American, Latin American and European archives, Offner has now published *An Unwanted War: The Diplomacy of the United States and Spain over Cuba, 1895–1898* (Chapel Hill, NC, 1992).

There are several good biographies of American political leaders. Richard E. Welch, Jr, *The Presidencies of Grover Cleveland* (Lawrence, KS, 1988) is concise and readable. William McKinley has attracted considerable attention from historians. Margaret Leech, *In the Days of McKinley* (New York, 1959) is highly informative and sympathetic to her subject. The President's skills and strengths are also expounded in Lewis L. Gould, *The Presidency of William McKinley* (Lawrence, KS, 1980); John Dobson, *Reticent Expansionism: The Foreign Policy of William McKinley* (Pittsburgh, 1988); and Paolo Coletta, ed., *Threshold to American Internationalism: Essays on the Foreign Policy of William McKinley* (New York, 1970). An excellent guide to further reading on McKinley is Joseph A. Fry, 'William McKinley and the Coming of the Spanish-American War: A Study in the Besmirching and Redemption of an Historical Image', *Diplomatic History* 3 (1979), pp. 77–98, which shows how historians have changed their views with the passage of time. The classic studies of the emergence of the 'yellow' press are Marcus M. Wilkerson, *Public Opinion and the Spanish-American War: A Study in War Propaganda* (Baton Rouge, LA, 1932), and Joseph E. Wisan, *The Cuban Crisis as Reflected in the New York Press* (New York, 1934). Charles H. Brown, *The Correspondents' War: Journalists in the Spanish-American War* (New York, 1967) is the best account of American journalists in search of sensational stories. Another readable work which brings the period to life is John E. Weems, *The Fate of the 'Maine'* (New York, 1958). Hyman G. Rickover, *How the Battleship 'Maine' was Destroyed* (Washington, DC, 1976) points to the likelihood that the explosion was caused internally. The wider historical debate is surveyed in Louis A. Pérez, Jr, 'The Meaning of the *'Maine'*: Causation and the Historiography of the Spanish-American War', *Pacific Historical Review* 58 (1989), pp. 294–322. Gerald F. Linderman, *The Mirror of War: American Society and the Spanish-American War* (Ann Arbor, MI, 1974) perceptively examines the attitudes of small-town Americans to the crisis over Cuba and the ensuing war.

The war

There is a vast amount of descriptive information on the course of the war in French E. Chadwick, *The Relations of the United States and Spain: The Spanish-American War* (3 vols; London, 1911), and Herbert H. Sargent, *The Campaign of Santiago de Cuba* (3 vols; Chicago, 1907). For many years the standard of secondary text has been Walter Millis, *The Martial Spirit: A Study of Our War with Spain* (Boston, 1931), which was a popular bestseller in its day. This work is still informative and entertaining, but it has now been surpassed by the more detailed and scholarly David Trask, *The War with Spain in 1898* (New York, 1981). Readable works which attempt to recreate the sight and sound of battle are Jack Cameron Diercks, *A Leap to Arms: The Cuban Campaign of 1898* (Philadelphia, 1970), and G.J.A. O'Toole, *The Spanish War: An American Epic – 1898* (New York, 1984). By citing extracts from letters and diaries, Frank Freidel, *The Splendid Little War* (Boston, 1958) highlights the human angle.

Among the many accounts of American soldiers and journalists who visited Cuba, I have found especially useful Theodore Roosevelt, *The Rough Riders* (New York, 1902), and Charles J. Post, *The Little War of Private Post* (Boston, 1960), which describe the life of the Rough Riders from opposite vantage points. Richard Harding Davis, *The Cuban and Porto Rico Campaigns* (New York, 1898) presents the views of a professional journalists with an eye for interesting facts and details. George Kennan, *Campaigning in Cuba* (Port Washington, NY, 1971) is the work of a fair-minded observer who showed particular concern for the medical welfare of the troops. The problem of race relations is raised in Willard B. Gatewood, Jr, *'Smoked Yankees' and the Struggle for Empire: Letters from Negro Soldiers, 1898–1902* (Urbana, Il., 1971). American soldiers are commended for their bravery in John Black Atkins, *The War in Cuba: The Experiences of an Englishman with the United States Army* (London, 1899). Among the memoirs of the American military commanders, Nelson A. Miles, *Serving the Republic: Memoirs of the Civil and Military Life of Nelson A. Miles* (New York, 1911) is disappointingly brief on the war.

Naval experiences are recounted in William T. Sampson, 'The Atlantic Fleet in the Spanish War', *The Century Magazine* 57 (April, 1899), pp. 886–913, and George W. Dewey, *Autobiography of George Dewey, Admiral of the Navy* (New York, 1913).

The mind-set of officials in Washington and the prevalence of inter-service rivalries is revealed in Russell A. Alger, *The Spanish-American War* (New York, 1901), and Lawrence S. Mayo, ed., *America of Yesterday as Reflected in the Journal of John Davis Long* (Boston, 1923).

By contrast, there are few Spanish memoirs. The outstanding exception is Victor M. Concas y Palau, *La escuadra del Almirante Cervera* (Málaga, 1992), which was translated into English and published as *The Squadron of Admiral Cervera* (Washington DC, 1900).

There are no full-length biographical studies of American generals, but Paul H. Carlson, *'Pecos Bill': A Military Biography of William R. Shafter* (College Station, TX, 1989), and Edward Ranson, 'Nelson A. Miles as Commanding General, 1895–1903', *Military Affairs* 29 (1965–66), pp. 179–200, are informative.

Historians have paid more attention to the activities of the American navy. Harold and Margaret Sprout, *The Rise of American Naval Power, 1776–1918* (Princeton, NJ, 1939) and William R. Braisted, *The United States Navy in the Pacific, 1897–1909* (Austin, TX, 1958) are standard accounts which only briefly discuss the Spanish-American War. These works have been superseded by the perceptive analysis provided in John A.S. Grenville and George B. Young, *Politics, Strategy, and American Diplomacy: Studies in Foreign Policy, 1873–1917* (New Haven, CT, 1967). Ronald Spector, *Admiral of the New Empire: The Life and Career of George Dewey* (Baton Rouge, LA, 1974) is an excellent biography.

The military strategies adopted by the United States and Spain are perceptively analyzed in the 'Comments' section which Herbert H. Sargent, *The Campaign of Santiago de Cuba* (3 vols; Chicago, 1907), includes at the end of each chapter. Alfred T. Mahan, *Lessons of the War with Spain, and Other Articles* (Boston, 1899) reviews the naval campaign. British military attachés were often highly critical of the implementation of American strategy. Their views are discussed in Edward Ranson, 'British Military and Naval Observers in the Spanish-American War', *Journal of American Studies* 3 (1969), pp. 33–56. The outstanding work on the organization and activities of the War Department is Graham A. Cosmas, *An Army for Empire: The United States Army in the Spanish-American War* (Columbia, MO, 1971).

The postwar scandals affecting Alger and the War Department are described in Edward Ranson, 'The Investigation of the War Department', *The Historian* 34 (1971), pp. 78–99. Jasper B. Reid, Jr, 'Russell A. Alger as Secretary of War', *Michigan History* 43

(1959), pp. 225–39, adopts a sympathetic attitude towards Alger.

American imperialism

The negotiation and ratification of the Treaty of Paris are illuminated in H. Wayne Morgan, ed., *Making Peace with Spain: The Diary of Whitelaw Reid, September–December 1898* (Austin, TX, 1965), and Paolo E. Coletta, 'Bryan, McKinley and the Treaty of Paris', *Pacific Historical Review* 27 (1957), pp. 131–46. The motivation of American expansionism is examined in Julius W. Pratt, *Expansionists of 1898: The Acquisition of Hawaii and the Spanish Islands* (Baltimore, MD, 1936) and David Healy, *US Expansionism: The Imperialist Urge in the 1890s* (Madison, WI, 1970). Robert L. Beisner, *Twelve Against Empire: The Anti-Imperialists, 1898–1900* (New York, 1968), and E. Berkeley Tompkins, *Anti-imperialism in the United States: The Great Debate, 1890–1920* (Philadelphia, 1970) explain the rise of the anti-imperialist movement. A meticulous study of the impact of the debate over imperialism on American domestic politics and the 1900 presidential election is Göran Rystad, *Ambiguous Imperialism: American Foreign Policy and Domestic Politics at the Turn of the Century* (Stockholm, 1975).

The establishment of American military rule in Cuba is superbly analyzed in Louis A. Pérez, Jr, *Cuba Under the Platt Amendment, 1902–1934* (Pittsburgh, 1986) and the same author's, *Cuba Between Empires*. This can be supplemented with the competent study by David F. Healy, *The United States in Cuba, 1898–1902: Generals, Politicians, and the Search for Policy* (Madison, WI, 1963). Edward J. Berbusse, *The United States in Puerto Rico, 1898–1900* (Chapel Hill, NC, 1966) deals with American attitudes towards Puerto Rico.

The broader question of American pre-eminence in the Caribbean region is highlighted in many historical works, of which Lester D. Langley, *The Banana Wars: United States Intervention in the Caribbean 1898–1934* (Chicago, 1983) and David Healy, *Drive to Hegemony: The United States in the Caribbean, 1898–1917* (Madison, WI, 1988) are recent examples.

The story of the extension of American control over Hawaii and Guam is briefly recounted in Thomas A. Bailey, 'United States and Hawaii during the Spanish-American War', *American Historical Review* 36 (1931), pp. 552–60, and Leslie W. Walker, 'Guam's Seizure by the United States in 1898' *Pacific Historical Review* 14 (1945), pp. 1–12. Thomas J. Osborne, *'Empire can Wait': American*

Opposition to Hawaiian Annexation, 1893–1898 (Kent, OH, 1981) shows that American political interest predated 1898.

Stanley Karnow, *In Our Image: America's Empire in the Philippines* (New York, 1989) is a highly readable and informative study of the historical relationship between the United States and the Philippines. The one-sided nature of the relationship is the theme of Leon Wolff, *Little Brown Brother: How the United States Purchased and Pacified the Philippine Islands at the Century's Turn* (New York, 1961). Wolff's emotive condemnation of American policy and racial attitudes is treated more dispassionately but no less critically in Richard E. Welch, Jr, *Response to Imperialism: The United States and the Philippine-American War, 1899–1902* (Chapel Hill, NC, 1979), and Stuart C. Miller, *'Benevolent Assimilation': The American Conquest of the Philippines, 1899–1903* (New Haven, CT, 1982). Informative studies which concentrate on the activities of the American army are John M. Gates, *Schoolbooks and Krags: the United States Army in the Philippines, 1898–1902* (Westport, CT, 1973), and Brian M. Linn, *The US Army and Counterinsurgency in the Philippine War, 1899–1902* (Chapel Hill, NC, 1989). Glenn A. May, 'Why the United States Won the Philippine-American War, 1899–1902', *Pacific Historical Review* 52 (1983), pp. 353–77, draws interesting comparisons between the Philippine-American War and the Vietnam War.

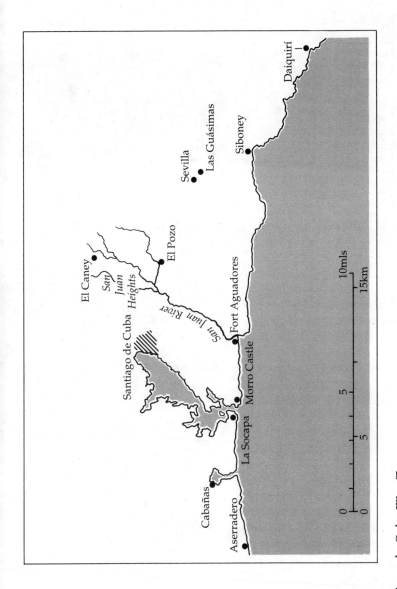

1. Santiago de Cuba War Zone

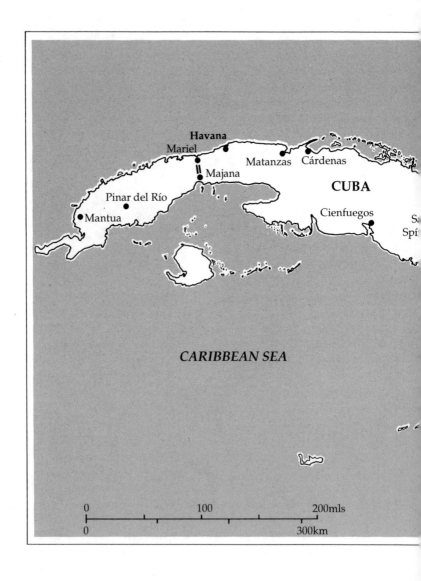

2. Cuba

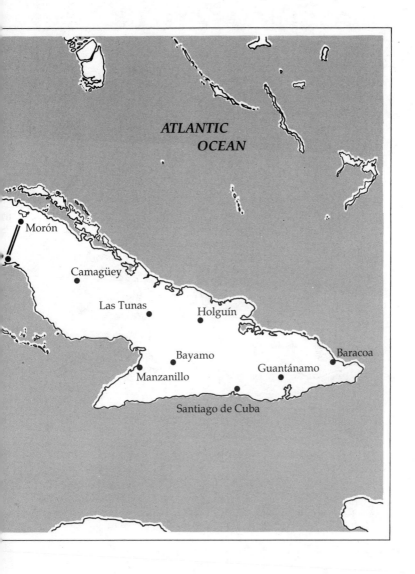

ATLANTIC
OCEAN

Morón

Camagüey

Las Tunas

Holguín

Bayamo

Baracoa

Manzanillo

Guantánamo

Santiago de Cuba

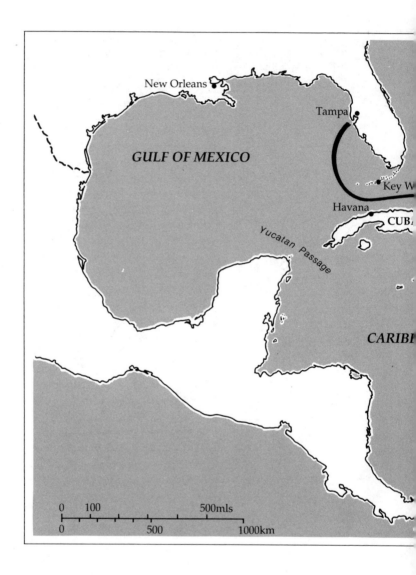

New Orleans

Tampa

GULF OF MEXICO

Key W

Havana

CUB

Yucatan Passage

CARIBl

| 0 | 100 | | 500mls |
| 0 | | 500 | 1000km |

3. The Caribbean War Zone

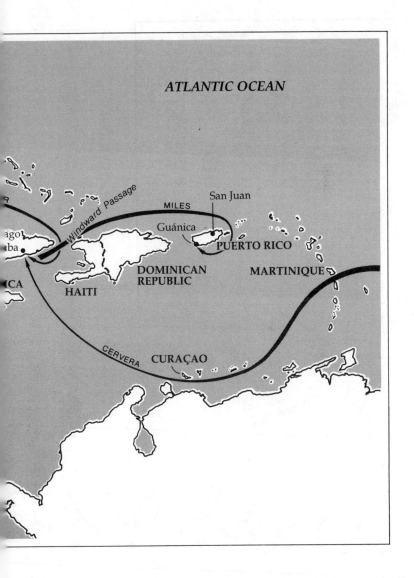

ATLANTIC OCEAN

San Juan

Windward Passage

MILES

Guánica

igo
iba

PUERTO RICO

DOMINICAN
REPUBLIC

MARTINIQUE

CA

HAITI

CERVERA

CURAÇAO

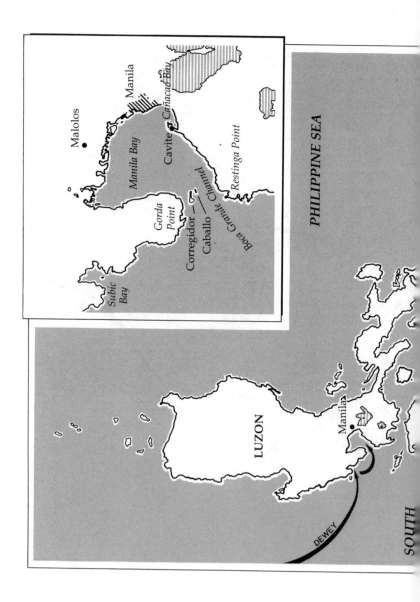

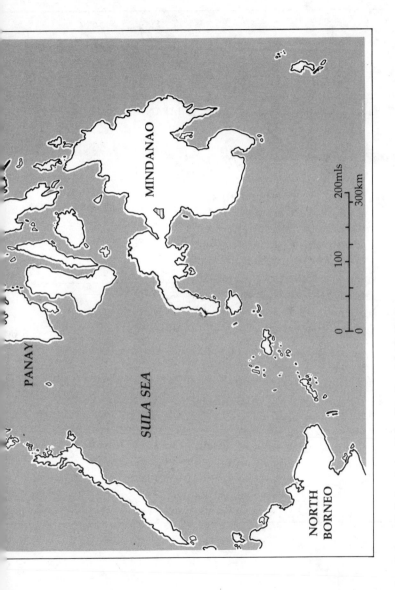

4. The Philippine Islands and the Battle of Manila Bay

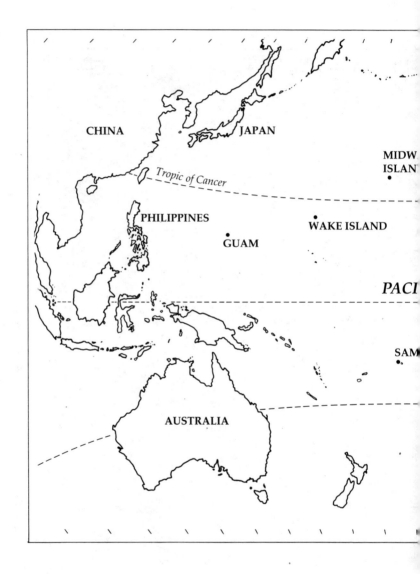

5. The Pacific War Zone

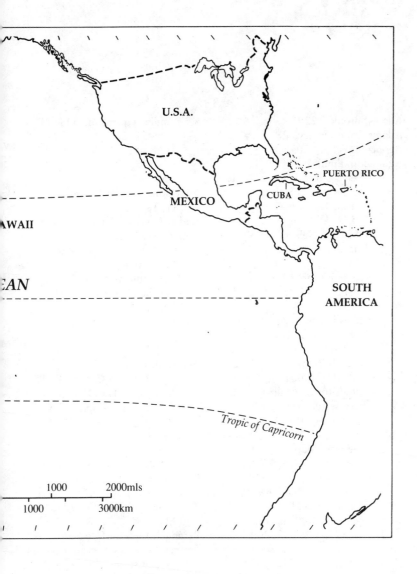

U.S.A.

PUERTO RICO

MEXICO

CUBA

AWAII

EAN

SOUTH
AMERICA

Tropic of Capricorn

1000   2000mls

1000   3000km

INDEX